the
impossible
first

the
impossible
first

the impossible first

colin o'brady

AN EXPLORER'S RACE ACROSS ANTARCTICA
YOUNG READERS EDITION

Simon & Schuster Books for Young Readers
New York London Toronto Sydney New Delhi

SIMON & SCHUSTER BOOKS FOR YOUNG READERS
An imprint of Simon & Schuster Children's Publishing Division
1230 Avenue of the Americas, New York, New York 10020

This work is a memoir. It reflects the author's present recollections of his
experiences over a period of years.
This young reader's edition is adapted from *The Impossible First*
by Colin O'Brady, published by Scribner in 2020

SIMON & SCHUSTER BOOKS FOR YOUNG READERS
and related marks are trademarks of Simon & Schuster, Inc.
For information about special discounts for bulk purchases,
please contact Simon & Schuster Special Sales at 1-866-506-1949
or business@simonandschuster.com.
The Simon & Schuster Speakers Bureau can bring authors to your live event.
For more information or to book an event,
contact the Simon & Schuster Speakers Bureau at 1-866-248-3049
or visit our website at www.simonspeakers.com.
Also available in a Simon & Schuster Books for Young Readers
hardcover edition
Interior design by Kyle Kabel
The text for this book was set in Miller Text.
Manufactured in the United States of America
1123SKY
First Simon & Schuster Books for Young Readers
paperback edition September 2021
2   4   6   8   10   9   7   5   3
ISBN 978-1-5344-6198-7 (hc)
ISBN 978-1-5344-6199-4 (pbk)
ISBN 978-1-5344-6200-7 (ebook)

Impossible is just an opinion.

—Paulo Coelho

Contents

CONTENTS

Author's Note

This is a work of nonfiction. To write this book, I relied on journals that I began in childhood, voice and video recordings as well as photographs that I took in Antarctica and on my previous expeditions, conversations with individuals who played a role in my journey and life beyond it, personal memories, and researched facts.

No names have been changed and there are no composite characters. Others may remember details or events slightly differently. Any misinterpretations or errors are my own.

Although I'm American and typically note temperature in Fahrenheit, all temperatures in this book are recorded in Celsius since that is how weather forecasts were shared with me via the international weather report. Keep in mind, at forty below zero Fahrenheit and Celsius meet and are equal to each other. During my journey I tracked progress in both nautical miles and statute miles, but in this book I report my progress solely in statute miles for ease and consistency.

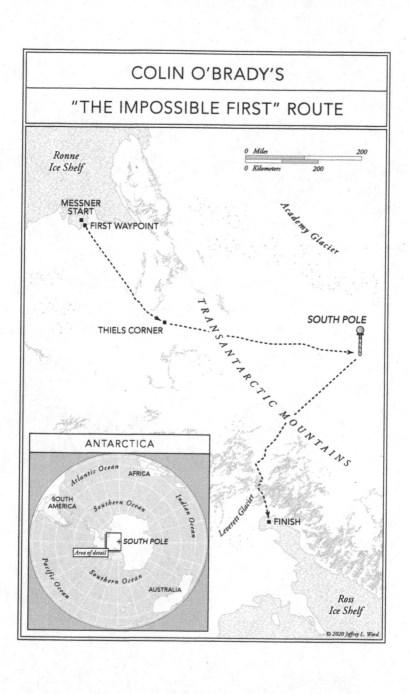

the
impossible
first

Prologue

I started thinking about my hands.

That was my first mistake.

After forty-eight days and more than 760 miles alone across Antarctica, the daily ache of my hands—cracked with cold, gripping my ski poles twelve hours a day—had become like a drumbeat, forming the rhythm of my existence. And that night the ache got to me. As I pulled my sled into a blizzard of cold and white—my jacket thermometer read thirty below Celsius, with blasting gusts of wind that made the windchill at least fifty below—I started picturing how intensely pleasurable it would feel to get out of my mittens.

I saw myself securely inside my tent, massaging life back into the sore, stiff, cold-battered knuckles, holding them close to the hissing flame of my stove, pressing them up against the little aluminum pot as it began to warm and melt the snow for my drinking water and dinner.

At about 8 p.m., with the twenty-four-hour sun just a pale yellow dot overhead through the thick clouds and blowing snow, I stopped to make camp. I unhitched from the harness that connected me to the sled, unzipped the cover, and fished out my tent.

Then I paused for a moment, hunched over in the cold, looking down at the tent in my hands. I'd made camp in storms and sun and wind, and always done it the same way, through muscle memory forged by repetition—anchoring one end of the tent to the sled, then driving anchors into the ice at the opposite end and around the perimeter. It was the most secure way.

But that night, in my fatigue, and with the cold ache of my hands crying for relief, I decided that a simple stake into the ice would be good enough rather than securing it to the sled. It was much faster. It would be fine, I told myself.

I rushed it.

That was my second mistake.

I drove in the stake, unrolled the tent flat, and walked back around to the far end. I knelt down on the ice and pushed the spring-loaded tent poles into their little metal grommets, popping the tent up. The next step felt utterly routine, too, at first. I inched back and pulled the tent toward me, straightening it out into a point of tension with the first anchor, preparing to put a second stake down into the ice.

Then it happened. At exactly the wrong moment, before my second anchor was secure, a monstrous gust came straight at me over the top of the sled, as though it had been taking aim from the farthest reaches of the continent. Between my yanking on the fabric and the sudden blast of wind, the first anchor I'd planted on the tent's other side lost its grip in the ice.

In the next instant, I saw the far side of the tent rise up, now unsecured and disconnected. The horror of the scene flooded through my body as though I'd stuck my finger in an electric socket, but it almost seemed like slow motion, too—as the tent, with each new inch off the ice, caught more and more of the oncoming wind from beneath.

And because I'd just pushed the tent poles into place, popping up the semicircle spine of the frame, there was more surface area to catch the wind. So as the tent rose it caught greater and greater force, like a kite or a sail. In a split second, I lunged forward and barely grabbed the edge of the tent, making me the tent's sole attachment to the planet.

What could happen next played out before my eyes like a waking nightmare: I lose my grip. The tent rises, I leap desperately for it but can't catch it, and I stumble and fall. The tent disappears almost immediately into the white. I get up and run for it into the storm . . . and then . . . and then . . . I am lost. The tent is gone. I turn back and see nothing but the full whiteout of the storm. I have nothing to guide me back to the sled and no hope of surviving the night.

The horrible vision kept playing out as I held on desperately.

I had no backup tent. No rescue party could ever make it through a storm like this, with zero visibility and rugged, uneven terrain that would prevent a plane from landing. I'd grow sleepy, then increasingly irrational, and finally I'd just lie down, thinking that the ice was a nice place to rest. I'd die alone, in the cold, my body temperature falling.

It wasn't the fear of death that really got to me—it was the realization that I'd never make it home. I'd never get back to Portland, never walk along the Willamette River holding hands with my wife, Jenna, never laugh around another campfire at the Oregon Coast with my parents and the rest of my family, never again smell the deep, peaceful aroma of a damp, bark-lined forest trail in the Cascade Mountains.

My hands were now everything. They gripped the edge of the tent as my airborne home yanked and jerked over my head. I knew that everything depended on what happened in the next few seconds—on how long I could hold on, and what I did or didn't do.

I knew I had to flatten out the tent somehow so that it wasn't catching so much wind. But the only way I could think to do that—pulling it down and crawling on top of it to hold it with my weight—might snap the tent poles. That would create a different crisis.

Aiming to save a bit of weight on the sled, I'd left my spare poles behind on a brilliant sunny morning that now felt like a lifetime ago.

As the wind blasted into my face, the cold deepening with every second, my panic increasing, I relived that sunny, long-ago moment of choice. I could feel those poles in my hand, see myself digging a hole in the snow and burying them along with other supplies and tools for later retrieval. All that equipment had seemed so heavy and so dispensable.

Maybe, I thought, *that* was actually my first mistake—the place where the great chain of error really began. Such a tiny thing, it seemed: tent poles. A few ounces saved, another mistake, and I was living the consequences.

Choices and consequences. Everything in the universe was simplified into those giant words. Overhead, my small tent seemed suddenly huge, a fluttering, flapping red monster, bigger and harder to hold with every passing second. And my cramping hands were starting to lose their grip.

CHAPTER ONE

The Captain

PRE-EXPEDITION

The Russian-built Ilyushin cargo plane that rumbled and rolled over Drake Passage toward the Antarctic ice had all the comforts you'd expect from its hard and pragmatic Russian design, which meant essentially no comforts at all. It was built to withstand the worst weather you could throw at it, land and take off on runways of pure ice or war-zone rubble, and deliver cargo where few other planes could go. It smelled like damp canvas, machine oil, and old sweat, perhaps with a hint of spilled vodka for good measure, and it was utterly beloved, or so said our pilot, a weathered, wiry Russian in his fifties who'd wrestled with the Ilyushin's cockpit controls over the ice for thousands of hours. This plane was a tank that would save you when other planes would fail and falter, he told us as we boarded, giving the fuselage a loving pat. That it was the only way to get to Union Glacier's windswept ice runway and base camp—and the starting point for just about anybody heading into the continent's interior—was also totally in keeping with the plane's lack of frills. "Take it or leave it" might as well have been written on the side.

On this morning in late October 2018, there were only a handful of paying passengers amid the jammed-together jumble of boxes, tents, generators, and mysterious crates being shipped south for the start of the summer expedition season. I was one of them, strapped onto an ancient, rock-hard Ilyushin bench seat, with the plane's big steel ribs arcing overhead. Strapped in next to me and sharing the same bench for this four-hour flight was perhaps the most intimidating man I'd ever met: Captain Louis Rudd.

Rudd was forty-nine and British, wrapped in a cloak of vaguely scruffy steeliness and BBC English. He sat firmly erect on his half of the bench and looked across at me with piercing hazel eyes. He spoke like a commander, in the crisp declarative sentences of the British military that had shaped and sharpened him for more than three decades. We were each headed to base camp to await further air transport out onto the Antarctic ice for the formal beginning of a historic race to try to become the first to cross the continent alone, unsupported, and unassisted. In planning our course, each of us had chosen different routes. But our paths, though neither of us could fully see it then, would become intertwined.

"Henry Worsley and I were on one team, doing Amundsen's route. The other team started from Scott's hut at McMurdo," Rudd said, leaning toward me as he described his astonishing Antarctic expedition in 2011, which replicated the great race to the South Pole in 1911 between Roald Amundsen and Robert Falcon Scott. Just the names of such giants, and Rudd's connection to them, took my breath away: Amundsen. Scott. Worsley. Frank Worsley had captained what was probably the most famous Antarctic ship in history, carrying Ernest Shackleton off into legend on the *Endurance* in 1914. Henry Worsley, a distant relative, had continued the family Antarctic legacy, with tragic consequences. Rudd had walked in the company of gods.

"It was a brutal expedition, sixty-seven days to the Pole," Rudd continued, his eyes boring into me. "Severe storms. Henry and I each lost more than four stone. That's something like sixty pounds to you Yanks. Anyway, we beat the Scott team by nine days, so I guess history repeats itself and the Amundsen route was better," he said. He finished with a wry smile that looked like he appreciated the irony: The 1911 race had been a national contest between Norway and England, and Amundsen's Norwegians had won, beating Captain Scott of the British Royal Navy to the South Pole. Scott and his men all perished trying to get home.

I mumbled something like "wow, that's amazing," but in truth I couldn't stop thinking about sixty pounds and sixty-seven days. My mind was suddenly back on Chile's southernmost windblown tip, in a tiny Airbnb apartment in Punta Arenas, preparing for my transport flight to the ice. Equipment and food bags were spread across every surface, from kitchen countertops to the bed and the floor between. The featured fare: oatmeal and protein powder, crunchy dried ramen and freeze-dried dinners. Deserving special attention, though, were wallet-sized protein bars that were piled high like decks of cards. They'd been made by a Wisconsin nutritional supplement company that had taken me into their food science lab and produced a one-of-a-kind calorie bomb they'd dubbed the "Colin Bar."

The checklists prepared by my wife and business partner, Jenna—the logistical road maps for the expedition—were laid out on a table, and she and I were scurrying from pile to pile, organizing, sorting, and weighing all the things I planned to drag across Antarctica in a sled, so absorbed that we nearly collided once in coming around a corner. In the eleven years of our relationship, she and I had been in more than a few exotic and challenging places, but at that moment the stakes had never felt higher, and we both stopped after our near collision, standing there in front of the refrigerator, arms full, leaning forward for a quick kiss.

We were redistributing everything so that I'd have less.

I'd planned on carrying seventy days of food and fuel, which put the sled well over four hundred pounds, a weight I'd realized I couldn't pull. So on a tight deadline before the flight south, we'd been stripping out what felt like surplus, reducing my margins. Seventy days of food became sixty-five. Now, on the plane, that number sounded suddenly and frighteningly a lot like sixty-seven, Rudd's number of days to the Pole on his previous expedition, losing around sixty pounds along the way. I started doing the math in my head. Sixty pounds was almost a third of my weight.

I didn't know what to say. My stomach was suddenly churning as though the whale-like Ilyushin had hit turbulence. Rudd had replicated Amundsen's route. He'd known Henry Worsley, whose amazing life and tragic death had so moved and inspired me. Worsley had died in 2016 attempting the very goal that Rudd and I were aiming for—the first ever solo, unsupported, unassisted crossing in history, something that many people after Worsley's passing had come to call "impossible." And the thought echoed through my head: Rudd is already ahead of me. He knows everything.

"Want to see a picture of me at the end?" he suddenly asked.

"Sure. Of course," I said, shrugging.

Rudd fingered through the photos on his phone until he found the one he wanted, and handed it over. I immediately wished I hadn't seen it. He looked almost skeletal—cheekbones bulging like baseballs from an emaciated face; dark, cold-weather wounds across forehead and nose. Rudd smiled broadly as he took the phone back, and I finally understood what he was *really* saying: "You don't know what you're in for, mate."

It was true. I admitted to myself that what I didn't know about Antarctica and polar survival could probably fill a book. I was far less experienced than Rudd, so much so that I probably looked like an imposter in his eyes.

He'd fought and been decorated in combat, and through various expeditions over the years had spent more time man-hauling a sled across the Antarctic ice than just about anybody alive. I was from a scruffy counterculture corner of the Pacific Northwest. Rudd? Probably hatched from a cannonball.

Yes, I was fit and strong, and at thirty-three years old, sixteen years younger than Rudd. I'd also been a professional athlete for years, racing triathlons around the world, and I'd climbed some of the world's biggest mountains, including Mount Everest. I'd even been to Antarctica before. But as I looked at the inimitable Captain Rudd, none of those things seemed very important, or even relevant.

I felt like we'd been dropped into the plane from two different planets. We had absolutely nothing in common but this moment where our lives had intersected, each of us gripped by the goal of being the first to do something that had never been done: cross Antarctica alone via the South Pole using only human power and without being resupplied. We each knew a little about the other's plans and preparations—mine in America, his in the UK—but we were going to start from different places on the Ronne Ice Shelf at the edge of the Antarctic landmass. Rudd was leaving south from the Hercules Inlet; I was leaving several hundred miles away at a place called the Messner Start. We might never even see each other again after our little jammed-in-together cargo flight to base camp.

But all that mattered was that Rudd was getting inside my head from the first minutes, and with every hour that the plane lurched south, and the beginning of what I already knew would be the hardest thing I'd ever thought of attempting, my confidence was sinking. I felt as if he were looking across the seat at me and thinking, *Working this guy is child's play.*

The feeling put me suddenly back in ninth grade on the first day of class at the big high school across town in Portland, Oregon. It was filled with kids I didn't know who were mostly from the cooler, wealthier parts of the city. I'd walked in looking for my homeroom and my locker and felt almost immediately like an imposter then, too, thrown into a place I didn't belong and didn't fully understand. Southeast Portland, where I'd grown up, is a hot corner of the city now, with some of the best restaurants and music venues. But in the late nineties, the kids who filled my new school, coming there from upscale neighborhoods in the West Hills, considered anything east of the Willamette River a wasteland of auto garages, machine shops, and small houses built for the old timber-town and dockworker crews of the city's industrial past. To them, the neighborhood where I lived was poor, uninteresting, and unworthy, if not downright dangerous.

My salvation came in finding a friend. David Boyer arrived for class from the wrong side, too, and like me was keenly aware of the difference that made. Together, we formed an alliance, each of us with something of a chip on his shoulder, and something to prove, if only because we were outnumbered. We'd each helped the other face the unknown.

And that memory brought on another realization: Rudd was facing the unknown, too, just as I was. He possessed reserves of deep experience that I didn't, unquestionably, but experience would only help so much in a place where the human imprint on the landscape was so shallow, small, and thin. He knew some of Antarctica's hardest, cruelest truths and had lived through them, but in Antarctica, I knew—from the grizzled veterans I'd consulted and trained with as well as the little time I'd spent there—unpredictability was the defining characteristic.

Antarctica would set the terms of what was possible, in all the unknowns and variables of wind and storm, ice and bone-chilling cold, and neither Rudd nor I knew what those variables would be, day-to-day or even minute-to-minute, or what strengths would ultimately matter.

Improvisation and resourcefulness would decide fates and outcomes—just as they had for the early polar pioneers who really couldn't know, before airplanes and satellites, even what terrain they'd face. Improvisation was crucial to me and Rudd since we didn't really know if the thing we were both attempting could be done at all and survived.

Captain Scott's attempt at motor-powered sleds in 1911 was an improvisation that didn't work given the technology of the day. The idea was right, just premature. Snowmobiles and modified all-terrain trucks are now the workhorses of the polar regions. Amundsen improvised around food; worried that he and his men would have digestive trouble eating a meat-heavy diet with no fiber, he'd added peas and oatmeal to the rations.

Shackleton honed improvisation to an art form after his ship, the *Endurance*, was caught in the sea ice and crushed in early 1915. In keeping himself and his men alive and fed on the Antarctic ice for more than a year, and then sailing an open boat hundreds of miles across some of the stormiest waters in the world to seek rescue, he embodied the idea that survival itself can be an act of heroism.

And going through all that in my head helped me straighten up in my seat and think of my own strategy in what had already become a bizarre kind of airborne chess game. Rudd, I decided, was genuinely, amazingly impressive with his military-officer bearing and his crisp monologue of astonishing feats. He was canny and probably brilliant. But I felt he was also working me, or playing me, or using some military mind trick in breaking down my resolve and confidence. And I decided to let him do it. That he knew nothing about me, and showed no inclination to ask, could be an advantage in a way I wasn't sure of yet.

So from that moment, I mostly nodded and let Rudd talk, keeping my own cards close. I was, in fact, truly intimidated—he could probably have sown doubt and undermined the confidence of anyone. But having him think me even more diminished than I was also felt like the best hand I had to play. The more he thought me unworthy or unprepared, a probably pampered American millennial with no business trying something like this, the more he might grow too confident himself. I had no idea where any of that might lead or how it might play out. But the lesson, in training for this moment—in seeking out mentors and polar veterans, in reading everything I could get my hands on—had been hammered into me by then like an ice anchor: In Antarctica, overconfidence can be as dangerous as fear.

THE ILYUSHIN SKID-LANDED on the blue-ice runway of Union Glacier just like you'd expect, like a flying tank—as though it had been hurled down from the sky, bouncing and rattling and heaving its cargo until it finally came to a squealing halt and I could take a breath. I was finally on the ice. After the long, intense confinement of the flight and the mind games that had played out across the bench seat, it felt like much more than just an arrival—more like I'd emerged from a long dark tunnel into a new world. In stepping down out of the plane, the tense hours of flying were instantly behind me. Antarctica, from the first seconds, lit up all of my senses. The bitter cold stung my face, yet the unbelievable brightness and the forever white landscape left me in awe. The emotional charge of finally being there made me smile so broadly that my cheeks hurt.

Union Glacier, which functions as a kind of logistical base camp for almost every nongovernment expedition into Antarctica, is a bustling place as the high season of the Antarctic's summer unfolds from November to January. The company that transports just about everybody and everything to the ice, Antarctic Logistics and Expeditions (A.L.E.), sets up a small town of food tents and camp offices. Wealthy adventurers chartering guided trips rub shoulders with ecotourists, scientists heading out to study ice cores, and people who've simply fallen in love with a strange, harsh place—like our hard-boiled pilot on the Ilyushin. Mountaineers embark from there to Mount Vinson, the highest peak on the continent. Tiny subcultures of Antarctic obsession blossom in the brief months of twenty-four-hour sunshine before dying back in the months of darkness—people coming to the world's emptiest and most extreme place just to say they've been there, or to run marathons, or to see the famous emperor penguins, imagining themselves to be Captain Scott himself, who made a famously arduous side trip to see the emperors and retrieve some of their eggs for science before beginning his sprint to the Pole in 1911.

On this day, camp workers were shoveling huge mounds of snow around prefab huts and steel-framed tents. I thought it was probably a normal start-of-season ritual—the summer cleanup of winter's mess—until I stopped to chat with a guy who'd paused to lean on his shovel for a smoke. He was from England—season on the ice, season off, and good paying work, he told me, if you could tolerate it.

"This snow is nuts," he said, blowing out a huge cloud of water vapor and smoke into the cold air. "Way more loose snow than normal and I've been coming down here a lot of years." He paused and took another drag. "The scientists tell us there could be more snow down here in a warming climate because warmer air can hold more moisture, so maybe . . ." He shrugged, then ground out his butt into a can he'd pulled from his pocket. "Whatever it is, something very different happened over the winter, that's clear enough," he said.

Rudd and I needed almost a full summer season, which in the Southern Hemisphere begins to unfold in November, to have even a hope of completing a crossing before the long winter darkness closed in. We were just as ironbound by the seasons as Scott or Shackleton had been, or Reinhold Messner, the legendary mountaineer and namesake of the spot I was heading for, where the sea ice met the continent. Nothing of modern life or technology had changed that fundamental fact: expeditions went out only when Antarctica allowed it.

So we each had to start at the earliest window of possible transport. And what that meant is that we were about the only non-A.L.E. people in camp as October rolled toward November. On the morning of the second scheduled smaller-plane flight that would take us to our different starting points on the Ronne Ice Shelf, we filed into the mess tent, the only people in there at that hour. We took our trays and sat down together, just the two of us. It was clearly becoming a pattern.

Rudd was digging into a huge plate of bacon and eggs.

"One last big load of fat and calories," he said.

Then he stopped, took a sip of coffee, and looked around the tent for a moment. I thought I saw a shadow of hesitation or indecision cross his face, but then some corner turned in his mind, it seemed, as he looked straight into my eyes and blurted his news.

"I'm starting at the Messner," he said, digging back into his breakfast.

I stopped mid-bite, my mouth hanging open. What had been, until that moment, two similar but not exactly parallel projects— different starting points, different attempts at answering the same question, whether this expedition we were trying could be done—had just fundamentally changed: we were now on exactly the same course. With Rudd's words, this journey each of us was taking had become truly a race. Apples to oranges had become apples to apples—same exact route, same goal. There'd now really be a winner and a loser.

I looked down at my own plate of eggs, then back up again at Rudd. Maybe, I thought, just maybe, I'd gotten to him a little, too. Maybe silence and nodding and saying hardly anything about myself and my plans, even if it mostly had come from a place of insecurity, had sent some message I hadn't intended. The experienced polar giant had flipped his plan to be like mine, not the other way around.

He wanted to beat me. That's what it meant. Rudd had inched his seat closer to mine. We were bound up together, for better or worse, in everything that would happen next.

CHAPTER TWO

Frozen Tears

DAY 1

The start of any great effort feels to me like a blank canvas of hope. Since my first swim meets in elementary school, those extended minutes before the buzzer goes off to mark the start have always been magical in their white-knuckled anxiety and completely uncharted sense of possibility. An unwritten story hangs in the air. The future beckons, full of unknowns. Winning or losing is the measure of how things go, but between those two extremes, a whole compacted life, it often seems, will unfold through the minutes to come. Anything is possible. Everything is possible.

That sense of magic, open-ended potential caught fire in me when I was seven, sitting on the couch with my mom watching the swim finals in the 1992 Summer Olympics in Barcelona. Seeing Pablo Morales of the United States win a gold medal in the 100-meter butterfly changed my life, firing a dream that blazed in me for more than two decades—that maybe I could one day stand on that medal podium, too. It turned me into an Olympic geek-child who, perhaps sometimes annoyingly, could rattle off the most obscure Olympic trivia, along with the backstories of my heroes.

The ferocious, uncontainable optimism that boils over inside me at the beginning of almost any new challenge or adventure is a result of that day: Morales in the pool, raising his arms in triumph, me screaming my head off in our living room, jumping up and down on the couch. It's also partly what had brought me to Antarctica—the idea of the blank canvas, of life unfolding with all its deep uncertainties and possibilities wrapped up together.

Antarctica felt to me like an untold story. Other than bases for scientific research, it's a place with no real towns or permanent residents or animals, once you get past the water's edge and its huge schools of fish, colonies of penguins, and pods of killer whales. It's the only continent never to have seen a war. Mapmakers routinely don't show it at all. It's a blank space in a world that is mostly filled up.

But as Rudd and I got ready to leave Union Glacier, flying out to our starting place on the edge of the Ronne Ice Shelf, he seemed bent on trying to fill the continent himself, if only with his bristly commando confidence.

"How many calories per day are you bringing?" he'd said as we were readying to load up the plane, a red-and-white Twin Otter turboprop—a workhorse of transport in harsh environments all over the world, from the Alaskan bush to the Sahara.

I hedged for a second, bracing myself for his reaction. I knew he'd have one. "Seven thousand," I said as firmly as I could.

"Seven thousand!" he spluttered. "I'm only bringing fifty-five hundred." His eyes narrowed into a piercing squint as he looked at me and then at my sled as though for the first time. "Fifty-five hundred is plenty," he added.

I thought about saying something about the research I'd done, the medical tests I'd undergone to see how my physiology worked and how my body burned fuel in conditions of stress and cold. I wanted to sound scientific and smart. And we both knew that we'd be burning through a lot more than even seven thousand calories a day—probably closer to ten thousand—so extreme weight loss was certain no matter what. But I was pretty sure he'd see that sort of thing—blood tests, nutrition, and aerobic analysis—as American and fussy rather than rational and scientific, and in any case not remotely British in the can-do toughness of the exploration and expedition world that he worshipped and called home.

"I think I know what works," he continued.

"You know what else works?" he went on. "Ice!"

I raised my eyebrows, unsure of where he was going.

Laughing, he said, "I saw you brought toilet paper. I never bother weighing myself down with something so luxurious."

Maybe he did know better. I was no longer sure about anything. More calories, however scientific they were, also translated into more weight, even a sheet of toilet paper added to the burden. Rudd was clearly beginning with a much lighter load.

Jenna and I had removed five days of supplies in the little apartment in Chile, taking us to sixty-five days, and then I'd subtracted five days more as I fretted and waited at Union Glacier Camp. That took me to sixty days, which was a full week less than Rudd had carried in his project duplicating the 1911 Amundsen route to the Pole. He'd lost sixty pounds in that expedition, and I'd be going much farther. The numbers were scary, but also just plain mysterious, since there was no way to check to see if I was any more correct, or incorrect, than he'd been back then.

The moment of truth came as we started loading the sleds. Our plane sat on its white-ski landing gear near the storage tent. Our pilot, an upbeat Canadian named Monica who'd told us her story of falling in love with Antarctica at first sight, climbed in and out of the cockpit, making preparations. The flight team had asked if we wanted to weigh our gear.

Rudd immediately barked a definite yes, and with help from one of the crew members, wrestled his sled up onto the big industrial scale beside the ice runway. I tried to look busy, pretending to be occupied even as I cocked an ear, desperate to hear what the scale might reveal. What I heard chilled my blood. One hundred and thirty kilograms, Rudd had repeated aloud—loud enough for me to hear, intentionally or not—as the scale numbers popped up. One hundred and thirty kilos translated into about 286 pounds, radically lighter than my sled, I knew.

Rudd looked over at me and nodded, saying with his eyes and gestures, "Your turn, mate."

And I couldn't do it. I couldn't weigh the sled in front of him. The look I'd get from Rudd at my astonishing load, which Jenna and I had estimated to be somewhere around 375 pounds, from just adding up the list of what was in there, combined with the weight of the sled itself, would destroy the confidence I had left. I couldn't risk it. Rudd might say nothing, probably would say nothing. But he wouldn't need to.

Our huge awkward difference in weight, open for him and all the camp to see, would reinforce and amplify all the smaller, subtler unstated things that hung in the air—his air of command, his vast knowledge. Even his terrific English accent was daunting. I'd look like the spoiled American who'd never learned how to pack a suitcase, and Rudd would be able to lay me out with an eye-roll. He'd know the vast difference in what we were going to try to pull, and I'd know that he knew.

I suddenly remembered a boy I'd faced in a swim meet when I was about twelve. I hadn't thought of him for years and can't even remember his name now. He was a breaststroke kid like me, and supposedly all but unbeatable. My coach, a tough former collegiate champion in her twenties named Beth, leaned down as the race was about to start.

"He's probably the best you've ever been up against," she said, nodding toward my nemesis in the far lane. I could hear the unspoken words she didn't say, the outcome she was preparing me for: "You might well lose this one, Colin."

I'd decided then as I stared across the pool—intoxicated as always by those pre-race emotional highs—that he was probably a West Hills boy who was ready to look down on me as an East-sider. I wanted to believe he didn't think much of me, that he was arrogant and superior and so deserved to be beaten. Seeing him that way, whether it was true or not, gave me a jolt of fuel. I liked the prickly, sharp feeling that victory would also be about righting some perceived slight or injustice.

But then, just before the start, I thought of my dad and the words he'd said to me that morning as we were heading to the meet.

"Colin, remember the most important thing . . . have fun!" he'd said, reaching over in the car and rustling my hair.

He always said that before a competition, the same thing every time, and usually I barely heard it. I don't think I'd ever really even understood it. But that day I felt something different.

I still wanted to beat West Hills Boy just as badly. He gave me something to prove. But my dad's positive spirit gave me a fuel, too, and as we took off down our lanes, the idea really jelled in my head for the first time that competition could be ferocious and joyous at the same time. I surged, moving through the water with a feeling of happiness that made my strokes all the stronger, and ended up beating West Hills Boy, swimming one of my fastest times ever.

But now, as Rudd's sled slid off the scale back onto the ice, things were much less clear. The scale beckoned. Rudd and the members of the flight team all turned to look at me.

"No, I'm cool, no need to weigh mine," I said. My Mr. Casual act was probably as phony as could be, and I'm sure Rudd saw through it, but I didn't care. I was limiting my losses, trying to avoid one more image that could get stuck in my head and weigh me down like the haunting photo from the South Pole that Rudd had showed me.

Then it was time to go. We hauled the sleds aboard and climbed into a plane that was narrow, tight, and cramped—my sled and Rudd's strapped down side by side, filling the entire space behind the open cockpit, two rows of single-file seats after that running to the back of the plane. Rudd and I were the only passengers.

The Twin Otter, unlike the Ilyushin, at least had a few windows, and as we took off, the view immediately took my breath away. I couldn't pull my face from the window. Mountain ranges anchored the far distance in mottled colors of blue and white. Deep black crevasses looked bottomless, as though they might lead to the center of the earth. The ice seemed timeless and permanent, but it was heaving with change. Recently, billions of tons had broken off from some of the continent's ice shelves into increasingly warm coastal waters, including a monster about the size of Maryland the year before. I squinted, trying to see the ice directly below the plane, then out as far as I could toward the horizon, and the same word captured both perspectives: limitless. I was heading into a place where the regular scales of measurement—in size and harshness of climate and so much else—didn't really apply, and so all the old ways of measuring myself wouldn't apply either. Down on the ice, I'd be the tiniest and most insignificant of specks.

And the plane droned on. Rudd looked out his window as raptly as I did through mine. But then as we were preparing to land at the Messner Start on the edge of the Ronne Ice Shelf to disembark and begin, we looked across the cabin at the same time and nodded to each other.

It doesn't sound like much, I guess. Strangers nod to each other every day in passing. Office workers scuttling off to meetings nod to each other in hallways.

But such a deep gulf separated me and Rudd—in who we were and how we'd come to be there at that moment—that our little nods felt almost like signal flares from distant mountain peaks, inarticulate but poignant at the same time.

With my nod, I sent his way all the wishes I hadn't been able to put into words—sure, we were both going to battle to try to be first, but overall I respected him and hoped only for the best in what would now come. And I felt that he'd sent the same to me.

* * *

AND THAT WAS IT.

The plane shuddered and shook as it landed, its skis rattling on the sea ice. The crew helped me pull off the sled, offered a few bang-bang handshakes of good luck, and jumped back in with a schedule to keep, taxiing off to deliver Rudd to his drop-off a mile away, the same distance as me from the starting line waypoint at the continent's edge.

With a few small steps from the cabin down the plane's little red ladder and onto the Ronne Ice Shelf, I'd left civilization behind. I'd exhaled the last breath of heated air I would know for two months and stepped down from the ladder's final metal step, my calf-high thick-soled polar ski boots crunching onto the ice for the first time. I pulled up the fur collar of the red-and-black windproof jacket that matched my overalls, and adjusted the face mask that left no inch of skin exposed, then arched my arms up overhead to stretch my muscles, stiff from the cramped ninety-minute flight.

They had dumped me off. One minute I was in the world of people, and the next I wasn't. There was no ceremony; there were no inspirational speeches; there was no starting gun. The motor roared, the skis rattled and bumped—off and away. It was a little like being the last passenger on a bus in a strange, forbidding city you don't know, and the driver suddenly opens the door and says, "This is your stop, buddy. Out," and you watch him drive away as you stand there with your suitcase—except that it's twenty-five below zero and your ungainly, awkward suitcase weighs close to four hundred pounds.

I was here finally, after a year of planning, and many years before that, starting in childhood when Antarctica first gripped my imagination, but even more than that, I was really alone.

That's the thing that hit me like a slap to the face as I watched the plane head away.

I'd been to Antarctica once before, climbing Mount Vinson and skiing the last sixty-nine miles to the South Pole from the 89th degree of latitude, a place called, with simple geographic majesty, "the Last Degree." But that effort—part of a world-record project to climb the highest peaks on each continent, with a roughly one-week expedition to both the North and South Poles—had been done with other people by my side.

Now, as I looked around me at a horizon of flat empty whiteness in every direction, glaring sun and ice and nothing else as far as I could see, the plane's buzz fading in the distance, it hit me what a completely different kind of thing this was that I was about to try. I'd understood that it had never been done, crossing to the South Pole and then to the other side of the continent without replenishing supplies or using anything to help propel you but your own body and muscle—that's a lot of what had appealed to me in the testing of my limits, endurance, and grit.

I knew now for certain how tiny and isolated I'd be on that vast expanse of ice through every day and night—twenty-four hours of daylight under a sun that never set, all stretching out before me to the horizon. And I knew that I'd have to dig deeper into myself than I'd ever gone, looking for reserves of energy I could tap and use.

My first grade teacher, Shannon Pannel, understood my energy. She saw a boy who couldn't sit still, and instead of trying to force me into some quiet conformity I probably couldn't have achieved anyway, she had a simple three-word prescription: Burn it off.

"Go and run outside around the playground for fifteen minutes," Ms. Pannel said to me and my best friend, Lucas, after we got into some trouble, egging each other on in some kind of classroom craziness. We went out and sprinted and screamed and jumped as high as we could, and when we came back in I could be, at least for a little while, Colin the student again, not Colin the problem child.

But the dividing line between worlds—where I'd come from and where I was now—seemed huge beyond measure. My life before Antarctica, through the months of training for the project, the fevered dreams in planning it with Jenna, and really my whole life extending back into Ms. Pannel's classroom, sat on one side. I was on the other side, alone in the coldest and emptiest place I'd ever been, and a door had just slammed closed.

I'd need it all if I was going to make it across the ice. I'd have to reach back and find the boy who needed to run, and also the boy who found he could focus and solve problems when the energy was burned off. I'd need to remember my failures and my victories because of what they'd taught me. Rather than needing to burn off excess energy, now I'd need every scrap of emotional and mental fuel I could pull together. I'd have to open the door to my own past to have any hope at all.

THE PLANE WAS GONE. It was time to start moving. That was the crucial thing, if only to stay warm. At twenty-five below, even under the brilliant blinding sun, the body's core temperature can drop fast. I needed to get the muscles cooking.

As I walked over to the sled, I glanced at my watch. Though what I was about to start would be measured in days and weeks rather than minutes or even hours, it seemed important somehow to commemorate the moment and give it at least a little more sense of ceremony than the see-you-later goodbyes from the plane crew. There should be an official starting time, I thought. The watch was silver and steely, a Rolex with a circling second hand, and I thought of my friend Marc, who'd pressed it into my hand and insisted that I borrow it to take with me to Antarctica.

In a visit to his house a month earlier, as Jenna and I were getting ready to go south, he'd looked down at my $10 digital Timex and gasped. "You aren't going to wear *that* down there, are you? Dude, this is a historic expedition. I don't think the Timex is gonna cut it." With his hands on his head in disbelief, he ran upstairs and brought back the watch that he got the day after his first child was born. The birth had been difficult. The watch had a story, he said. It carried good luck.

The Rolex felt good and solid, something human-crafted and fine. I gave it a pat on the glass with my mittened thumb. But just noting the time also seemed inadequate somehow, so I reached into the sled and pulled out my little rectangular GoPro camera, which sat perched at the top of a lightweight tripod. I then pulled off a mitten long enough to grab a tiny battery from my inner jacket pocket—I'd already learned that the camera could function no longer than a few seconds unless the battery was kept warm, kept close to my chest—popped in the battery, and hit the record button.

"Well," I said, looking into the lens, about two feet from my face at the end of the tripod, which I held out like a selfie stick. Then I stopped. I was incredibly excited, charged with adrenaline, but the moment seemed serious, too, and I wanted to get it right. I thought of the old polar explorers glimpsing the ice for the first time as their ships approached the continent, writing the first words of their expedition journals.

"So, here and now on November 3, 2018, at 3:22 p.m. I officially begin," I said, staring into the lens. "Beginnings are simple. You take a step forward. If you're going a thousand miles or a hundred yards, it's the same. And maybe endings are simple, too—my finish line, should I succeed in reaching it, is a post pounded into the ice by the United States Geological Survey at the continent's far side, on the edge of the Ross Ice Shelf. The post even has a name—LOO-JW. I have its coordinates entered in my GPS, as my beacon." I gazed out over the ice, trying to summon something more, something Shackleton or Scott might've said.

"And so it starts," I added, tilting the camera down to my legs as

I walked over toward my sled, then tipping it back up to my face. I shrugged. "So, yeah. That's it."

I switched off the camera, re-stowed the battery, repacked the tripod, and bent down to check the cover and the straps on the sled and make sure all was ready. There were four straps, about two feet apart, used to secure my gear. I'd opened and closed them and cinched them over and over in the previous days, packing and repacking and then checking all over again.

But when I pulled on the very first one, the buckle immediately snapped in my hand, broken into pieces. I leaped back in shock, and instinctively glanced in the direction of the plane, as if I could summon it back. The words I'd just said into the camera about journeys and starts seemed suddenly ridiculous, too, and as I stood there stupidly holding the pieces, the terrible thought whispered in my head: I haven't even taken a single step and things are already breaking.

The buckle had been weak and probably already cracked, I immediately told myself, trying to reset from the shock. It was part of a hand-me-down used sled with a lot of miles on it—nothing more than that, and definitely not any kind of a sign that things were going sideways already. I had a bungee cord in the sled and could make do by tying it to the other straps.

But the other message from the buckle couldn't be sidestepped so easily: Worse problems than this would surely come, and I'd be on my own to solve them. I needed to adapt and improvise and be ready to do those things at any given moment. The buckle was a symbol of my new reality, in which I'd be self-sufficient or I'd fail.

So I tried to banish it from my mind. I'll deal with the next problem when I come to it, I told myself. Turning back around, sled behind me, harness in place, I consulted my compass for due south, straightened my spine, shook my head to clear it, clicked into the bindings of my cross-country skis, and took my first steps.

Because I was pulling a 375-pound sled, the skis weren't there to be used in their traditional way, to glide effortlessly through the snow. Rather, they were really just glorified snowshoes—ones that dispersed my weight and minimized the risk of falling into a crevasse. On the skis' bottom, instead of the slick waxy surface found on a ski racer's equipment, I'd adhered full-length synthetic fur skins. The traction they provided prevented me from sliding backward. Long before synthetic materials were invented, pioneering polar explorers had used sealskins.

Yet even with the traction of my skins, with those first steps it was immediately, horrifyingly clear that I could barely budge the sled at all. A stupid little buckle was the least of my problems. My sled felt anchored and unmovable on the ice. I managed to inch it forward a few yards, but then had to stop, go back, and check it out. Maybe there was something wrong with the harness or the runners. But there was no easy answer.

Whatever we'd done in removing weight, in Chile and again at Union Glacier, and whatever I'd done in training back in Portland, pulling heavy loads up grassy slopes at local parks, enduring endless minutes of planks with my fists in ice buckets, hadn't been enough. My crossing of the Greenland Ice Sheet as a training exercise—four hundred miles in twenty-seven days—hadn't been enough either.

I leaned in and managed a few more steps forward before I had to stop to catch my breath. I had more than nine hundred miles to go, and getting even twenty feet from where the plane had dumped me was already painful.

I became, with every next step, aware of my body—the harness yanking deep into my shoulders, my lower back arching forward to help my legs, which should not, I knew, hurt this much this soon. Something was very wrong and I couldn't help but cry, mostly because, pitifully, I was feeling sorry for myself. I quickly learned how Antarctica dealt with such pity; the tears immediately froze to my face. More ice in a world of ice, and now I was even making it myself.

My entire expedition felt as if it was unraveling and I'd only just begun. I didn't think it could get any worse. And then I saw Rudd.

On the now empty and silent landscape he appeared to my right, heading at an angle from his starting place and moving along smoothly and steadily, it seemed—a military man in full march. He had me in his grip all over again.

He'd found a rhythm and was striding across the snow. He looked strong. More to the point, he was actually moving, and just as with the disappearing plane, I couldn't look away. But then he gradually grew smaller, too, pulling away until he disappeared entirely into the glare.

I was stuck in place. The feeling of being confined and immobilized triggered a memory that suddenly began rolling through my head.

I was in a wheelchair. I could feel the pressure of it against my back, so familiar and strangely comforting even though I despised it to the bottom of my soul. I was twenty-two years old, sitting in the kitchen of my childhood home in Portland.

My mother stood at the edge of the kitchen counter, leaning casually on one elbow. The kitchen lights were on though it was mid-morning—a Pacific Northwest monochrome loop of gloom, drizzle, and gray having settled in outside.

And Mom had placed a chair there in front of her by the counter—straight-backed and wooden, simple and functional, pulled out from the table. The chair was facing me, seat out, and she had her hand on its back.

Up until that moment, I hadn't taken a single step in over a month, and my tightly bandaged legs hung in front of me against the wheelchair.

"It's time, Colin," she said, softly but firmly. "Your entire goal for the day is to get out of that wheelchair and take one step to sit down in this chair instead. Show me that you can do it."

"I'm almost ready," I said with bright phoniness, gazing out the window to the Portland gloom, which felt easier than looking into Mom's eyes. "I'm going to do it."

I wasn't ready, though. I spent three hours staring at that chair just a few feet in front of me. I thought that being in a wheelchair was, in fact, kind of a milestone and I'd come pretty far already after so long in a hospital bed. I thought that I'd be stronger and more healed tomorrow, really ready *then* to get up and try to walk.

Fear is a strange beast, because so often it hinges not on the things we know, but the things we don't. And the what-if fears are the worst, the ones that wake you up at night, half in dream, fearing some wildly irrational possibility that has bubbled up while you slept. What if I can't do it? What if the ankles, tendons, or knees seize up? Worst of all, what if that Thai doctor with the bad skin and broken English was right: "You will probably never walk normally again," he'd said.

Mom wasn't having any more of my delay tactics.

I'd glimpsed her intensity before, and heard plenty of tales about it growing up. I'd pictured her strong, defiant posture at age eighteen standing before a federal judge and being sentenced to a month in jail for an act of civil disobedience and protest that she wasn't about to apologize for. I knew the depth of her commitment to the political and environmental causes she still believed in. That formidable mom was now staring me down across the kitchen.

"One step, Colin, that's all. Just one step," she repeated, this time without as much of a smile as the last time. That told me she was losing patience with me after all these weeks.

I knew she was not going to let me off that easily. One step was, after all, really only one step. The chair would be farther away next time, farther still after that. And I'd declared a month earlier from my hospital bed, legs bandaged to the hip, that I'd do a lot more than walk. I'd vowed to one day complete something I'd never done before or even talked about—a triathlon of swimming, biking, and running. Mom hadn't questioned, just nodded and promised to help, however unrealistic the goal seemed, or in truth really was.

And now she was living up to her half of the bargain, and I could hardly complain. The can-do part of me stirred, pushing me to grip the chair's arm, rustle my legs, and put a tiny bit of weight onto my feet. The what-if part then stilled everything back into place with fear. Surging with new resolve, and wanting so vehemently, so ferociously hard to please my mother, I slowly rose. The what-if Colin was still in there and talking, resisting until the last second putting any weight onto my legs and feet. But I'd finally managed to silence him. I took my first step.

I STRUGGLED ON, with Rudd now long gone in the distance and my skis and sled runners still sinking into the powder. But after three hours, one grunting step forward after another, I'd made it only two miles, and finally I just ground to a stop, feeling like a failure and a fool. The strength to take another step had left me. The frozen tears were making matters worse. Not only did they make me feel pathetic, but they also raised my risk of frostbite. Even worse, despite the cold I was sweating from the hard exertion, which on this Antarctic twenty-five-below-degree day could bring disaster all by itself. "If you sweat, you die" has been a maxim of polar exploration since before the days of Amundsen and Scott, based on the hard reality that damp clothes can freeze against your body in minutes in subzero temperatures, causing hypothermia.

I needed my wife. That's really all I could think. Jenna would be able to see something in this that I couldn't, some way to change course. She'd thought through the project more than I had, more than anyone had. I saw the big picture, but she saw both the picture and the brushstrokes that might make a work of art. She planned better than I, organized better, and saw three steps ahead of me most of the way.

She was flying home from South America to Portland that day, I knew. I pictured her on the plane, reading her book. I saw in my mind how her hair was probably pulled back into a ponytail; I could see her graceful stride walking across Portland International Airport's wonderful and weird teal-colored carpet. I imagined the upstairs office in our house with its view overlooking the Willamette River, the wall maps of Antarctica, and the desk from which she'd be running the expedition. Every image I could grab onto felt far away, untouchably remote from where I stood.

The satellite phone, which I kept in a jacket pocket on my chest— accessible even should I fall into a crevasse or get separated from my sled—managed to catch a signal, bouncing from the bottom of the world, and she answered. I could immediately hear her surprise, even through the crackling static of the connection. The pitch of her voice went up a notch as she heard my voice, clearly bracing herself for something.

But she immediately also announced she was in the car with my mom, which sent its own sharp signal back to me: Colin, don't freak out your mother. If there's disaster to relate, save it, please.

"She just picked me up at the airport," Jenna said brightly. "We're almost to her house."

More code was embedded in that sentence: Save it. Hold on.

So for the next few minutes, as Mom negotiated traffic from the highway into my childhood neighborhood, we talked in generalities. The weather was good, I said. Rudd had passed me, not so good. At the house Jenna jumped out of the car, and I could hear slamming doors and the voice of my stepfather, Brian, in the background, welcoming Jenna home.

Jenna paused, then was back on the line, serious now.

"How's it going?" she said evenly.

"It's really hard," I said quietly, still crying. "The sled is so heavy . . . it's cold and I'm sweating . . ." I rambled on in partial sentences, which were further garbled at Jenna's end by the poor connection.

"What did you say?" she said, though at my own crackly end it sounded something like "Wha . . . ay?" So I repeated the main point, that I was in trouble, and it sounded even worse a second time, because I knew it pointed even more emphatically to a worst-case scenario I wanted to avoid: that I was done, that it was over. I could already imagine the grim message we'd have to put out to friends, followers, and sponsors. Colin O'Brady, who set out to achieve a never-before-completed feat and dubbed it "The Impossible First"— to trek more than nine hundred miles across Antarctica unassisted and unsupported—announced today that Antarctica had done him in after about two miles.

"I think we named the project the right thing, babe," I said. "It looks like it might really be impossible—three hours into a thousand-mile journey pulling the sled and telling everyone I'm going to do this and I'm already having doubts. I think we need a new plan."

"Where are you?" Jenna said.

"What?" I shouted back.

"Where *exactly* are you?"

I told her I was still on the sea ice, not even yet on the landmass of the continent, where the first waypoint, a GPS point of latitude and longitude, marked the actual start. I'd planned on blowing past the place where sea ice met land ice and making another seven miles or more inland before stopping for the night, but now even getting to the waypoint—which I was sure Rudd had blown by—seemed hard to get my head around.

Jenna said she was outside the front door of my parents' house. I imagined her pacing, then sitting on the front step. I'd sat on that step a thousand times. I knew how weak it sounded that I wasn't even to the formal starting place and was already blubbering.

"Okay, Colin, how far are you from the first waypoint?" she said.

My reply sounded labored, even to me. "Point five-four miles," I said, looking at my GPS, though it sounded and felt like a million right then. "We'd figured that ten-hour days would get me across—"

"So we'll reboot," she said briskly. "You're half a mile from the waypoint—let's just get you there for now." She paused for a moment, either thinking what to do next or letting me process what she'd just said. I couldn't tell.

"We're going to come up with a new plan, Colin," she continued. "Tonight you just need to make it to the first waypoint, just that little half a mile. That's all, just the waypoint. If you can do that, you'll feel like you've made some progress."

She stopped again for a second, letting me digest that last bit. Progress. Yes, I nodded to myself. That would help, however miniscule it was.

"And you should eat your full ration of calories, a whole dinner," she continued. "Then call me after you're in your tent and you've checked in with A.L.E. Are you remembering to put on your parka when you stop?"

I could hear in her voice that she was testing me, checking the stability of my mental compass.

That Jenna was concerned enough about me to throw in that gentle nudge—"Hey, you haven't lost your mind entirely yet, right? You're remembering to stay warm?"—made me wince that I'd worried her, and smile that she loved me. And her giving me a little goal to make, however pathetically small it was, meant she was also seeing inside me. She knew what made me tick. Goals were how I functioned, and she'd thrown me an easy one. She knew that I'd grab it and use it to push myself, and at that moment the size of the goal didn't matter.

"The weather is clear and sunny," I said quietly, staring out at the horizon, the sky brilliant and blue, hoping to see Rudd, somewhere out there, slowing down himself. She thought my weather comment was a positive note, I think, because I could hear her brighten up.

"That's great!" she said. I'd meant the exact opposite, and started to say so. If it was this hard pulling the sled on a day that was just bitterly cold—no storm, no whiteout, no ferocious wind—the prospect of truly bad weather was utterly terrifying. I'd thought of telling her that I might've cried myself into a bit of frostbite, but I pulled back from that as well. She had too much on her shoulders already. "Yeah!" I replied back, trying to harness her upbeat energy, sitting there on the front step of the house, a place I knew as well as any in the world and much better than the place I was in now.

It was about 8 p.m. Chilean time in the time zone my watch was set at to coordinate with A.L.E.—so 3 p.m. in Portland—by the time I got to the waypoint, set up camp, got into the tent, and called her.

Across thousands of miles, bouncing up to a satellite and back down to me in my tent, the details poured into my head as she talked—how she'd walked into my mom's house after our earlier conversation and sat down with her around the kitchen table to scribble out thoughts about weight and mileage, food and fuel. Jenna had been hesitant to involve my mom, not wanting to worry or burden her, but couldn't hold it in when my mom saw the signs of trouble in Jenna's face. Mom wouldn't let up, and it all came out.

That I hadn't weighed my sled now really felt like a failure. If I didn't really know for sure how much I was pulling, then a new plan was clearly far harder to calculate. But I didn't know what to say, feeling as if I'd let her down in my weakness back at Union Glacier.

"Okay, Colin, clean slate," Jenna said. "Expectations, disappointments with the day, whatever—put them aside. When you wake up in the morning, you'll see a text outlining everything—how much weight and supplies I think you can cache on the ice at the waypoint," she said. "But right now you need to think about getting a good night's sleep and making six miles tomorrow, if you can. That's your first target."

Sitting in my tent for the first time, I imagined Mom and Jenna, bent over their spreadsheets, side by side, heads almost touching as they consulted. They were sitting in those wonderful plain wooden kitchen chairs—maybe even the one that I'd just been remembering in thinking of the day I'd taken the first step from my wheelchair. Jenna said she'd needed my mom that night, needed to have someone else looking at the numbers, a second pair of eyes. She'd wanted help in bearing the responsibility of the decisions she was making on my behalf.

"Six miles," I repeated. "That's what I need to think about tomorrow."

"Yep, just six miles. You've got this. I love you," she said.

"I love you, too."

I PRESSED THE BUTTON to end transmission and lay back in my bag, listening to the soft rustling of the tent and staring for a long time at the bright red, diffuse spot on the roof, marked by the midnight sun. My tent was big enough to sit up in, barely, but also small enough that when I stretched out, my head and feet were only inches from the tent's opposite ends. It felt claustrophobic but comforting at the same time, lying there anchored down—first night on the ice, first night alone. Around me, the continent stretched out in one direction, sea ice in the other. I was in Antarctica's embrace, separated from the ice by an inch of pad and an inch of sleeping bag.

But everything had just been shifted, subtly but profoundly, by the events half a world away in Oregon.

The two most important women in my life were thinking about how to help me get through this thing, and that made me feel deeply grateful, as I lay hoping for sleep but not finding it. Tomorrow they'd advise me how much of my precious supplies I should leave behind so that I might be able to pull the load I had. They were expressing their love in helping me achieve my dream, while at the same time reducing my margin of safety by reducing the amount of food I'd be taking and narrowing the window through which I might pass to the other side of the continent.

I'd put Jenna and Mom in a terrible position of responsibility. But, in itself, knowing that their decisions were ferociously difficult and painful gave me a new reason to push hard starting tomorrow, if only to honor them in return. And they'd know that I'd push harder precisely for that reason, because they knew me so well. One day at a time was probably all I was ever going to be able to picture of my journey in the days and weeks to come anyway, and the new plan took that fact into account. Six miles. One day. That much I could get my head around.

As I pulled down my sleep mask to block out the sunlight, I felt a wave of confidence based on almost nothing except trust, but that was enough. I was sure the new plan would be precise, strategic, and carefully thought out on my behalf, even though I had only the slightest clue what it would contain.

CHAPTER THREE

You Are Strong, You Are Capable

DAY 2

don't know where it came from, but I woke with a phrase. My
alarm beeped, I pulled off the eye mask that helped me block
the sun, and there it was, and it had to be said aloud. "Colin," I
shouted into my tent to the empty, cold continent around me. "You
are strong! You are capable!"

No matter how loud I shouted it, the sentiment was still mostly
blind optimism. But I have always believed that we are the stories
we tell ourselves. This mantra was a story I would have to tell myself
over and over again to believe it. It seemed like everything in my
little universe of tent and ice should know the phrase, too. "Colin,"
I said to my stove as I lit it. "You are strong! You are capable." My
shoulder muscles still aching from the first day's effort, and my row
of mittens, masks, and neck warmers, suspended the length of the
tent on a clothesline, needed to get the message too, loud and clear.

The new Colin was roaring into the day, leaving the disaster of
yesterday behind, and embracing a new plan and new hope. Even
my bowels seemed to get the strong and capable signal, I thought as
I clambered out into the little vestibule at the end of the tent. The

vestibule-bathroom, which was sort of like the tent's front porch—ice for a floor, only a single layer of nylon overhead—was much colder than inside the tent, where solar radiation could sometimes heat the air to just above freezing, which was balmy compared to the well-below-zero temperature outside. But on that morning of new commitment, the cold front porch air felt almost welcome and invigorating as I dug a hole to squat over.

Then it came down to choices, which weren't as easy.

The text from Jenna had arrived, as promised, and I sat there in my sleeping bag, reading it over and over on my inReach, feeling my heart pounding in my chest. The inReach, a handheld electronic device, which also functioned as my GPS indicator, was the only way to reliably send and receive rudimentary text messages via satellite transmission on the ice—cell phones being useless and satellite phones not much better in their often static-filled connections. In a few terse sentences, she said she thought I could remove five more days' worth of food off the sled, which would take me down to only fifty-five days of supply.

Fifty-five! The number shouted in my head. After the horrible first afternoon, struggling to make barely two and a half miles, then in the tent gobbling down a whole day's rations as though I'd earned them—fifty-five gave me the shivers beyond the deep cold that had penetrated into me through my first night on the ice. I read the text again, then looked down at my supplies. I had six dry bags, each with ten days of rations, each day in its own one-gallon Ziploc bag, which made it easy to feed myself—one Ziploc's worth per day, every one exactly the same, day after day. About half a day's calories came from things like oatmeal, ramen, soup, and freeze-dried dinners that I ate inside my tent, and half from the protein-dense Colin Bars I ate in small bites through the day while pulling my sled.

"Take out ten Ziploc bags of daily rations, keep the Colin Bars from each bag, and cache the rest of the food from those bags at the waypoint," the text said. "The net result leaves you with five days of food weight off the sled, and on your final days of the expedition you'll have to depend more on the bars, which are the most calorie-dense and efficient food you've got anyway. But, don't worry about that now—we'll cross that bridge when we come to it."

Five days' worth of food laid aside seemed like a huge amount. But then came the troubling thought of how many miles I had to go on those now more limited rations. Jenna had said yesterday that she and Mom were doing new numbers on a mileage plan, so I shouldn't think about that, but I couldn't help it. From where I sat, more than five hundred miles were left just to the South Pole, and the Pole was just another waypoint, not even close to the finish line at the continent's other edge. Divided by fifty-five . . . even if I managed six-mile days . . . I started to do the math and stopped myself. No, the day-by-day plan was what I needed to focus on now, the one Jenna had worked through last night. Six miles I could imagine, so I said it to myself again, aloud. "Six miles!" I shouted in the tent.

"We worked out ten-day sections," Jenna said in her text. "The sled will get lighter as you go, as you eat and burn fuel. The 375 pounds we figure you have now is temporary, Colin. You'll be able to go more miles per day in each section, pulling less weight behind you. It'll be more like Greenland, eventually."

Eventually. I liked that. It was something to look forward to. I'd successfully pulled a much lighter sled for four weeks across the Greenland Ice Sheet earlier that year in training for Antarctica, and the idea that my dead-weight behemoth here on the ice with me now could slim down at some point to a Greenland weight was tantalizing.

But the margins were clearly tight. The new plan, if it worked, would get me across the continent with exactly the amount of food I needed and no more. It had me arriving at the edge of the Ross Ice Shelf, 930 miles away, in fifty-five days with little cushion for down days, blizzards, error, or injury.

But her text then went further.

"Is there anything else in your other supplies that you want to rethink?" she wrote. "This is the last, last chance to leave anything, Colin. You should think about all of the gear in the sled and decide for yourself what you can really do without."

I stopped and looked around the tent—at the crucial little circle of things from stove to extra clothes that all felt, just then, really important—then back to the text to read it again. I knew what she was saying. There were clearly other things she'd thought of that I might cache down in the snow at the waypoint. And she'd known, too, that crews from A.L.E. would return to the Messner Start, to drop off or pick up people on future expeditions, and could pick up the cache. But in the leave-no-trace ethic of the Antarctic expedition world, and the ethic I'd been raised with, by parents who'd taught me that public lands were sacred, she was right—this was the last, last chance. After this, there'd be no other place to leave anything behind.

But Jenna—and my mother, I suspect, in consultation—had been afraid to put specific suggestions on the list. They were already reducing my margin of safety in telling me to cache food. To then go beyond food, and urge me to get rid of gear that could be crucial in other ways—that was clearly a bridge too far, which I immediately understood. It was another step I'd have to take by myself.

I ate my protein powder–fortified oatmeal without really tasting it, thinking through which of my belongings would be critical. There were no clear scientific answers. There were traditions and handed-down nuggets of wisdom about equipment and supply on the ice, but anything never before done—whether it's a previously unclimbed mountain or a new way of attempting to get through and across an ocean or a continent—brings with it the possibility of old answers not working for new questions.

As I packed my stove, grabbed my thermos, and braced myself for the day, I started to picture everything that was out there packed and folded on the sled. It had all seemed important once. That's why it was there. Now I needed to reset, start over, throw out the decisions that had seemed easy back in our garage in Portland when we'd laid out everything.

And I wanted to have as many decisions made as possible before I unzipped the tent and headed out, knowing that the brutal cold could make me rush. I was afraid I'd tilt too far in my haste and anxiety and make mistakes, pulling things off the sled I shouldn't, or leaving things on the sled that would drag me down.

As soon as I was out in the elements, I knew my fears about rushed decisions had been well founded. The cold hit me with a body blow—almost thirty below zero according to the little thermometer clipped to the bottom of my jacket—and it felt as though it was trying to get at me, claw through the layers of parka, mittens, mask, and then to the base layers beneath. I stiffened with the force of it, feeling my muscles clench, as though trying to hold in the heat. I took a deep breath and felt the cold grip my lungs.

The tent was my first priority, and so I methodically set to work on that, pulling the stakes up from the ice, folding the poles, rolling it all up in preparation to pack on the sled. I wanted all the things I absolutely had to do done before tackling the hard things, the decisions that from this moment would certainly ripple out in importance.

I chose the ice axe immediately. I could cache that. In bringing the axe, and insisting from the very beginning that I'd need it, I'd been thinking of mountain climbing and crevasses, and forty-five-degree slopes—places where one bad step will take you to your death. Only toward the end of my journey across Antarctica, on the Leverett Glacier, should I make it that far, would I hit terrain where blue-ice crevasses were common, running down deep into the ice.

But as I held the axe there in my hand, I had second thoughts. It felt so reassuringly solid, sitting there in the palm of my mitten, its silver blades gleaming in the sun. An axe had saved me before, when I'd slipped on Mt. Hood in Oregon when I was sixteen. Back then, I'd been able to dig the tool into ice and arrest my fall, saving my life, and now I was getting ready to leave behind the only one I had, with more than nine hundred miles of unknown terrain ahead.

I could hear Jenna's voice in my head as I laid it down in the pile by the five bags of food. "You sure?" She'd remember my insistence back in Portland that the ice axe was a must-have, and she knew from experience herself, in her own climbing, that an axe could be the most unnecessary and burdensome of things until suddenly it was the most important.

The Leverett has been mapped pretty well, I said to myself. I think I'm fine. At that moment the Leverett felt sort of theoretical, too, so far out into the distance it felt almost like an alternative future that might or might not happen. I'd face the Leverett—and whatever risks came with it—if and when I got there, eight hundred miles from now.

I'm going to leave my spare thermos, too, I thought, grabbing it from inside the sled. That one was scarier and harder, partly because I knew Rudd had specifically mentioned having a backup. If a thermos breaks, or its seal gets compromised in some way, you're finished, he'd said, because the water inside will freeze solid, and once it has you'll never get it out. Then you have no way to store any melted water, he'd said, which would mean having nothing to drink during the day when you were outside and couldn't stop to melt snow. Antarctica's cold, dry air would suck the moisture out of you. Dehydration would be imminent.

By then, I was rushing, just as I'd feared I might. I'd put on my extra parka layer, but even then—masked and goggled up in my layers and mittens—I was getting colder by the minute. It was crucial to get my decisions right, and just as crucial that I finish the task as quickly as possible to preserve my body heat. Kneeling on the ice, pawing through the sled was precise and detailed work, better suited to a warm living room or a kitchen table, and didn't use the big muscles in my legs, arms, and torso that kept me warm in pulling the sled. Worse still, the wind had kicked up, sending a stab of cold that felt like ice water had been poured through a tiny gap in my neck warmer and down my back.

But bit by bit, I added tiny things to the pile. Most, I knew, made almost no difference in weight. An extra stick of lip balm. A small tube of sunscreen. Half the needles from my repair kit. But taking them out felt like simplification, as if I was stripping down more than weight. I was unburdening myself of entanglement, of things and possessions, civilization itself. Things were in my way, and the fewer I had of them, the better, at least for my mindset, if not the actual physical effort itself.

I stopped for a second when I got to the bag with cleaning and first-aid supplies. There'd be, of course, no way to bathe or shower in Antarctica—any liquid water, made with snowmelt on my stove, was too precious to use for anything but drinking and cooking. So back in Portland, we'd put in seventy days' worth of little prepack-aged wet wipes—one per day in cleaning up whatever part of me needed it. At Union Glacier, I'd pulled out half of that, to thirty-five. Now I grabbed most of what was left and threw them into the pile, too. Ten wet wipes and a roll of toilet paper would do for the next two months.

Jenna had led me to this path, stripping down and stripping out, without ever saying anything directly. And there was a sweet and delicate history to that back-and-forth. We'd both known that any decisions compounding my risk at this moment had to come from me. But I also knew from experience that she was the great anchoring backstop of logic and reason in our relationship. If she thought I was going too far too fast along the edge of a cliff, she'd pull me back—not so much in fear but in clarity because she could see where the drop-off was and I often could not. And yet she found that place at the edge of things attractive, too, in her own way, and it was in that complex swirl of chemistry that we'd met, twelve years earlier, on an absurdly tiny island in the middle of the Pacific Ocean.

I'd landed on the main Fijian island of Viti Levu—twenty-two, fresh out of college, and off to see the world with savings from my summer job painting houses—but had decided on an impulse to take a boat out to one of the smallest nearby islands, a beautiful little patch of sand and palm trees about the size of a city block. It had some shacks with bunks, great waves offshore, a bar, and nothing else. So the waves called out to me, and then the bar did.

And in the bar was a girl. She was with a group of female friends, none of whom I noticed for even a second—just her. Sipping my budget Fiji Bitter, I watched how she brushed the hair back from her face, and how she seemed to pay such close attention to her friends when one spoke.

Okay, I thought, taking another sip. I'm here in the most unlikely of places, and so is she. What have I got to lose? So I just walked up and said hi, and after a few minutes of small talk about incredibly tiny Polynesian islands, asked her name.

"Jenna," she said as she stood, looking me straight in the eyes and drawing me in with her infectious smile. She was tall and slender, had sun-kissed brown hair, and was wearing a white bikini. "And you're the surfer dude—I noticed you down on the beach."

"It's a small beach," I said with a nervous smile, unable to take my eyes off hers—her left iris had a little diagonal line running across it and it looked almost like a tiger stripe. But what I was really thinking was that she'd noticed me. On a speck of sand in the middle of a vast ocean—a place I'd stumbled onto by mere chance—something had happened, and a spark had jumped between us. Over the next couple of days hanging out in paradise, I learned she was from Massachusetts and that she was studying in Sydney, Australia, for a semester abroad from college, and when I left the island, I stowed in the bottom of my bag the paperback book I'd been reading on the island. I was traveling without a cell phone so I'd asked Jenna to write down her phone number on the back cover.

I wanted to make sure the book didn't somehow get lost. It was a number I knew I'd call.

BUT NOW I WAS HERE, kneeling on the ice trying to figure out what I needed, and Jenna was far away. The pile grew.

When I got to the extra tent poles in the bottom of the sled—a full replacement set for the ones threaded into their sleeves that sprung the tent into shape, now on the ice, rolled and ready to load—I paused for a few seconds, weighing them in my hand. I gave them a bounce, up and down, making another little calculation of cost, benefit, and risk. The spare tent poles can go, I said to myself. I don't think I'm going to need them.

Choices are complicated. I stared down at the pile I'd made. It felt as if I'd drawn an invisible line on the ice, separating things that were utterly crucial to my life from things that would soon be gone forever and out of my reach, and I'd been forced to dig around somewhere deep inside myself to see the difference.

It felt strangely familiar, like "Switch Day."

The every-Wednesday ritual of Switch Day, which shaped my life from the sixth grade through high school, was a product of my parents' divorce when I was ten and my sister Caitlin was twelve. The shared custody arrangement—going from Mom's house to Dad's and then back the other way—was amicable and easy, with Mom's new house just eight blocks away from the family house where Dad still lived. But shared custody also meant we were always either coming or going, with Switch Day approaching or just over.

Things, possessions, objects—what to take, what to leave in one house or the other, and how to travel as lightly as possible—had defined the rhythm, as my sister and I were driven back and forth by Mom or Dad, then later by Caitlin herself, in her beloved hand-me-down Mazda 626. Two laundry baskets always rattled in the backseat. Mine had a week's worth of clothes and shoes jammed and stuffed into it in no particular order, with my book-stuffed school backpack plunked down on top like a lid. Caitlin, two years older and already more precise than I—in the process of becoming, in a small way, the exacting scientist she'd become in college—actually packed her Switch Day things. Her clothes were folded and laid down in layers, which always impressed me because I couldn't imagine doing that.

The Switch Day drive became an anchor of how I came to understand and experience the idea and reality of divorce. Switch Days taught me to travel lightly, to live lightly. Take the things you need, what will fit into a basket, and no more. I loved the weekly hand-off partly for that reason, being forced to choose the things I'd need and realizing as I did how short the list really was. That extra pair of jeans? Unnecessary. One would do. A second hoodie or sweater? Extra weight that would just sit there unused.

But even before their divorce, my parents—in living the values they'd built their lives around as organic farmers, then health-food store workers—had instilled in my sister and me the idea that choices would shape our lives. That started with food. Whole grains and organics, they taught us, were the yellow brick road of righteousness, and lots of corporations were out there making and selling the exact opposite—unhealthy things that my parents said exploited human weaknesses for sugar, fat, salt, and artificial ingredients of every sinister kind. Around our kitchen table "the industrial food complex" was a kind of whispered curse phrase.

Choosing became a parlor game in our house, often centering on the bags of mysterious free product samples my dad, the natural food store's purchasing manager, would bring home. They'd been sent from manufacturers hoping to get their products on the store's shelves, and my sister and I were enlisted, over and over, as food-testing guinea pigs. "Five new kinds of alternative nondairy milk, kids!" my dad would say cheerily. "Tell me which ones you like, or hate!" Snack time came from the sample bag, in the form of high-fiber crackers, odd nut spreads, and fake cheese. "Alternative non-wheat cereals for breakfast, kids! Dig in and give me a report!"

I only realized gradually as I got older that the choices game, and the bag after bag of product samples that rolled into our kitchen and onto the table, were also part of a hard calculus of choice by my parents. They were living their values in the work they did at the store, which paid very little, and also living those values in feeding us bulk rice and beans multiple times a week. Making free samples fun disguised a truth that they were often, in fact, dinner itself, a necessary component to make ends meet. My parents were doing their best to feed us, and making some of the toughest choices themselves along the way.

AFTER ABOUT TEN MINUTES of deciding what to leave behind, the cold was seeping its way into me. I needed to get moving. I could feel it creeping around the edges of my mittens and boots, looking for gaps. So I gathered my little pile of choices on the ice, and was instantly full of second thoughts. A part of me feared I'd need it all and it should go back on the sled, while the other part of me thought what I'd extracted was minimal and that I'd gone through the struggle and cold for nothing.

But I was also quickly learning that Antarctica doesn't allow for indecision. You do or you don't. You act and you move and you hope for the best. Pondering takes time, and time spent in indecision can freeze you. So I dug a little hole, picked up the little cache of items in my arms—about twenty pounds' worth, I'd estimated, mostly from the food—and, without ceremony, buried it under the snow at the waypoint coordinates. There was little else to do by then but stuff my extra parka into the front of the sled, strap down the cover, and harness up.

I'd tried to lower my expectations as I prepared to actually start for the day and begin pulling, but I still hoped and imagined that twenty pounds—all those things I might potentially need, now gone—would be worth the nagging worry they'd caused.

When the harness straps dug into my shoulders and waist with the first lunge forward, though, it felt precisely the same as yesterday, like the straps had hands—strong, cruel grasping hands that wanted to drag me back, and fingers that dug into the flesh around my stomach and shoulders.

After a few puffed breaths, I stopped and looked back. The sled, six feet behind me at the end of the rope connected to my harness, looked sadly the same, too, its yellow cover bulging with what were now clearly absolute necessities. What could be stripped out was gone, and before long I found myself, as I had the day before, crying into my goggles again, if only from the frustration. Another day, with more ice where you didn't want it. Despite all of the training and preparation to pull this heavy sled and survive in these brutal conditions, my body felt weak. In that moment I understood that the outcome of this journey would ultimately be decided by the strength of the muscle six inches between by ears, my mind.

The waypoint, I knew, even as I struggled to move past it, was hugely significant—in the struggle to reach it on that first day and in the potentially momentous decisions I'd made there. It marked the beginning of the continent, but also, in a way, the end of what now felt like a prelude. The long arc of events that had landed me in Antarctica—the trek across Greenland, the panicky, nervous insecurity about my preparations, the strange interludes with Rudd on the plane and at Union Glacier, in some ways the entirety of my whole life to that point—had brought me to the waypoint as a first test, a hurdle to be cleared in preparation for the real challenges in the days and weeks ahead.

And as hard as it still was, with the snow still deep, full of soft, unstable drifts that would collapse down under me and the sled with deep groaning crunches from my weight and the sled's weight behind me, the words that really started swirling in my head were gratitude and humility.

Whatever happened from this morning on, I told myself, I was standing on the shoulders of giants. The inspirational path of the polar pioneers before me, and what they'd taught the world about endurance, strength, and perseverance, was the foundation of everything I was attempting.

Those early explorers had mostly started with questions. Norwegian pioneers like Nansen and Amundsen had reached out in humility, asking native Inuit villagers across Greenland and Canada the simplest and most profound questions: How do you survive? What do you wear and eat and how do you protect yourself from the cold in an environment that can kill you so easily?

When they headed to Antarctica, where human civilizations had never managed to penetrate at all, those pioneers concluded that the great white continent was essentially a giant math problem. Weight was part of the equation, but the deeper and more challenging part was how much food and calories they'd get for the weight of the food they carried, and what methods and means they'd use to cross that landscape, which in turn would affect the other variables.

In the modern era, the distinctions got even finer grained, often relating to whether an effort on the ice was supported or unsupported by resupplies of food or fuel cached or provided along the route, and/or assisted or not by any means other than muscle. The Norwegian adventurer Børge Ousland in many ways defined the terrain of astonishing modern Antarctic feats, becoming the first person to cross Antarctica solo when he traveled eighteen hundred miles alone in sixty-three days from late 1996 to early 1997. Not only did he cross the entire landmass of Antarctica, but he also crossed the full Ronne and Ross Ice Shelves from the ocean's edge. Ousland's expedition, which had deeply inspired me, was unsupported in that he'd hauled all his food and fuel with no resupplies, but, importantly, *assisted* in that he'd used a parachute-like kite called a parawing, harnessing the wind to pull him across on the ice. His team proudly announced that on one day with particularly favorable winds—parawing deployed—Ousland had sped 125 miles in only fifteen hours. A single-day distance unfathomable without wind assistance.

Rudd and I now, Henry Worsley in 2016, and Ben Saunders in 2017 set a different goal. Each of us was trying to become the first person to cross the landmass of Antarctica via the South Pole completely alone with only what we could carry behind us, with no resupplies, as Ousland had. But unlike Ousland, Rudd and I were relying on human power alone. Without the assistance of a kite like a parawing, the math of what I had to carry with me was even more unforgiving.

The equation was at the very heart of everything, and it was one of the reasons why no one had ever been able to do what Rudd and I were attempting, and why so many people thought it impossible: If I carried too much food, my load would be so heavy I probably wouldn't make it across without assistance. And if I carried less food, I could go faster but then I might run out.

And as I pushed into the morning after the unburdening at the waypoint, as I thought of that first morning on the ice, I flashed back to a hotel room in Whistler, British Columbia, a few days after Christmas the year before. Jenna and I had just come in from a long day of skiing. We dumped our gear by the front door of the hotel room, and Jenna walked over to the fireplace to get warm and check her phone. I was pouring water in some glasses when she suddenly gasped.

"Oh my God," she exclaimed, looking over at me. I tensed, braced for some family news or a disaster unfolding somewhere in the world. Her mother had only a few weeks earlier been diagnosed with cancer, and Jenna had just come back for New Year's Eve, after being by her mom's side through the surgery and post-op over the

Christmas holiday. Jenna had a special bond with her mom, who'd raised Jenna, her only child, as a single mother. If there'd been some sudden bad turn in the prognosis—my mind started reeling off the possibilities—we'd need to get back east immediately. I started thinking flight schedules and airport logistics.

"Ben Saunders is ending his expedition," Jenna said quietly. "He just posted to his blog."

She looked back down and immediately began to read aloud: " 'Standing here with less food for the remainder of my journey than I'd planned, with a safety margin that I felt was too slim, I have decided at this time to end my expedition at the Pole.' "

"Oh my God is right," I said, slumping onto the couch.

Jenna and I had been rooting wildly for Saunders, and we'd followed every twist and turn of the plot on his blog as he pushed relentlessly toward the South Pole, aiming to fulfill the dream that Henry Worsley had chased to complete the first solo, unsupported, and unassisted crossing.

He seemed invincible. He'd been invincible back in 2013–14, retracing the steps of the Scott Expedition to the South Pole. But in this latest effort the math of food and supply had tripped him up, as it had so many Antarctic explorers. He'd arrived at the South Pole fearing he didn't have enough food to make it all the way across.

There was more, though, as I learned when I found his blog on my own phone and began to read.

Saunders, writing as he awaited a flight to take him home, said he'd become fearful. He'd fallen so many times in passing through the twisting canyons of sastrugi—as the parallel wind-carved hills of ice are called—that his mind had begun to roll through dire implications and potential consequences. As I read, I knew exactly the place Saunders's mind had gone: the fear loop. I'd been there, feeling trapped in a maze where every option feels dangerous and escape seems impossible. And sastrugi zones aren't just places where you can fall—they're also off the map in a way, places where rescue would be difficult and delayed, if not impossible, because planes can't land there.

"I slipped and lost my balance many times in the 450 kilometers or so of sastrugi I encountered," Saunders wrote. "And I recall the moment I suddenly imagined falling and breaking an arm or a wrist. How would I put my tent up? What if I fell and knocked myself out?"

Staring out the hotel window, looking at Whistler Village, I felt dizzy, as though I'd just fallen on the ice. Saunders had seemed so close to finding the secret, solving Antarctica's brutal math problem, bashing through the physical and psychological barriers of a solo crossing.

I joined Jenna at the window, and we looked for a long time out at the ski slopes, and the light snow that had begun to fall. She could see where I'd gone, knew the wheels that had begun spinning inside my head. Saunders, as much as I'd wanted him to make it, had left a thousand questions lying on the table. If anyone was capable of a truly solo, unsupported, unassisted continental crossing, it was Ben. So did that mean it was really impossible? And where would you even start in trying to figure the answer one way or another?

As usual, Jenna was ten steps ahead of me, answering questions to herself I hadn't even said aloud or even thought of.

"Yup, here we go. This is it," she said with a faint smile, reaching over to take my hand. "I think I know what we're going to be working on for the next year."

THROUGH THAT AFTERNOON after the first waypoint, I felt rattled by the choices I'd made that morning in pulling things off the sled, decisions I could no longer go back and fix. I kept picturing the hole I'd dug in the snow. I saw the food down there, now frozen solid, and the ice axe and thermos, covered in darkness and snow. And that mental loop of images made the physical work I was doing in pulling the sled feel even harder. By midday I felt every muscle in my back and shoulders from the harness.

But I got to my allotted and assigned six miles, as my GPS told me, and then decided I could, and must, keep going and add some more. I ultimately pushed on to cover just over nine miles. By the time I stopped to make camp, I was almost as exhausted as I'd been that first night. I was feeling stupid and slow, stumbling around, thick in my thinking and clumsy in my movements as I set up the tent.

When I crawled inside, I knew I had only a few minutes before I'd almost certainly pass out, and there were two crucial things to do: I texted Jenna that I was in the tent and safe, and set my alarm. Then I fell facedown onto my sleeping bag wearing all my gear and was gone, falling instantly to sleep as though into an abyss, bottomless and dark.

I woke with a jolt, in the same facedown position and drooling, when the alarm beeped me back into consciousness. It was 8:50 p.m. I hadn't overslept, but it was right at my deadline: The Antarctic logistic transport company, A.L.E., required a call every night at exactly that time to give them my location—back at Union Glacier, Rudd and I had been told that under no circumstances should we ever forget. If you missed two consecutive nightly check-ins, A.L.E. would assume you were incapacitated or injured and would scramble to send a rescue, attempting to get to your last-known location, *if* weather permitted. My GPS location was also being tracked live to the world—anyone with internet could check to see where I was—but in my nightly required call to A.L.E. I felt like a buoy in the middle of the ocean. The mother ship needed to know I was still afloat.

I dialed in. The person who picked up, an Australian in his early twenties named Tim, wasn't interested in conversation, or me in particular, just the facts. It was, for him, simply another shift inside the Comms Box, which is what A.L.E. called the tiny, modified cargo container at Union Glacier that served as information central. If

A.L.E. had brought you to the continent, and you were out there somewhere, Tim or one of the other two workers who manned the box around the clock was your contact.

"Ready?" Tim said, getting right down to business after I identified myself. I gave him my latitude and longitude and miles traveled that day, picturing him at one of the tiny desks, fingering a laptop, phone maybe crooked up to his ear by a shoulder, thinking about home maybe, or Bondi Beach on a sunny summer day outside Sydney. He had a life off the ice, and that thought suddenly brightened my mood.

He was real, and I'd become, it suddenly felt, a bit less real. In my stripped down post-waypoint life, the new strong and capable Colin was also far smaller than he'd been before, as though the stripping down had gone farther than intended. I'd become, to Tim and the world, a digital blue dot on a computer map, blinking my little existence on a website tracker. Tomorrow, my dot would move a bit or it wouldn't, and that was as basic as it got.

After I hung up, that idea kept resonating. As I melted my snow and ate my reconstituted Thai noodles, watching the tent flutter around me, it occurred to me that maybe the simplified, stripped down life—the life of a digital dot—had things to teach.

My life was certainly not uncluttered, I thought, as I looked around my jammed living space, where just about every square inch, from the tent floor to the clothesline running end to end, had a hard pragmatic function. It was a smelly, drippy world of bags and boots and coats.

But at that moment, it also felt like a palace of wonders since, undeniably, it was shelter in a place of brutality. I was out of the wind. I was out of my harness. I was fed. In my forty below zero–rated sleeping bag and my hat pulled down low, I'd be warm through the night to come. And that seemed, just then, like more than enough.

CHAPTER FOUR

The Suggestion

DAY 3

I didn't want to do it. I really didn't. I knew, in trying to think rationally, that it was a tiny thing, a little pinprick and a few drops of blood. Big deal. I'd experienced far worse pain than that in just the last hour, like the pain that had built to a fever pitch in my neck and shoulders from the strain of my harness as I trudged across the ice. Every day so far had offered a menu of large and small pains greater than a little needle jabbed into my finger.

But the finger prick did seem like something I could put off, if I chose to, in a sea of hurts and aches I couldn't. So I sat there staring, needle in hand, feeling a little ridiculous and weak, but also sort of powerful—in a pathetic way. The weakened, hurting self could take a stand, there in the tent: Look at me. I am strong. See me avoid pain.

Finally the absurdity of it got to me and I jabbed. Four red blots went onto four swabs. I scrawled the date on a slip of paper, and tucked it into the tiny plastic envelope.

I flashed back to that day in Dr. John Troup's office when that part of the journey had begun. It was the understated office of a

54

man who mostly worked from his lab—the domain of a scientist clearly more passionate about what he did than where he sat. He was square-jawed, with short gray hair, and had a warm presence. I liked him immediately. "Remember, the samples have to stay frozen, they can degrade pretty quickly," he'd said, glancing up from his papers at his desk in the lab.

Jenna and I, in chairs across from him, glanced at each other and tried to keep a straight face, holding our silence. Finally, after a brief, puzzled look, he'd gotten his own set-up punch line: Keeping something frozen in going across Antarctica would be the least of my problems. "Oh, right," he said with a smile.

Dr. Troup, who has a PhD in nutrition science and metabolism, knows a universe of things about food, but when we met him, not a lot about polar exploration and the weird history of Antarctic dining that echoes down to this day. As a vice president of clinical science, education, and innovation at Standard Process, the Wisconsin whole-food supplement company that was sponsoring my project, his goal was to figure out what I should eat, and definitely not eat, once I hit the ice.

"Some expeditions have subsisted on things like salami and crackers," I told him. "There's a whole weird mystique about dried meat, probably because the old polar heroes ate it."

"No, no, no," he said emphatically, waving his hand as though salami represented some evil spirit that had just stomped into the room. "Very inflammatory, especially for how long you're going to be out there—I think we can do something better."

I told him what I knew about pemmican, a kind of meat paste that European polar explorers had adapted from old Native American recipes, and Amundsen's special formula for pemmican in 1911. He'd added oatmeal and peas to the mix, providing some fiber, which was considered a crucial element in keeping him and his men healthy and regular. Scott and his men carried ordinary pure-meat pemmican, sometimes mixed with hard navy biscuits.

"Oatmeal and peas," Dr. Troup said, looking up sharply. "Yes. Antioxidants. B Vitamins."

Standard Process had promised to build me a super-food that would be compact, nutrient-rich, and—most intriguing of all—designed entirely around how my body worked and processed food. The blood samples had begun that day in the lab along with the first of a battery of treadmill stress tests and skin-prick examinations meant to tell him and his team what compounds my body reacted negatively to. About seventy different food compounds ultimately popped up on the no-no list, many of which I'd eaten for years seemingly without any bad results or allergic reactions. But in Antarctica, Dr. Troup said, food would be different. Extreme physical effort in an extreme environment could elevate the tiniest of things to huge importance. "Inflammatory" was one of Dr. Troup's scary words. The way he wielded it reminded me of my parents and their fears of industrial food.

"Personalized nutrition. That's what it is. The food we create has to *choose* you in a way," said Dr. Troup, who was in his mid-fifties, a hiker and former collegiate swimmer. He knew the world of exertion, not just chemistry. "The calories it contains have to burn clean," he said. "Specific to how your body burns calories."

Through the months that followed, I made repeated visits to the Standard Process Nutrition Innovation Center, their dedicated whole food science lab in North Carolina, for medical follow-up tests and taste tests. Eventually a little brown thing Dr. Troup and his colleagues dubbed a "Colin Bar" emerged.

In contrast to most other historic polar expeditions' food supplies, this solution was entirely plant-based. Coconut oil was the main ingredient, partly because of what was revealed about my gut and how my body worked—and what was, God forbid, inflammatory—but also partly because of the temperature at which coconut oil solidifies and melts. If I kept a bar with me as I worked on the ice, in a pocket close to my skin, my body heat would thaw and soften it and make it edible by the time I reached for it. The combination of seeds and nuts was also fatty, and added some protein without a lot more weight. The texture and flavor was then tweaked again and again. Dr. Troup's team went for slightly grainy, but not crumbly, slightly chocolatey, but not so much that I'd get sick of it, and above all, by the bucketful, calories. Four thousand calories' worth of Colin Bars, cut up into bite-sized pieces, could fit into a jacket pocket, amounting to more than half my daily total.

But Dr. Troup was no salesman.

"It's a slurry of whole food—nuts, fruits and vegetables, plus our proprietary blend of plant-based supplements customized to give your body the exact phytonutrients it needs," he said proudly, then stiffened a little as he heard his own words. "Sorry, that doesn't sound very appetizing, does it?"

I laughed. "Regardless of your description, they actually taste really good. I'm impressed." I was fascinated to be learning so much about the science of high performance and nutrition, but the trade-off for all that science was that I became part of the science project. Standard Process wanted results in the field. Eating the bars in volume, day after day through the expedition, made me a perfect candidate for their research, hence the request for blood samples. So I'd dutifully started stabbing myself, once a week starting on one of my first nights on the ice, as the good doctors had ordered.

What Dr. Troup and his team couldn't test, or know, was what that huge load of fat, day after day, would do to my system when I wasn't used to eating like that, or in those conditions. There was no timeline or stress test to show how my body, and my gut, would adapt to eating thousands of calories of super-high-fat Colin Bars day after day for weeks. Trying to crack the code on this solo Antarctica project was a step into the unknown; there was no playbook. I asked Dr. Troup if he thought the Colin Bars would work, and he simply replied, "The proof will be in the pudding."

*   *   *

OVER THE NEXT FEW DAYS, as I struggled to follow Jenna's mileage plan, it often felt as if I was dragging an anchor behind me rather than a sled. Runners built to slide on the ice, weighed down by all I carried, seemed instead to be digging in with every step I took, trying to drag me back and pull me down. I also knew, because Jenna was tracking Rudd's progress by monitoring his nightly blog posts, that he was still moving along steadily, which didn't help my state of mind.

But it was only when I experienced my first real Antarctic white-out that I began to realize how much my perception of physical things—aching shoulders and legs, cold that creeps in and jabs you like a knife—was tied up with what I could or couldn't see.

Whiteouts aren't just about the strange blank light. I was pre-pared for that. What startled me was how much the whiteness grabbed onto me, pulled me in, and closed up the world even tighter, down to the little bubble of me and my sled. The light flat-tened completely, erasing the horizon of every defining boundary and eliminating all the contrasts of light and subtle differences of ice.

Almost instinctively, I felt the need to bundle up even more, as though the cold could penetrate more deeply under such conditions. I pulled my hood up tighter, checked my mask for gaps, and grabbed my snow skirt, which extended down onto my thighs, adding an extra layer of protection to my legs.

And gradually my mind began to fill the empty space around me, too, not with visions or things that I knew weren't real—though I'd prepared myself for that as well—but with memories. As I went deeper into the textureless landscape, it began to seem that the tex-ture of memory was everywhere, and that I wasn't merely recalling events and conversations but real and starkly observed scenes as if in a waking dream.

Then it went beyond even that, and I found that in the vacuum of sensory deprivation, I was able to recall with sharpness and detail a whole tapestry of my life that in the blur and distraction of the normal world I'd never had access to. It felt as if a file cabinet of memory had emerged, ready to be opened, begging to be opened.

And as I moved through the whiteout the world disappeared; the things I *could* see and feel became the keys to that memory cabinet. I glanced down at my knee and, in a flash, relived an entire afternoon at the playground when I was five, scraping a knee in a fall from the monkey bars, which caused Lucas to run over to make sure I was okay.

Then I glanced at my hands, which moved back and forth with the poles, and I was suddenly—with startling clarity—able to remember a specific morning when I was six, walking into my first day of grade school, holding my big sister's hand. Caitlin's hand was cool and dry while mine was sweaty with anxiety. She was wearing purple pants with cuffs. I'd insisted, with great passion, on wearing gray sweatpants and Velcro sandals. The school's big blue metal doors had a little line of rust running down below the hinges.

I felt I could close the Caitlin-first-day file and open up another. The second-day file and third-day file were easily accessible. Reliving any school day and really any day of my life was just as powerful and vivid, just as available to fill the void in what I couldn't see around me.

Other parts of me, though, were disappearing. I'd had a shadow once, in the days before, which I could sometimes use to help me navigate when the sun was behind me. Shadow Colin moved on the ice ahead of me and felt sort of like a companion, moving as I moved, distorted and unrecognizable when the terrain under him changed with a snowdrift or sastruga. But the whiteout erased him, so it was just me again and my compass to guide me south.

And then, just after breaking camp on the morning of my sixth day, seventy-four miles from the start, still enveloped in the whiteout, I saw a ghostly image in the distance that quickly became real and clear as I approached: a red tent.

I'm pretty sure there isn't anyone else out here, I said to myself as I stopped in my tracks, overwhelmed by the strange and almost comic oddness of bumping into someone, here of all places. It could only be Rudd. Of all the people in the universe it could only be him. Antarctica stretched out around us, as big as the United States and Mexico combined, and on a vast and remote swath of the continent at that moment he and I were the only humans for hundreds of miles in any direction.

I didn't know what to do. Though I'd certainly fantasized about the moment I might catch up to Rudd, and gone through in my mind all sorts of imagined scenarios of what I'd say and do and how he might respond, I'd always pictured a gradual sort of thing—seeing him in the distance, pulling his sled as I slowly closed the distance.

Staring at his tent, I felt suddenly claustrophobic, as though in all the vastness of Antarctica, he and I were trapped all over again in a tiny, tight little world that I couldn't escape, just as we'd been on the Ilyushin.

I immediately decided that I'd quietly sneak by, hoping that he wouldn't wake up or notice.

But then I heard a cough, and I froze in place, unable to take my eyes off the tent as the front flap slowly unzipped and a head popped out, looking stark and round against the red fabric about fifty feet from where I stood. An arm wriggled out from the flap and Rudd began to wave.

In dead silence that made it feel all the more surreal, Rudd's slow, deliberate wave—mostly in his hand, the way I've seen the Queen of England do on television, saying hello to her subjects from a royal balcony—looked formal and dignified, but in the middle of the Antarctic ice also extremely odd if not downright disturbing.

I was so stunned by the whole bizarre scene that I couldn't think of anything to do but wave back.

After that, there seemed little else to do but keep going. Execute the plan.

I wasn't thinking at that moment that I'd passed Rudd, only that I'd just been through one of the most bizarre experiences of my life, and was a little afraid that the image—the head, the wave—would get stuck in my memory like the photograph of his skeletal body at the Pole.

But executing the plan of pushing on south through a whiteout also took just about all the concentration I had, and pretty quickly I wasn't thinking of Rudd at all. My compass, strapped to my chest, jutting out about eighteen inches from my face, became the central focus of everything as I tried to stay on course. The compass's black-and-silver box, with the little mirror lid that stood up vertically facing me, black needle indicator pointing south, was the only guide I had. Because I had no other visual cues, I'd almost immediately veer off my heading if I glanced away. It was like walking down a pitch-black hallway and bonking into the wall after five steps—human beings, with our reliance on sight, just aren't built to walk in straight lines without visual cues to help us.

After about an hour of that, though, I happened to glance back and saw that Rudd was now exactly in my tracks, about a hundred yards behind me, just visible at the edge of the whiteout.

It felt just as dreamlike and strange as stumbling onto his tent. I'd been utterly alone, and now here we were together once more in the emptiest of places, seatmates all over again in a way, jammed together and jostling, and a part of me wanted to shout back to him, "Hey, get your own continent!"

But because it was Rudd, I decided pretty immediately that he knew what he was doing. There was strategy at work. Had to be. It was another grizzled veteran polar trick, I thought, similar to how bike racers tuck behind the rider directly in front to reduce wind resistance. Because he could see me, I was functioning as his navigational beacon, which meant he could relax a bit and not need his own compass so much. I slowed my pace and he eventually came up beside me.

"Good morning, mate," he said immediately. "I've got a bit of a suggestion for you."

That in itself was enough to stop me short, and I stood there staring at him for a few seconds. Middle of nowhere, middle of absolute emptiness, only two people for hundreds of miles, racing history both bundled up head to toe in subzero cold, and one guy steps up to the other to offer advice?

I couldn't see anything of his face at that point, behind goggles and mask, so there were no further clues about what he was talking about. My skiing form? My sled? My food supplies? My personality?

He was trying to undermine my confidence. That seemed unquestionably true to me at that moment. Something in his eyes implied I was committing some error. I decided I'd had enough.

"We've both announced to the world that we're each trying to be the first," I started, then paused, wanting to say something more, something deeper. This might well be the last conversation I'd have for the next two months with a living, breathing person in front of me. Rudd deserved more.

"I know that your dear friend Henry Worsley died attempting this. We both know the stakes out here," I said. "Worsley was a hero and an inspiration." I was almost about to go on, and say how much Worsley had inspired me personally, but I stopped myself. Worsley's memory and honor were Rudd's to carry as his friend, not mine. "Look, I hope we both make a safe crossing," I finally said. "But we're doing this solo, so let this be the last time that we speak until this is over."

I stopped, feeling like I'd thrown down a challenge. I hadn't intended to pick a fight or antagonize, but simply to establish a dividing line, to say we should each go our own ways, down our own roads, come what may. Rudd said nothing more, but simply reached up and lifted the bottom of his mask, revealing his face. He then gave me a silent look that was as mysterious as his wave.

There was something of a scowl in it—I got that much. "Fine, suit yourself" is how I read it. But there was also almost a kind of deep, knowing smile, as though he'd just looked into the bottom of my soul or I'd been tested. As always with Rudd, I wasn't sure that in his eyes I'd passed the examination.

It was also extremely difficult after that, and through much of the day, making my own words a reality. To say, "Okay, we're parting ways now, Lou, this is it, we're splitting up," sounded good, but with two guys slowly dragging heavy sleds across the ice, really splitting up quickly wasn't just hard to do, it was nearly impossible. It was the world's slowest race; the tortoise versus the tortoise.

He trudged, I trudged, always in sight of each other because neither of us could go faster. We were each also clearly pushing much harder than we would have without the other, hovering out there in the white, and by mid-afternoon I felt close to falling apart from the effort. My back and shoulders ached from the jerking pull of the harness, and I could feel, down in my right boot, a blister beginning to form on my big toe, which could be problematic if it started to get worse.

But something had changed. I needed to keep going in a way I hadn't before. Rudd had awed and intimidated me through those days at the beginning, and I'd come up with no defense against it. Now, in knowing he was watching me, it almost felt as if it was my turn to shine, not to intimidate him—I knew I could never do that and I'm not sure *anybody* could—but for him to just understand me a little better, and maybe even respect what he saw. I vowed to myself, even as the hours wore on in what came to feel like a race within a race, that I'd go on as long as he did, and then an hour longer. If he went nine hours, I'd go ten. If he went ten, I'd go eleven.

Rudd seemed unstoppable. Eight hours passed, then nine, and then ten, and still he pushed on, about a hundred yards or so to my left. Had there been even a single witness on the planet watching us that day, from above or from the ice, I'm sure it would've seemed strange beyond description: two lumbering southbound figures, bundled head to toe against the cold, traveling almost side by side, each ignoring the other and yet abjectly focused on the other at the same time. And as our strange grinding, utterly silent slow-motion standoff continued through the flat white afternoon, I found myself more and more thinking beyond the blustery, hard-edged Rudd that I'd seen back at the start.

I saw for the first time his dogged determination, his vulnerability, his humanity—the Rudd of the eleven steps, of lost friends and old wounds.

For years, when he talked about his various Antarctic expeditions, Rudd had described the moment at the end of every day when he was about to stop to make camp, but took an eleven extra steps beyond that.

However tired he was, the eleven steps were sacrosanct, an homage to the Scott expedition. Scott and his men, heading back from the South Pole in early 1912, Rudd said—citing a Scott biography from years ago—might've survived to their famous last cache of food and fuel, called "One Ton Depot," if they'd taken just eleven more steps each night before camp in their brutal, months-long effort. So Rudd, in their memory, had committed himself to the margin they didn't or couldn't make—a small salute to their spirit of sacrifice and honor.

Rudd's nightly tribute of the eleven steps had given me chills from the first time I'd heard about it. And maybe, I thought, he was taking those eleven extra steps right now in a way, in vowing to stay on my heels. But the idea that one bit more is always possible and can make a difference was now perhaps ironically fueling me, too, inspiring me to push further and harder. It felt like my own little tribute, to Scott and those long ago days on the ice, and to Rudd himself.

And as I kept glancing back, I also thought I began to understand a bit more of the enduring mystery of Lieutenant Colonel Henry Worsley of the British Army.

My first exposure to Worsley, long before I'd ever met Rudd or heard about their friendship and adventures together, came through a stunning black-and-white photo I saw taped up on a whiteboard inside the food tent at Union Glacier on my first visit to Antarctica in 2015. Worsley grinned into the camera, mouth clamped on a giant cigar, wearing a wool neck warmer and a set of round snow goggles that looked straight out of 1912. He looked like a time traveler, a proud Antarctic survivor from the heroic age of Shackleton, with a proud and perfectly square missing front tooth to complete the picture.

It was my first morning ever in Antarctica in late 2015. I'd thought, until walking in for breakfast and encountering a room of people obsessed with Worsley and wanting to talk of little else, that what I was trying to do there was a pretty big deal. I thought of myself as primarily a mountaineer in those days and was just then beginning a world-record attempt on something called the "Explorers Grand Slam," a challenge in the global climbing community to climb the highest peak on each of the seven continents, "the Seven Summits," and trek to both the North and South Poles from at least the 89th degree of latitude, a distance of about sixty-nine miles each. At the time fewer than fifty people in history had ever completed the Explorers Grand Slam, most knocking off the separate challenges over five or ten years, climbing a peak, then going home to rest and plan for the next one. I was trying to become the fastest person to ever complete the Grand Slam, by finishing all nine expeditions in one continuous four-month push, no breaks between mountains other than a plane ride to the next trailhead. Antarctica was my starting point—the only continent with two items to be checked off, having both the Pole and a highest peak, Mount Vinson.

So as I always am at the start of things, I was pumped with energy that morning, surging with adrenaline, barely able to sit still with my eagerness. But as I walked by the whiteboard with

Worsley's picture, and a scrawled line of numbers below it about his location out on the ice, I found myself completely swallowed up by the grandeur and audacity of what he was trying. I hadn't even heard of the idea of a solo, unsupported, and unassisted crossing until that moment—and the decades-long, never completed dream of it—and my own goal suddenly felt smaller in comparison. I was going for speed, but Worsley was attempting what had never before been done: climbing a "mountain" that people said couldn't be climbed at all.

"I think he actually might make it—it's unbelievable," barked one of my breakfast mates, a ruddy Scot with red curls who was also heading for Vinson.

"I met him in 2011, in the Amundsen trek," a Russian woman offered up between deep swills of strong camp coffee.

"Who is he?" I asked the table I ended up at, which was lined by a United Nations array of faces from around the world—A.L.E. staffers and guides, climbers, adventurers, and wealthy birders bent on ticking off an emperor from the penguin list.

Heads swiveled as one toward the ignorant new guy.

"Henry Worsley is the best there is," a Brit to my left said simply. There were shrugs around the table as though such a sweeping generalization couldn't be topped or improved upon. I looked back at the whiteboard, at Worsley's face, hoping our paths might cross.

A week later, I arrived at the South Pole after my relatively short sixty-nine-mile ski traverse across the Last Degree. The Pole was a bustling place of expedition travelers and scientists, with about 150 men and women there full-time through the Antarctic summer, many working and living in a long, low building, that—like my tent every night—was aligned to take the least force from the prevailing winds. But I was still thinking of Worsley and the vast and amazing goal he'd set for himself in attempting to cross one thousand miles alone.

Worsley had already passed the Pole. He'd come and gone only a few days earlier, crossing north toward the other side of the continent, and I stood at the Pole, gazing in the direction he'd gone and cursing my bad luck in arriving too late.

Only a few weeks later did I get the news. I'd moved on by then to the next continent in my sprint around the world that year, South America, where I was climbing Aconcagua in the Andes, near the border of Argentina and Chile. Worsley had run into trouble after the Pole when he'd fallen ill and had called for emergency evacuation. But it was too late. After seventy-one days alone on the ice, and just one hundred miles from becoming the first man to complete a solo, unsupported, and unassisted effort, he died in a hospital in Punta Arenas, Chile. I'd climbed for a long time in silence after that, mourning a man I never met but might have, thinking for some reason of his great missing front tooth and wondering about the story behind it.

THE HOURS OF THAT STRANGE, tense race with Rudd dragged on and on—just him and me and our sleds, each of us, I knew, groaning inside as we pulled through the cold, blank light. Finally, after eleven hours, I glanced back and saw that he'd stopped. He was putting up his tent.

I felt certain he was still watching me. He had to be. He was a competitor, a man who wanted to win this race across the continent as much as I did, and so I knew he would be studying me and guessing where my body and mind were at, even as he seemed to be nonchalantly going about the business of making camp.

In truth, I was utterly wrecked. But I refused to let it show. I dug in and tried to find the reserves of energy I might still have left. As long as Rudd could see me, I decided, I'd be strong, and I wouldn't let up, or look back.

The weirdest thing of all about that deep internal dialogue was that somehow it pulled me deeper inside myself to the zone where the reality of my race with Rudd could be stilled. Trying to quiet the voices of fatigue, doubt, and craziness somehow led to quieting all the voices entirely, and I found that for long stretches, I surrendered, hearing only the shuffling of skis and sled runners on powder. Effort and breathing and the forward-and-back swing of my ski poles all swirled into a place that was deeply silent, too, muffled under a layer of stillness, synchronized and natural, mind and body moving together.

My borrowed Rolex beamed back up at me as an extra ten minutes became twenty and then thirty, until finally the sixty minutes I'd demanded of myself was completed and I unharnessed and fell to my knees, as exhausted as I'd ever been. I'd completed twenty miles, the longest and hardest day by far. The extra hour, I calculated, had put me about two miles past Rudd's camp.

More than that, as I crawled into the tent, lit my stove, and tried to stay awake for the evening tasks and check-ins, I felt I'd turned a corner. I realized that the day had been far more than just surreal. I'd been changed by it in some way. Before, through the days leading up to the start, from the Ilyushin cargo plane ride through the anxious days at Union Glacier, I'd been measuring myself against Rudd. It had felt inevitable, and to one degree or another, I think he'd also encouraged it. The stark contrasts between us were mostly to his advantage.

But that first chapter of our shared adventure, as I now thought of it, was over. Going forward from this moment, now leading this historic race for the first time, I'd have a new standard of measure for comparison: myself. Rudd was still out there, literally just beyond view. I pictured him in his tent, thinking about me and our neck-and-neck day—he'd posted to his blog that night a powerful declaration in describing it. "The race is on," he said. But I had strengths, too, and I could kindle them into a flame that would propel me forward. If I could push once through a twelve-hour day, longer than I'd ever thought possible, I could do it again, and maybe again after that.

I wasn't Rudd, and that was okay. I was me.

CHAPTER FIVE

Commit to the Break

DAY 6

C hewing and swallowing when you're famished is the most natural and basic of things. Food is the focus and down it goes.
Babies do it long before they walk or talk.

But in passing Rudd that day, the hour-after-hour of slow, straining grind, had left me so exhausted that even lifting the spoon to my
mouth seemed like work. I needed the freeze-dried chili that was
there in my mug, steaming up from the boiling water I'd just poured
into it. I wanted it. It smelled wonderful and its aroma filled the
tent as I sat, legs thrust down inside the sleeping bag, back wedged
into my little roll-up chair, beanie on my head.

The need for sleep, though, was just as intense and insistent
as hunger. I'd take a mouthful, slowly start to chew and realize I'd
halfway dozed off, my head drooping toward my chest.

A sudden, ferocious blast of wind, slamming the tent and warp-
ing it around me, brought me back to instant attention. Instinctively,
my mouth still full, I reached up to check my solar panel as the winds
rattled and shook the tent's fabric. The solar charger, a flat panel of
cells about the size of a hardcover book, was as crucial to my safety
as food, water, and shelter because it powered my satellite phone,

which was my means of rescue should I need it. Every night, in one of my first tasks on getting into the tent, I slid the panel into the little sliver of space between the roof and the wind shell that I cinched down over the tent's top. The shell was thin enough that sunlight could penetrate through while I slept, and the battery inside the panel would be charged by morning, at least on a sunny night. In a whiteout like today, I wasn't sure how much light would get through.

The solar panel, and the uncertainty of how much juice I'd have tomorrow to charge my devices with the sun so shielded by clouds and blowing ice, made me think I'd better check my other tools, too. Another little task would also take my mind off the hard work of eating dinner with exhausted jaws. The sat phone, most essential of all with its mandatory required nightly communication back to A.L.E., was fine. My iPhone, which was virtually useless down here other than as a camera, was good, too. But as I held it there in my hand, my eye was drawn to the icon for my music catalog, and I had to click on it.

It was all but empty. Thousands of songs and albums that had been a hugely important part of my life back home were gone.

Spoon in one hand, phone in the other, the rattling wind outside—I thought of the afternoon, back in the little Airbnb apartment in Punta Arenas, Chile, when I'd deleted almost everything.

I was on the couch, and Jenna was leaning against my shoulder. We were both tired after a day of packing, repacking, and questioning ourselves about what I'd need on the ice or would not. Two cups of tea were growing cold on the coffee table in front of us.

"I'm doing it," I said, giving her head a little nudge with my shoulder.

She sat up and looked at the phone, then at me. "Yeah? You ready for that?" She gave me a poke back on the arm to tease me. "Sure you can live without Bob Marley, or whatever the forty-year-old reggae is that you listen to?" she said.

"I'm actually taking a Marley, one of the few things I'm keeping,"

71

I said. "But that's mostly in honor of Mom. Just about everything else? Going, going, gone." I began to delete, and delete, and in a few seconds, it was done.

"Empty," I said, putting down the phone and grabbing my luke-warm tea.

Jenna knew what I was doing and why, and she reached up and kissed me.

"Empty," she repeated. "This is going to be interesting."

WHEN I WOKE UP the next morning, the tent was still rattling hard. There was something different going on outside for sure. But in my little red-fabric-tinted world, the rhythm clicked in—the sequence of steps and moments that were coming to define everything, and shape my every waking moment, all repeated in more or less the same order. I'd wake up, say my morning mantra, *You are strong. You are capable.* I'd light my white-gas-fueled stove, then put on my socks—always the right before the left. I'd crawl over and unzip the door to the vestibule at the foot-end of the tent—a kind of porch space, covered by the tent's wind flap—dig a hole in the snow, and take care of my morning business. Then I'd come back and squeeze into my little chair with my legs stretched back into my sleeping bag. I'd reach over to my stove, which sat in the snow in the tent's other vestibule—at the opposite end from the bathroom—and pour boiling water into my oatmeal. I'd put a hand in my left pocket to get the ChapStick that was always in that exact place, and put it on my lips. I'd get out of my tent and pack my sled, and then I'd resume my push south exactly as I had the day before and as I would tomorrow and all the tomorrows I could glimpse in the distance.

When I finally crawled out—immediately scanning for any sign of Rudd, though he could've been a hundred feet away and invisible in those whiteout conditions—the wind hit me directly in the face.

I hadn't been able to tell the wind's direction during the night—the tent's rattle seemed to come from every side—but I now saw what kind of day it would be. The wind felt like it was coming directly from the South Pole, as though it were anchored to a compass point, and I'd have to push into it. My thermometer said it was twenty-five below, and the windchill would drag it down far below that. Bare skin could be frostbitten in minutes.

Drifts had all but covered the sled by then, too. It was simply a mound that looked like any other drift, but for a smudgy glimpse of its yellow cover. And instead of the grainy ice crystals that had been blowing around in the last few days, the coating was powdery and light and felt freshly fallen. As I took down the tent and rolled it up, the drifts were soft and deep, and I thought again of the puzzled, head-shaking workers back at Union Glacier, shoveling out the camp and talking about climate change. Fresh snow blown here could only mean that a storm had struck somewhere ahead of me to the south, where this wind had originated.

And what that meant was that the real test had probably not even begun. Whatever was ahead, on the other side of those winds, would likely be worse.

But a few things were certain. I was ahead of Rudd. I'd have to go out into this fierce headwind, into cold that required great caution. And most important of all, I'd commit to the break.

"Committing to the break" was a phrase I'd loved as long as I could remember, since I first became an Olympics freak at age seven. If you pull away from the pack in a race, don't squander it. Dig in. Push. That's the definition. When staying longer in the tent could've been so appealing, I went out into the whiteout that day fueled by that thought.

Galen Rupp and Mo Farah had defined the commitment personally for me, amazingly and brilliantly, in the 10K final on the track at the London Olympics in 2012.

Jenna and I were in a noisy London bar that evening, just outside the stadium at Olympic Park where the race was to be held—unable to afford tickets to get in and feeling bitterly disappointed. It was one of the events we'd come to the Olympics most eager to see because I knew Rupp, who was from the US—he'd grown up just a few blocks from me in southeast Portland—and because he and Farah, a Brit, trained together in Portland, both Nike athletes. I'd seen them running together.

So we'd settled for a TV in a pub as close as we could get, jammed with enthusiastically drunken Brits at our elbows and British flags on every wall. It turned out to be one of the greatest races I'd ever seen—a ferocious, jostling crowd of runners dominated by the East Africans, shoulder-to-shoulder lap after lap. Rupp and Farah hung back through the race, just two men in the pack, then with a breathtaking surge, they moved forward together in the final lap, Farah winning the gold and Rupp the silver.

The bar went absolutely crazy as the live TV coverage melded with the screaming roar of the stadium crowd outside, which spilled into the bar's front door at the same moment.

I saw now that passing Rudd in the first day of the whiteout had been my breakaway moment. I hadn't deliberately surged or tried to catch him. That had seemed, in fact, unlikely, as strong and powerful as he'd looked that first day, striding off into the glare, marching in his soldier's rhythm.

I just kept going, and it happened. There he was. Seeing his tent suddenly in front of me had been more shocking than triumphant. And surviving yesterday—the two of us lumbering forward, anchored down by heavy loads—had been more a matter of gutting it out and getting through.

Now I was committed to holding that lead, if only to live up to the example of the heroes from that amazing 10K final. I wasn't sure I could actually stay ahead of Rudd for the hundreds of miles ahead of us. He was astonishingly experienced and resourceful. Bad or good luck could happen to either one of us at any time.

But the commitment, and the effort to follow through on that commitment with whatever was in me, felt crucial.

And it wasn't just competition and wanting to beat Rudd that drove it. The hundreds of miles ahead would be challenging beyond anything I'd ever done and would require a measuring out of physical and mental energy for the long road. I feared, based on the day before, that having him nearby—or seeing him at all—would be distracting, draining, and emotionally exhausting. It might even push me to a level of effort that would cause something to snap. But that didn't matter, I had to give it everything now. I was all in, fully committing to the break.

THE WIND AND THE WHITEOUT got worse through that morning. My wind-streamer flags zipped and snapped back toward me on my ski poles, and the compass, strapped to my chest, became the center of my focus, the center of everything. Everything about it started to seem even more concrete and real because it was the only thing I had to look at, and because it was the most important thing—taking my eyes off it even for a minute could mean veering off in the wrong direction.

And I trudged forward in silence, the snow muffling my steps.

Deleting my music catalog had been a choice, a deliberate commitment of its own. I'd decided, in working through the details of the project with Jenna, that the profound silence of the world's emptiest place was a gift that I shouldn't run from or fill up with sound. Music can be a great distraction on a long run or a drive, but Antarctica was the world's biggest sensory deprivation tank, a whiteboard waiting to be filled with scrawled thoughts, and maybe inspirations, and I'd decided I wanted to embrace the blank canvas and see where it led. I wanted nothing that could block, or even dull, what seemed like Antarctica's most distinctive gift.

Silence doesn't come naturally to me. I can talk. And I like to talk, sometimes too much. My stepfather, Brian, knows that all too well. The day he drove me to my first ten-day Vipassana silent meditation retreat, in late 2011, he wasn't about to let the opportunity pass for some teasing.

I'd told him the basics of how the retreat would work, on the drive north from Portland on I-5, toward the rural, wooded Northwest Vipassana Center in the little town of Onalaska, Washington, in the shadow of Mount St. Helens.

"No talking, no reading, no writing, no eye contact," I said. "They wake you up at four a.m. with a gong, and you get two simple vegetarian meals per day, with twelve-plus hours spent in meditation."

Brian laughed for a long time, wiping his eyes, then laughed again. He's had a hugely positive influence on my life, always supporting and encouraging me, but this time he was skeptical.

"If I made a list of all the people in the world I know who couldn't possibly shut up for ten days, you'd be right at the top, Colin," he said. "Seriously, though," he added, turning to look at me across the cab of his truck, "you've never meditated for even a minute in your life, and you're going straight to ten days?"

"Yep . . . I guess I'm diving into the deep end again. Hopefully I'll figure it out," I said.

I'd been encouraged by a friend to try Vipassana for the mental discipline and focus that she'd said could boost athletic performance. But I was curious, too, and nervous as well that the spartan diet of the retreat would leave me famished, and that ten days without conversation of any kind would be difficult or impossible. I made Brian stop at a Subway off the highway where I ran in and bought a giant sandwich so I wouldn't arrive already hungry.

"Vipassana means to see things as they really are," I said, wolfing down the sandwich, halfway fearful that his teasing was on the mark, and I'd have a hard time. "So I guess we'll see."

As we pulled into the parking lot, I grabbed my bag and hopped out of the truck, and Brian rolled down the window.

"I'll keep the motor running! My guess is that you'll only last ten minutes," he said with a wink.

At the center's door I turned back for a look and saw him wave to me as he sped out of the lot. For all the ribbing, he clearly believed in me, and hadn't even waited for me to get inside.

But that day on the ice, from the force of the whiteout and the wind, my sensory deprivation felt complete. As I pushed south, the crunch and squeak of my skis, which I could barely hear over the roar of the wind earlier in the day, seemed to grow louder in volume. My breathing, in and out through the mask, fell into sync with the motions of my legs, moving the skis. Up, back, breathe. Up, back, breathe. My arms, swinging the poles, melted into the flow of movement, and even my wind flags—ribbons attached to the handles of my ski poles to indicate the wind's direction—fluttering straight back toward me in the headwind, seemed to be part of the dance.

And then the rhythm swallowed me. The cumulative force of repetition, from those first socks-on, stove-on moments of the morning through all the hour-to-hour, minute-to-minute tasks of movement and survival, became a kind of song that carried me and lifted me.

As a little kid swimming laps in the pool, sometimes I'd stumble into that flow state, the timeless space where thirty minutes would go by and it would seem like two minutes or something like that. I never really knew how I got there. It just happened or it didn't. But I'd come to Antarctica with the deliberate intention of finding that space and exploring it. If ever there was a corner of the earth where the flow state should flourish, I thought, it was here on this endless, empty landscape.

I'd trained my body for this moment, through the years of competition and climbing and training, and now in a way my body knew what to do without being asked. I became a witness to myself and my thoughts, and I flashed back to my coach Mike McCastle and what he'd put me through in his gym in Portland during the previous year, in preparing for Antarctica.

"Hold it, Colin. Hold it," Mike said softly, standing above me as I held a plank position with my hands in buckets of ice. I'd surrendered completely to Mike by that point, in my awe of him and his amazing physical achievements and charitable work. A navy veteran and endurance sports legend, he'd broken the world record for doing the most pull-ups in twenty-four hours—5,804 of them, all while wearing a thirty-pound pack to represent the burden of the wounded warrior, in a benefit event. He'd pulled a Ford F-150 pickup truck for twenty-two miles in nineteen hours across Death Valley to raise awareness for veteran suicide. He pulled it with a harness. If ever there was a guy to help me train to pull something heavy, it was Mike, and I'd do anything he asked. If he said hold the plank as my hands ached in the ice, I'd hold it, no matter what. If he said release the plank and stand in these buckets of ice water while putting together a Lego puzzle—another of his training demands— then I'd do that, too.

Now I saw that he'd also been toughening my mind, honing it, or breaking it down so that when a moment like this came, I'd know not to resist but surrender.

I'd been thinking about the ideas of mindset, performance, and endurance for years, and working on them through things like meditation, but as I continued through the afternoon, I felt that Mike's training tools, and all those hours with him at the gym, were clicking in. Time felt like it was speeding up and slowing down at the same time because I felt so completely present in the moment and the movement. Every breath, every stride, every yanking jerk of the harness against my shoulders became part of that moment.

It certainly wasn't like time had stopped or that I wasn't aware of my muscles and cold hands, and how the harness dug into my shoulders with every forward pull. Exactly the opposite. I felt aware of everything, all at once, as though it was some kind of symphony.

I felt I would eat and drink exactly at the moments my body needed food and water, because I felt I could reach down inside and know. I'd know how the tips of my fingers felt inside my mittens, and the tingling that would hit them at the end of a bitterly cold day, and the sled's little squeak when I had to inch it up and over an obstacle.

When I finally looked at my watch, I was stunned. Almost two hours had gone by in what seemed like minutes. I ultimately pushed for twelve hours on the ice, the same workday I'd put in the day before, in passing Rudd. I was committing to the break, I realized, by stopping my mind from thinking about it. By not searching so desperately for the way forward, the way had found me.

AND THAT NIGHT THERE WAS NEWS. My mom had cracked the code.

Rudd, somewhere behind me, was sending messages to his blog, phoned in and recorded daily so that his followers around the world could know how he was doing, where he was, and what he saw and thought about when he gazed out on the Antarctic horizon.

But tactically he'd chosen not to put the signal of his GPS unit into the website itself so that people could track him in real time, as they could me, on my website. And his daily blog posts never referred to any precise location at all, only to a loosely referenced daily mileage that felt deeply uncertain if not downright suspicious—perhaps another clever deception by a wily veteran competitor.

I knew he was behind me, but couldn't with any certainty say where.

But my mom, for her own reasons, had gotten it into her head that we should know exactly where Rudd was. The inReach unit he was using, like mine, functioned as a GPS locator, but could also send short texts by satellite to his expedition manager back in England.

I was sharing with the world, not because I was better than

Rudd, but because I had a different goal regarding what the project could be. So I'd linked my GPS to my Instagram profile and my website, and then Jenna and I had worked to get schools involved, with students tracking me in real time and maybe getting excited about Antarctica, or their own goals and dreams. I wanted it all public, all out.

In any case, Rudd's inReach had to have a unique web address, a URL, just like mine. Mom and Jenna, in talking about the information gap, knew this—they just didn't know what URL Rudd had chosen. Finding the hidden URL became my mom's quest.

"She reached out to some of her tech friends," Jenna told me when I called her for our nightly medical check. "And they said that Lou's signal was probably encrypted—couldn't be broken. But then she found stuff from his past expeditions, which had the full URL address, so she figured this one was probably not encrypted either and she just started trying different variations."

"And she just stumbled on it?" I asked.

"What?"

I repeated the question through a thick wall of static, and lay there to wait to see if the line would clear or the call would drop, staring up at the roof of my tent. My battery was up there, and as I thought of Mom and Rudd, I reached up to tap it lightly again with a finger through the tent fabric, wanting one more bit of reassurance. Antarctica tolerated modern technology only to a point.

"No, I think it was more like just whittling it down," Jenna finally said when the static subsided. "It was incredible—she realized that because his GPS was running through a European network, rather than an American one, it would have a different label. Then she assumed it would have some personal touch, so she started trying names he'd mentioned in past interviews—wife, children, parents, whatever, but that didn't work."

I couldn't help but smile, there nestled in my bag on the ice, because I could see everything that Jenna was telling me so clearly.

Once unleashed, my mother's ferocity and determination was an awesome thing.

"The final piece," Jenna continued, "was seeing that he'd named all his past expeditions and put the expedition name in the URL for that trip. So when she got that, and typed the magic words of his project, 'The Spirit of Endurance,' it all clicked. Boom. She was on her laptop in front of the TV when it happened."

Jenna paused for a beat. "*Survivor*," she said.

She knew the effect that would have on me. *Survivor*, the long-running reality show about a group of people on a tropical island competing to be the last one standing, and so win the $1 million prize, had been a ritual family night in our house from its beginning when I was in high school. I'd gone off to college and life and mostly stopped watching the show, but my mom and Brian kept the tradition going. It was about the only television show they regularly watched—a guilty pleasure, they called it, never missing an episode through thirty-eight seasons. That Mom would crack Rudd's code in the middle of a tribal council or immunity challenge or some other old *Survivor* ritual was perfect because the effort itself, sitting there with her laptop, was a *Survivor*-like strategic move. It had required patience, guile, and determination. Outwit, outlast, outplay. That was one of *Survivor*'s constantly repeated catchphrases, and Mom had done all three. I could almost hear her scream when it all clicked, startling Brian half to death.

Learning Rudd's code, which would give Jenna the ability to calculate and report Rudd's exact distance from me every night, felt like a secret advantage, a mystery story of ruse and subterfuge. Antarctica's history was full of tales like that—explorers concealing their plans, veiling their intentions until the last minute, even keeping the mix of their food rations cloaked in secrecy. I lay in my bag, smiling for a long time until sleep took me, thinking of Mom's tenacity and cunning.

CHAPTER SIX

More Hospital

DAY 8

I pushed another twelve hours the following day, with the whiteout still socked in around me. My body felt the strain of that, for sure, in my aching shoulders and back, but the whiteout had a mental impact, too. With no visual evidence, minute to minute or hour to hour, that I was actually moving anywhere or making progress, I felt as if I were trapped inside the belly of a Ping-Pong ball, white in every direction.

Early in the afternoon, I took a bad fall, too, making things worse. Because I couldn't see much farther than my ski tips, ridges and bumps in the ice could appear out of nowhere, and the wind-carved sastruga that took me down was too big to avoid, at least three feet high.

Sastrugi are the ocean waves on a frozen continent, ice formations that are sometimes beautiful—they can look like meringue on a pie or sand dunes in a desert—but always rock hard, chiseled by wind. They can be modest or monstrous in size, and they're always irregular in their recesses and ridges.

My ski tips jammed into this one at the same instant I saw it, and I lurched forward. Momentum did the rest and I fell to the side, smashing my right hip onto the ice and pulling the sled along with me to the sastruga's edge, where I had a brief moment of panic that it would keep coming and fall on me.

But the sled stopped, and I got up and moved on, though I was definitely more tentative and cautious after that, fearing another fall and straining even harder to see what might be ahead of me.

So by the time I stopped, around 8 p.m., my mind was probably even more wiped out than usual. I felt the bruise on my hip when I pressed down on it. My eyes, even with my goggles, burned with fatigue from the hours of looking and seeing nothing. I was weakened by the day and feeling vulnerable, which probably made everything that happened next even worse. Like the sastruga, I didn't see it coming.

MAKING CAMP ON THE ICE starts with unpacking. There's a whole chain of events that unfolds after that in a certain set order, from unrolling the tent, to putting down the stakes to secure it, to getting inside and starting the process of melting snow for my water supply.

But it all revolves around the sled. And I began as usual. I unharnessed. I checked the wind direction and grabbed the sled's front to pull it around ninety degrees so that it would be less likely to move during the night. I unbuckled the straps on my sled one by one until the cover was loose, then unzipped it and pulled it up toward me.

That's when it hit: *Gas!*

The smell wafted up from inside the sled and through my mask. I froze, instantly rigid with fear, still gripping the sled cover. From the overpowering smell I instantly knew gas must have spilled somewhere down inside, and the possibilities of what that meant were all horrible. If it had spilled into my food supplies, they were ruined. If I'd lost too much fuel, I would be in just as much of a crisis, unable to melt snow for drinking.

The smell got stronger as I began pawing through my supplies in panic. Without warning, and with a power that only smell can create, the inhaled scent triggered a memory and I was transported: *Kerosene*. The thick, sickly sweet smell was suddenly swirling through my head, bringing a flood of dark images and sensations. In a flash of memory I was on a beach. It was dark and steamy hot. Torchlight flickered from a breeze off the ocean. A circle of people in bikinis, shorts, and sandals stood before me, mouths open, looking shocked, their faces starkly illuminated by the firelight. And I began to scream.

IT WAS 2008. I'd been traveling for five months by that night, and life felt open-ended with possibilities everywhere I looked. I'd graduated from college the previous year. The years of joy and grind, swimming competitively at Yale, were over. And I had slowly saved $10,000 from my summer job of painting houses since high school with my best friend, David. Contrary to many of my classmates, I was more interested in depositing adventure into my life-experience account than a paycheck into my bank account while racing up the corporate ladder. So I'd set off to see the world, starting west from Portland out across the Pacific, with the plan of traveling for a year or until the money ran out. Adventure without itinerary.

I was also going alone, and I was going on the cheap—peanut butter and jelly by the jarful, hostels by night. Chance events and serendipity, which I'd been ready to embrace from the beginning in having no firm plan, had already touched me by then. I'd bought an airplane ticket to Auckland, New Zealand, from Hawaii, where I'd been visiting my father at his organic farm, a patch of grass he'd moved to after I graduated from high school. Standing at the travel agency ticket counter, the agent had said, "Hey, ever been to Fiji? You can get a layover there, no extra charge."

"Why not?" I said, unclear at that moment even exactly where Fiji was.

Fiji, in my meeting Jenna there in that little beach bar, had defined everything about serendipity and chance, and my trip had continued on from there, hitchhiking through New Zealand, and then flying on to Sydney, from where I intended to surf my way along Australia's east coast. But as I got off the train from the airport in downtown Sydney, there was a phone call to make that I'd been thinking about for weeks.

I walked to the first pay phone I could find and pulled out from my backpack the book with Jenna's number written on the back cover, then reached into my pocket for the Australian gold dollar coin I'd acquired while changing money at the airport. I stood for a second, looking at the coin in my hand and the book, and was struck by the same thought I'd had that day at the bar in Fiji: nothing to lose. She might be gone, she might not answer, she might not want to see me. But I had to try. I dropped the coin into the slot.

And she answered. She was still in Sydney. My luck had held.

"Hi," I said, holding the book in my hand. "It's Colin, from Fiji."

"Oh my God!" she said. "Where are you?"

I looked around. "Somewhere in Sydney . . . haven't figured out the city yet. Just landed . . . and you're the person I wanted to call."

She paused for a second and I realized I was holding my breath.

"We're headed out tonight to a bar in Bondi—bunch of friends," she said. "Join us?"

The bar turned out to be a pizza place near the beach, which immediately reminded me of Fiji, and inside, Jenna was sitting at a big table, surrounded by friends, again just like that first time. She jumped up and hugged me and shouted introductions over the pounding, loud music.

"Let's take a slice outside!" she yelled in my ear.

I nodded and with two slices on paper plates, I followed her out toward the beach, and then to the Bondi Seawall, where we slid down, facing the ocean under a full moon, our backs to the cool concrete. I wanted to know more about her than I'd been able to learn on what now felt like our first date on the little island six weeks ago.

Thrilled to be alone with her but not knowing where to start, I grinned and said, "It's so good to see you!"

She reached over and touched my cheek. "You too . . ."

"So . . . Australia?" I said, struggling to take it all in: the beach, us together again, the electricity of the moment.

"I always dreamed of coming to Australia after my mom told me about her first trip here in the mid-seventies. So when my college offered a study abroad program here, the first semester of my junior year I jumped on it."

As the waves crashed in front of us and the bar music echoed somewhere behind, I peppered Jenna with questions and she told me about her life—growing up in small-town western Massachusetts, only child of a single mother.

"Mom grew up working class. She was one of seven kids in a family where nobody had ever flown on an airplane. She broke away, leaving home at eighteen in search of more, eventually becoming a flight attendant in the early 1960s, the Pan Am days of flying," Jenna said.

I nodded, curious to hear more.

"She had a thriving career for over twenty years, working her way up into the airline's management. But then I came along"—she looked over at me with a slight smile—"and she moved back home to rural Massachusetts, giving up her career and her global life to raise me near family. She sacrificed for me, but she always said I was worth it." I suddenly saw a depth in her that I hadn't seen before in Fiji, and I reached over to take her hand.

"So no siblings then, how about your dad?" I asked.

She took another bite of pizza. "Never met him," she said, not avoiding my eyes but, rather, looking right at me.

The serendipity of having no plan unfolded again from there, beginning that night. Instead of surfing up the coast, I explored Sydney with Jenna for most of the next month. We shared cheap dinners and took long walks along the water past the Opera House, talking more about our lives and families and dreams, and by the time I left to continue my trip, intending to head toward Southeast Asia, I'd fallen for her completely. We began talking about the future, vowing to get together again once we were both back home.

Outside the train station as I headed toward the airport—only a few feet from the pay phone I'd called her on—I kissed her goodbye and reached down into my backpack.

"I want to give you this—it's a book that's meant a lot to me," I said, holding out a copy of *The Alchemist*, by Paulo Coelho.

She bit her lower lip. "We seem to have a trend here—another book!" she said, looking like she might cry.

"You wrote your number last time, and this time I wanted to write," I said, opening the cover. "To Jenna," I read. "The time we have spent together has been absolutely amazing, from the endless laughter and smiles to the thousand kisses a day, you have captured my heart. The road of life's great adventure is full of surprising twists and turns—and luck, too, the kind I had in meeting you in the least likely of places. I hope our roads lead back together."

I looked up and saw that she was crying, and we hugged again, and I kissed her tears and turned for the train.

"Thailand!" I shouted as I turned for a last look.

THAILAND, IN ANOTHER SWEET COINCIDENCE, meant a reunion with David, who was doing his own year on the road. He'd become almost like a member of my family over the years, and through the course of dinners, hikes, and parties had met and fallen in love with my stepsister Lili and was traveling through Asia with her.

But she'd peeled off for a side trip with other friends, and so David and I had decided to meet up in Thailand to hang out for a couple weeks. Whenever I was around him, I felt as if there was a lot to celebrate, especially our years of friendship stretching back to high school, when we'd bonded over soccer, who we had a crush on, and our roots on Portland's eastside.

We'd ended up at a scruffy, $10-a-night diving resort on the island of Koh Tao, in the gulf of Thailand, intending to get scuba certified, but mostly just being twenty-two, and being together.

The beach resort, though that's probably too grand a name for it, served food at tables that sat out on the sand, and the rice noodles we ate that night were spicy to the point of being barely edible.

In the flood of memory that washed through me as I knelt on the ice, pawing through my sled in panic looking for the spilled gas can, I could taste those noodles again, feel the cheap wooden chopsticks in my hand, and see the waitress carrying plates across the sand to our little table.

Every detail of those moments before everything changed was ingrained into me. There were brightly colored Christmas lights strung out from the café, and the waitress had emerged through the lights, a dark silhouette lit from behind by a kind of rainbow that shimmered through the edges of her coal-black hair, frizzed up around her head in a tight bun. The two drinks she'd thunked down in front of us on the flimsy table were sweating in the steamy night. David and I clinked our bottles, enjoying the moment and our first sips.

The details are vivid because of what came after. Searing memories force the mind to reach back and look for patterns, ways that a thing could've been avoided, signs that were missed. Like searching the ripples of a rock thrown into a pond, you have to look for the source moment, the place where things began.

That café was just down the beach from where we were staying. As David and I sat there on our cheap plastic chairs, listening to the sound of the surf behind us, we saw that they were setting up for the hotel's evening entertainment. A small crowd was gathering and two big torches on stakes had been jammed down into the sand. The torches flickered in the breeze as two men squatted over a long rope, soaking it with fuel.

David grabbed my elbow and nodded toward the scene.

"Fire jump ropes again," he said.

We'd seen the fire ropes from a distance every night through the five days that we'd been on the island, and I'd deliberately ignored the ritual every time. I pictured a cheesy Hawaiian luau sort of scene, with jugglers and dancers. The rope would be lit on fire, and the rope guys would whirl it around like a jump rope.

"Should we do the fire ropes?" David said. "We're heading out of here soon. Might never be back. Last chance."

Being twenty-two that night, with all the strengths and weaknesses that come with it, I saw no danger, not even the possibility of it. Adventure was an intoxicant, and David's logic, in the footloose way we'd both been traveling, was compelling. Hey, something we haven't done! That means we should do it!

So we dropped some tip money on the table and headed toward the torches. The crowd mostly looked like us—young people doing Asia on the cheap—Americans, Europeans, and Australians for the most part—and a few scruffy older hippie couples who looked like they'd arrived on that beach around 1980 and never left.

The rope men, both in their twenties, in ratty shorts and T-shirts, had doused the rope with fuel, lit it, and stepped back by the time we got there. They stood about twenty feet from each other and with a practiced, even rhythm began swinging the rope in great, swirling, mesmerizingly beautiful loops of flaming rope that went up in a huge arc, and then brushed against the white sand and back around. It was hypnotic to watch.

Two girls were jumping as we walked up, both giggling like crazy. And when they were done and had jumped out, falling in hysterics onto the sand, there seemed to be an opportunity and David leaped in.

I watched his first couple of jumps, the burning rope brushing the sand beneath him as he leaped, then going high over his head, his face a radiant grin that I'd known so well and seen so many times since that first day in the ninth grade when we met. We'd both felt like outsiders back then, kids from the eastside with something to prove, and bond over. And now here on this beach together, thousands of miles from home, his friendship felt just as important and powerful.

I watched the timing of the rope, which was long and steady—the rope guys were practiced and smooth—and waited for my moment.

Then I jumped in, and decided David had been right. It was intoxicating and beautiful, and through the first few rotations, I found myself grinning back at him, and at the crowd.

Then it happened. I mistimed a jump and the rope tripped me, wrapping around my legs and feet. In a tangle of fire and sand and shouts, I fell, and the sudden twisting of the rope tripped David as well. I saw him going down, rolling safely out and to the side. But I wasn't as lucky, or as fast on my feet. My body slammed onto the kerosene-soaked rope. I could feel the thick oiliness of it, and smell it there suddenly in my face, as the impact sprayed fuel all over me, soaking my shorts and T-shirt. In a single horrifying instant, I was on fire to my neck.

I was also still tangled in the rope, which added its own horror, the feeling of being trapped. I had to escape, and I had to put out the flames. I knew that much. So out of some survival instinct, I grabbed with my bare right hand the very thing that was burning me, the flaming rope itself. With my surging adrenaline I didn't feel it burning my hand as I threw it off me. Rising up from the sand with no thought but survival, my body engulfed in flames, I ran directly toward the ocean and dove. The water was warm, bath-like and calm. It tricked me into thinking I'd simply had a bad scare.

When I came out, still not having looked down at my legs, David was there on the sand looking confused. Things had unfolded so fast for both of us—him rolling out, me untangling myself and sprinting to the water—that he wasn't even sure what had happened until I emerged from the ocean.

Now he stared at the charred and dead skin that hung off my legs as the salt water dripped off me, and I followed his gaze down to see it all for the first time myself. The flickering light from the torches reflected back from every surface, making everything, including the beads of water that clung to my burned skin, stand out in stark contrasts of black and white. The crowd of onlookers, so exuberant and happy a few minutes before, had fallen dead silent, staring at me in a circle. No one, clearly, had any idea what to do. But I knew I needed immediate medical help, as I stood there dripping, woozy, and becoming more aware of the pain every second.

"David, I'm going into shock," I said. "Help . . . please . . . do something."

David sprang into action, running up toward the café and finding a guy about to head out on his moped.

"Hospital!" David shouted and gestured to me down on the sand.

"Hospital," the driver repeated—maybe one of the few words of English he knew—gesturing to the bike. Carefully, David lifted me up and put me behind the driver, then climbed on behind me. I had no choice but to wrap my legs, with skin hanging off them, around the driver's lap, soaking his clothes in blood and salt water. And that awkward angle forced my face into his back. His T-shirt smelled like the sea, like rotting fish and salt water. Or maybe I was just smelling myself. But the reality was starting to hit either way: I'm in Thailand, in the middle of nowhere, on a beach, on an island. And now I'm on a moped, riding down a dirt path with God knows who to God knows where. I'd gone off to see the world, but now I was really far from home.

*   *   *

I'D THOUGHT OF THAT NIGHT and relived it in memory many times over the years, but never so vividly as I did hunched over the sled in Antarctica, pulling item after item up to my face to sniff for gas fumes before throwing it aside onto the ice. And each sniff seemed to trigger another wave of memory, in recalling—and really almost smelling again—the stench of burned flesh, general anesthetic, and sweat. I sniffed one food bag and recalled the odor of bleach, washed into coarse white hospital sheets. I grabbed another and remembered the smell of ancient dried, crumbling paint that came off in pieces on the corridor walls outside the operating room.

The "hospital" turned out to be more of a makeshift one-room clinic, squat and grim, plunked down next to a vacant lot, filled with garbage and abandoned appliances. As the moped pulled up and David and our moped driver each took one of my shoulders to help get me in, I saw old refrigerators, tilted to crazy angles with their doors gaping open. Cans and broken glass seemed to be everywhere. It did not inspire confidence.

Everything seemed surreal and strange as they laid me down on the steel exam table. The fluorescent lights buzzed loudly over-head. The nurse, when she came in, wearing jeans and a T-shirt, looked way too young, not much more than a child, it seemed to me as I lay there. And the pain, which hadn't seemed so bad on the beach, and through the moped ride—maybe because I'd gone into shock—suddenly hit with brutal force.

It radiated up from my legs in a wave and didn't stop. I felt my stomach clench and my chest tighten with it. The burned skin was screaming.

But they had morphine, which the child-nurse immediately pumped into me, and after that I mainly looked at David's face, scanning his reactions to see how scared I should be myself. I saw him flinch when the nurse grabbed a pair of scissors to cut off my burned clothes, and his whole body stiffened, jaw clenched, as she began cutting off pieces of loose and charred skin.

I was afraid to look down, afraid to look anywhere, and David looked like he was going to faint. So I grabbed his hand, and in my fear and pain, I'm surprised I didn't break it. "David, I need you to be strong for me," I said.

And then I saw a ray of hope cross his face when she cut off my shirt and everyone realized I'd only been burned from the legs down. My sprint to the ocean had probably saved my life, putting out the flames before they penetrated through my shorts and shirt to the skin.

But I really knew nothing for sure, and the language barrier didn't help. Despite the nurse's kindness, the only certainty we'd gotten out of her was that I needed to get to a larger hospital on another island, that the next ferryboat going there wouldn't leave until the following morning, and that David and I would be on our own to somehow make all of that happen.

"More hospital," the nurse said several times emphatically, though I wasn't sure whether that meant "better hospital," on the next island, or "more hospital treatment," or all of those things, or none of them.

But in her broken English, she got the point across that a ferry-boat was needed, but that it wouldn't come until the morning. Then she left the room, me still lying on the table.

David and I were both scared—both of us, I think, feeling like lost little boys, alone on the other side of the world. He stood there for a minute, blinking back his own tears, hands jammed into his pockets. And he did the only thing he could think of: He climbed onto the table with me, about the size of a twin bed, and held me in his arms for the long hours of the night, telling me we'd somehow find a way through.

The pressure was on David the next morning, just as it had been the night before. Through the heaviness of the morphine, I wasn't much use for anything. But he made it work, with muscle and love. I leaned on his shoulder as he got me out of the clinic and into the back of a pickup truck, which was crusted on every surface with red dirt, and then to the ferry dock. He wrestled me up the ramp onto the boat and laid me gently down on an empty patch of floor where I could stretch my bandaged legs out flat. Then he leaned up against a wall next to me for the two-hour ride, as tourists and locals walked by, staring at me, or trying not to.

By the time we finally docked and David had wrestled me into a taxi, the pain meds had long since worn off, but he did his best—and his best was pretty good—to keep up my spirits. Through the jolting taxi ride as I kept my teeth clenched and my eyes clamped shut, trying to think about anything but the pain, David ran through a monologue of the sights as we passed, making up total nonsense in trying to sound like a know-it-all tourist-bus operator. And when we pulled up to the hospital and I saw what looked like another tired and run-down building, he even managed to make me laugh.

"Hey, it's bigger at least," he said, jabbing me in the arm. "More hospital!"

THE NEXT DAYS AND NIGHTS were blurred by morphine and uncertainty.

Sometimes I found myself just staring at the walls of the little room between visits from David, unsure even where I was, looking down to find my legs completely bandaged and feeling a wave of shock as though seeing them for the first time. What have I done? I thought.

One night I woke up in the hospital's makeshift ICU, sick from anesthesia, after one of the eight surgical sessions of debriding my wounds to remove damaged tissue, and found a cat running across my chest and around my bed, hammering home the fact that nothing here was probably sanitary or safe and that just lying here was probably dangerous. I knew enough about burns to fear infection. The searing pain was unimaginable, but the morphine they kept giving me made it feel as if there were insects crawling over my skin. I couldn't tell which was worse.

And then the day came, four days after the fire, that made all of that seem utterly unimportant. A doctor walked in. He was skinny and unhealthy looking himself, with a bad complexion and thinning hair—not one of the usual doctors, which made me think he was a specialist or something.

Maybe now I'll know when I can get out of here, I thought hopefully. I imagined going on with my trip, or at least sitting by a pool. Anything beyond this hospital would be an improvement.

Without saying anything, the doctor unwrapped my legs. He grabbed my feet and moved them, which sent a jolt of pain running up through me despite the morphine. He prodded and poked around my knees with the same pain-surge effect.

Okay, I told myself, this is normal. Healing from burns hurts. I know he'll have something positive to say when he's done hurting me.

But then he straightened back up and crossed his arms in front of his chest.

"You'll probably never walk again normally," he said in Thai-accented English. He then ran through my damage as though it were a shopping list. The ligaments, knee joints, and ankle joints were all "affected," he said.

Then without another word or any attempt at bedside manner, he abruptly turned and left the room, leaving me feeling more alone than I'd ever been in my life. The physical pain suddenly seemed like nothing compared to the spiral of emotional darkness his words had thrown me into. My life was over. It was the end of everything, the end of the world as I'd known it.

*   *   *

MY MOM ARRIVED ON THE FIFTH DAY of this ordeal, not knowing how bad things were, or how deep I'd gone into despair, but only that I needed her.

I learned later that she regularly cried in the hallways at the hospital, pleading with the Thai doctors for good news. I can only imagine how scary it was for a mother to see her child so broken and helpless. But she never showed me that fear, and instead came into my hospital room every day with a smile on her face and an air of positivity. She saved me just as much as David had, and her arrival marked a handoff in my care. She wrapped David up with a hug of gratitude and encouraged him to continue on his travels.

"Colin, what do you want to do when you get out of here? Let's set a goal!" she said that first day after David and I had said our tearful goodbyes.

"Mom, are you kidding me? My life is over," I said, looking up at her from the bed. All I could see at that point was darkness, and hear the echoing words of that doctor: "You'll probably never walk again normally."

She leaned in. Behind her, I could see paint chips peeling from the cinder-block walls of the room. "Do me a favor," Mom said. "Close your eyes."

I shrugged and played along. Better to close my eyes than look at the crummy hospital room and its peeling paint. "I want you to set a goal for after you get out of here, Colin," she said. "Visualize it, picture yourself doing it. Grab onto it." And in that moment, for whatever reason, but mostly, I think, because athletic goals have always been how I function, I saw myself completing a triathlon, something I'd never done before. She could have easily looked down at my bandaged legs and told me to set a more "realistic" goal, but instead she wrapped me in her arms and said, "I can already see you crossing the finish line."

BY THE TIME we got to the even bigger, modern-looking hospital in Bangkok, via a medical airlift on the eighth day after the fire, the idea of a triathlon was starting to feel like something from a morphine-induced dream. And through the next month at that hospital, as I lay there incapable of taking a single step, things felt as if they were sliding even more. The power of those first moments of Mom's infectious energy, when she bounded into my room, demanding a goal, was fading.

But I gradually realized, as more days passed and she began to make arrangements to get me home to Portland, that one version of Mom, that first-day big-idea architect pushing me to envision my future, had transformed into another version, Mom the patient and painstaking bricklayer. She was there at my side, almost always. She slept in the room on a cot. She was there when I went to sleep and there when I woke up.

She didn't put a sunny face on everything, or gloss over my injuries. She just never left, and the message of love that conveyed was immense. She was a constant in a world that seemed turned upside down, and that became something I could cling to. But she also never stopped asking about the triathlon, and how exactly I intended to execute my plan for doing it—what steps needed to be taken to make it reality, and how soon I thought it might happen. She mixed open-ended love and support on the one hand with inspiration and relentless focus on the other, and she swept me along with her. One day I woke up and found out she'd convinced the doctor to bring me a set of dumbbell weights that I could start using in bed. Given my diagnosis, the doctor looked at me like I was crazy to be training at a time like this. I didn't care. I immediately started lifting for all it was worth. Mom had been emailing with a doctor back in Oregon by that point as well, and he'd told her to fatten me up. Rebuilding tissue, he'd said, requires thousands of extra calories a day, and the hospital might not be providing enough. So along with the weights came a torrent of snacks and treats and Thai street food. My upper body, at least, got stronger and stronger.

The homecoming trip, back to Portland, when doctors said I could finally fly without fears about what the air-pressure changes might do to my burns, was bittersweet. I'd fantasized, back in my hospital bed, about continuing my trip around the world. And when that clearly wasn't going to happen, I'd started to picture the good things about getting home. Portland, on some of those days in the bed, shimmered in my mind like a perfect place, magical and beautiful and full of things I knew and loved. I pictured Mount Hood in the distance, and the old steel Hawthorne Bridge I'd biked and walked across so many times, and the steep bark-covered trails of Mount Tabor Park near my parents' house.

Traveling as an invalid was definitely not part of the fantasy.

The passengers on the flight from Bangkok stared at me as I was being carried aboard, or looked away, just like the ferryboat passengers had on that long day with David. And the Portland airport, which I'd been through so many times on my visits home from school, was utterly different seen from a wheelchair. I'd loved that airport in the past and always felt a lift in my spirits from its homey charm. Now, being wheeled by my mother through customs and then to the arrivals curb, I hated it intensely. I was no longer me and neither was the airport, it seemed. I hadn't forgotten my triathlon dream, but the long list of humiliations in getting home made it seem more and more like a mirage, another morphine fantasy.

Mom's mix of love and relentlessness continued after we finally got to her house in Portland. The triathlon dream was real, and would *become* real, she kept saying. Her optimism and will became the great anchor and constant of everything, and I drew strength from them.

On that first gray Pacific Northwest morning after returning home from Thailand, when she stood there in the kitchen, her hand resting on the back of that wooden chair, eyes drilling into mine, she'd convinced me to take that first step out of my wheelchair. Her strength and belief in me hung in the air, strong as the smell of chai tea from the stove.

Despite my breakthrough the previous day, my mom didn't take it easy on me. Instead she moved the chair five steps away and the next day ten steps away. Each day I could take a few more steps on my road to recovery. And on it went.

I walked. Eventually I made it all the way around the block. One day I broke into a jog on a wooded trail in Mount Tabor Park. Barely faster than walking, but right then, jogging felt like flying, and I almost immediately stopped and broke down in sobs from the joy and power of it, startling a neighbor and her dog half to death.

The wounds slowly healed. I had to wear compression garments under my clothes and couldn't expose bare skin to sunlight for over a year, but those things seemed tiny and insignificant. I had less range of motion in my left ankle than before, but I could move. That was all that mattered. The Thai doctor was wrong. Tiny steps and life-changing leaps, love and commitment, pain and perseverance— they all brought me to a new place.

IN LATE 2009, about a year and a half after the fire, and the endless rounds of physical therapy, I stood on another beach, in Chicago. Needing to escape my parents' basement after the long recovery, and get my life back on track, I figured it was time to put my Yale economics degree to use. I'd moved to Chicago to take a job as a commodities trader. It was my first real job, if you don't count painting houses with David in the neighborhoods around Portland, and the money was good. I could afford a nice Chicago apartment. Things were on the upswing. But the dream of completing a triathlon, which I'd promised myself and my mom back in the hospital, was even more potent.

So I'd signed up for the Chicago triathlon, which started with a 1-mile open-water swim in Lake Michigan, followed by a 25-mile bike ride and a 6.2-mile footrace. And I'd trained my brains out, swimming before work, running circuits through the streets when I got off. In the middle of a training ride on my bike, I met a guy and told him the story of the fire, the wounds, the goal hatched in a hospital bed—and he said, "Hey, I've done a triathlon, maybe I can help you train."

And as the date of the race approached, I found more and more that being at work, watching the little disembodied prices of crude oil and corn futures flutter across my computer screen, was simply the interval when I couldn't be training. I trained in fear that my body was permanently compromised and weakened and that only a ferocity of effort could overcome the wounds and scars. But I mostly trained in joy that I could, more and more, move with the freedom I thought I'd lost forever.

When race day finally came, I stood there in my swim cap on the edge of the lake with more than four thousand other competitors— the city's staggering skyline rising up behind us—I felt once again the passion of my seven-year-old self, the Pablo Morales worshipper who fell in love with the Olympics. He was still alive, still in there, ready to leap, jump, fly, and dive. But as the countdown came, and the collective adrenaline of the racers around me rose to a fevered scream, I suddenly realized that I wasn't that boy at all. I had a different fuel burning inside me now: hope. I felt stripped down to a leaner place in body and mind—lighter from having shed a heavy burden.

I was there because I *could* be there, and that was a huge and powerful force. It propelled me out into the water, and then out of my wetsuit and onto the bike. I raced down Lake Shore Drive, feeling the wind across my face and the wonderful hard pull of the pedals. And the running felt best of all. I ran in joy, fueled by a power that seemed to surge up out of the ground and into my legs. I glanced down at them more than once, almost like I wanted to pinch myself that they were there and whole, and then I ran all the harder. I ran with an optimism that I wanted to shout to the sky, through the concrete canyons of the city that stretched out behind me, across the lake, to the kitchen in southeast Portland and my mom and that wonderful wooden chair—the one toward which I'd taken the single step that had led to this moment.

And I roared. And part of that was knowing that in a way it didn't matter—when I crossed the finish line it would be a victory no matter what. And I think maybe that made a difference. So purely was I running my own race, so driven by the momentum of what had come before, that I couldn't be stopped.

When I crossed the finish line, the world itself seemed to open up and cry with me. It had happened, the dream from that Thai hospital bed had become real. But then as I wandered through the crowd, dazed with euphoria, an even stronger thought hit me: The dream hadn't just happened. Through overcoming my fears, I'd built the dream, hammered the scaffolding around it, and made it mine.

Only hours later, walking up to the scorers table, did I learn what had happened. I'd collected my bike by then and grabbed brunch with Grandma Sue, who still lived in the Chicago suburbs where my mother had grown up. "We've been calling your name," a guy behind the scorers table said, squinting up at me.

"What? Did I do something wrong?" I said, fearful that something of what felt like such a glorious moment might be taken away.

"You won," he said.

"What do you mean?" I still didn't get it. The race had been run in multiple waves, so there'd never been any way of knowing who was in the lead.

"It means that more than four thousand people started and you came in first—you won the race," the guy said, speaking as though I was a little slow and needed an explanation of what winning meant.

THAT NIGHT, BY TOTAL COINCIDENCE, I'd been invited to a summer barbecue at my friend Jenny's parents' house, whom I'd met through David.

"Brian Gelber," the host said at the door. He was a fair-skinned, slightly freckled man in his fifties who shook my hand with a strong grip and a big smile, and he took me around to a beautiful backyard where his large family was gathered. In my finance job, I'd certainly heard of him—his firm was a major force in the Chicago-based commodity trading business—but his warmth and charisma instantly put me at ease.

"So what'd you do today?" he said, handing me a drink. It was a beautiful Sunday evening, full of the sounds of laughter and the wonderful smells from the grill.

"Well . . ." I felt sort of funny saying it; it hadn't sunk in yet. "I actually won the Chicago Triathlon."

Mr. Gelber stopped, his own drink halfway to his lips.

"You won it? Like first place, first place?"

"Yeah," I nodded. "Kind of surprised me, too."

He looked at me closely for a long time, but then his wife called out, "Dinner is ready," and after giving me a little touch on the shoulder, he walked over to the table and sat down. Platters of sweet corn and bowls of potato salad made the rounds. The sharp, intelligent conversation around me ranged from the global financial crisis to sports and family life. I was just finishing my plate when he wandered back over and took a seat next to me.

"I've been thinking about this triathlon thing," he said, looking serious. "Not everybody can do what you did today, Colin—hardly anybody in fact—especially considering what you went through with your . . . accident." He stopped and clenched his jaw. "My daughter told me about it. Anyway, here's the thing," he added with a little smack on the table with his palm. "Have you ever thought about what you might accomplish if you put in a full-time effort training?"

I sat back in my chair, thinking about my commodities trading job, and how much I was starting to hate it.

"I've been a competitive swimmer since I was a little kid," I said. "So . . . yeah, that dream has always been out there, to one day be a professional athlete, maybe even make the Olympics." I sighed, reached for my drink, and took a big sip. "But it's not really an option at this point in my life. I need my job."

Then Mr. Gelber was quiet for what seemed like a long time, clearly thinking, and finally he reached out and touched my arm. "I think I'd like to help you," he said.

"What do you mean?"

"Well, like a sponsor."

I sat up.

"Financial support so you can do what you should be doing, what your dream says you should be doing," he said. "Won't be as lucrative as trading, for sure," he added, shrugging. "But I'm seeing a guy who should not be sitting in an office."

I stared up into the pale summer midwestern sky over the Gelber backyard and realized that everything had just changed again. The ripples that had begun that night on the beach in Thailand—the rock thrown into the pond—were still spreading out and leading me to places I couldn't yet imagine. But I could tell already that those places were calling to me, asking what else I had inside, what other reservoirs might be tapped. I'd been guided by my mother from a place of abject darkness into brilliant light. And now this strange and unlikely moment in a backyard had opened another door. I had to walk through.

The next day, I went into the office, knocked on my boss's door, and quit my job.

CHAPTER SEVEN

All In, All Gone

DAY 8

The thick, sweet smell of the white gas had taken me down a rabbit hole of memory, evoking images of the burn and the road after, but the panic from the spill inside the sled, on that tumultuous eighth night of my crossing, had its own effect, too.

I'd hurled all the critical pieces of my life onto the ice around me as I struggled to find the spill and determine the damage. But then as I continued to paw down into the sled, breathing hard, feeling every muscle tighten up with the fear of what I might find—destroyed food, fuel supplies depleted—it suddenly struck me that my anxiety had led to yet another mistake. In throwing things onto the ice, I'd forgotten to secure them down. I turned back and gasped as I realized that my tent and arctic bedding sack with my sleeping bag and pad inside—two of the lightest but most crucial things to keep me alive—were just lying there. A sudden gust of wind could've taken them while I'd been bent over the sled, with implications as bad as or worse than spilled gas.

I immediately grabbed my orange and black duffel bags and piled them on top like paper weights along with my Kevlar kitchen box with the stove inside. I pressed the pile down with my mittened hand, just for reassurance.

Then I turned back to the sled. Food was a crucial worry. Historically, food spoiled by gas had ended expeditions. When I found the food bags, I immediately brought them to my face to sniff the outside, then opened them up and sniffed again. But they seemed secure and sealed. I threw them onto the pile of my gear. My gas cans also seemed, in hefting them up, about as heavy as they should be.

Only with it all cleared could I see the thin film of liquid, pooled in the grooves of the sled runners. The one-liter fuel bottle that had spilled, cap improperly screwed back on when I'd been refilling it, lay down there on its side. The loss of one liter of cooking fuel would erode my margin of safety, but not enough to trigger a crisis. I'd dodged a complete disaster. But the horrible rainbow sheen of petrochemicals reflecting back up at me told me how close I'd come. I fell back onto the ice, still gripping the side of the sled, shaking from head to toe.

I STILL HAD TO MAKE CAMP AFTER THAT. But just as crucially, I knew I needed to find my center again, catch a breath, search for a new place of calm. In addressing one problem I'd almost caused another. I needed to refocus.

I laid down the tent, first anchoring it to the sled so it would be absolutely secure on the ice even in the strongest winds, and then on the other side to put down an anchor there, and on around the perimeter, smashing the stakes down with my boot as I went—trying to visualize the process, to reinforce my certainty that I'd done everything right. I carried my kitchen box to the tent vestibule at the back—canopied over by the wind flap—dug it into the snow, and zipped it in with the same intent. And then in the final step, shoveling snow around the tent's outer edge to keep the wind from blowing up underneath it, I began counting the shovelfuls. It was unnecessary, but somehow it felt both soothing and precise. A one-foot-high snow barrier, piled along two ten-foot lengths of tent, with three feet across each end, twenty-six feet in total. That added up to about twenty-six shovels of snow, more or less, so I figured. I started counting that number down as I shoveled, each shovelful assumed to be about a square foot . . . 26, 25, 24 . . . until I completed the task.

There was a hypnotic rhythm to that, a feeling that I was relearning lessons, bringing myself back down from an anxious moment, and I heard Dixie Dansercoer's voice in my head as I worked.

"The best way to deal with a crisis is not to have it in the first place," he'd said to me when I'd met him in Longyearbyen, a tough and treeless little dot of a coal-mining town on Spitsbergen Island off the northern coast of Norway. I was preparing to cross to the North Pole in 2016 during the Explorers Grand Slam expedition, and Dixie, a Belgian explorer, was heading to the Pole on his own expedition, guiding a family of Brits.

As one of the most accomplished polar explorers in modern history, Dixie was steeped in survival wisdom about cold and ice, and starting that day, he became my mentor.

"All things wet are disasters at thirty degrees below zero, Colin," he'd said that day, another Dixie-ism that I'd kept and tried to absorb in coming to Antarctica. "So staying dry, or knowing what parts must never get wet—this must be your goal, always."

Dixie had taught me to put plastic bags on my feet in brutally cold weather, as a middle layer between thin liner socks and thick warm wool socks, and as I shoveled I wiggled my toes inside the boots thinking about him.

This concept had confused me at first. "But the feet will sweat in a plastic bag, and when they get wet, they'll freeze, right?" I asked Dixie, sipping a hot drink as a cold wind blew into town off the fjord that cuts into the island.

"No, the boot is the true thing to worry about, Colin," he said. "The plastic bag trick will make your feet and liner sock damp, but the moisture will stay there, right around your foot and not go into the boot. Because a frozen boot over the course of a long expedition? Phfft!" he said with a sweeping motion of his hand. "A frozen boot never thaws in the deep cold. It cannot be thawed. And that's it. Frostbite. Toes goodbye."

When the tent was secured, I stared down at it for a minute, rechecking my mental list of things to worry about or put aside as completed. The sum of my possessions, my life, and my existence on the ice was all in there, compacted in one place—the space inside barely bigger than your average coffin, but representing at the same time everything about safety and home.

But it also represented, beyond the eventual sleep I'd try to get, the second part of my workday. I still needed to get myself fed, get snow melted for water for the next day, check in with A.L.E. and Jenna, and on down a list that would take me another two or three hours to complete, and as I crawled inside, a wave of comforting familiarity rolled through me. The first thing I saw was my clothes-line dangling out before me, running the length of the tent. My face mask, banged to clear the icicles, went immediately onto the line, followed by my mittens. Then the boots came off, along with my three pairs of socks—the heavy wool outer layer, the plastic bag, and finally the thin inner liner against my skin. One of Dixie's added nuggets of wisdom was that a foot bag should also have been, in a previous life, a food bag. The container for a morning's oatmeal ration could be recycled as footwear, and that night as I held the bags up to my face to look, I saw that one of my oatmeal-turned-foot-bags had developed a hole and was done. I wadded it up and stuffed it into my jacket pocket.

All the pieces of my life were in motion. Mittens and steaming socks bounced on the line. The tent fabric fluttered as though it were alive. My overalls scraped on the tent's floor, fabric on fabric, as I crawled forward before turning back to zip up and close myself in.

STARTING THE STOVE, to begin snowmelt and make hot water to rehydrate my dinner, was always the first step once inside, and by then it was time for my nightly 8:50 p.m. check-in call to A.L.E.

But after that came a part of the day I always looked forward to, a moment that was soothing and comforting even when I wasn't trying to recover from some freak-out or trauma, when I'd feel, for a few minutes, like I was standing in front of a classroom of boys and girls—something I'd come to love in the nonprofit work Jenna and I had begun with the Explorers Grand Slam.

I grabbed for the inReach device from my bag, and there it was: The nightly text from Jenna had arrived, with a question from one of the thirty thousand students who were following my Antarctica project in their classrooms at 104 schools around the world. In a day of constant motion, answering questions about Antarctica or my life on the ice—often extremely thoughtful, always interesting—felt like a release, a few minutes when I was freed from the sometimes claustrophobic confines of my day and my routine.

Jenna was the facilitator in making it work: Every night, I'd send her a photo and recap of my day—transmitted through a glacially slow Iridium GO! satellite modem, thirty minutes or more to send one low-res image—which she'd post to Instagram, while I responded to the nightly question she'd forwarded on the inReach.

That night, an eleven-year-old sixth grader from Atlanta, Georgia, who had been following The Impossible First journey through the curriculum in his classroom, wanted to know about wildlife.

"How do you protect yourself from polar bears?" he asked. "Do you see them very often?"

I read it again and smiled as I did, picturing the boy and his school, hoping the curiosity that had prompted his question would always burn, pushing him to keep learning.

"Here's a riddle: why don't polar bears eat penguins?" I wrote back. "Because they live in different parts of the world! There are no polar bears in Antarctica at all, which is lucky for me, and the penguins. The bears all live on the opposite side of the globe in the far north near the North Pole."

I FOUND A RHYTHM the next day, and the next, and on through a string of twelve-hour days in the harness. That I could go days without an incident or accident or crisis of some other kind restored some of my confidence, and by the time I woke up on my fifteenth day on the ice, I felt in some ways like a well-oiled machine.

A bad headwind had developed during the night. I'd heard it growing in force, whipping the tent, and as I began my two-hour morning routine of chores—putting on the water to boil, pooping in the vestibule of snow at the foot-edge of the tent, pouring water into oatmeal, then filling my two-liter thermos for the day's drinking water—it seemed to only grow stronger. I pulled on my three sock layers, my red-and-black overalls and jacket, listening to the growing howl, and by the time I climbed out, it was really whipping, by far the strongest wind I'd experienced on the ice, coming straight north toward me from the high polar plateau.

I stiffened instinctively and involuntarily as the first real gust blasted into my body, feeling the deep cold of it even through my bundled layers, my mask, and the fur collar of my parka hood—and as I harnessed in and began, I realized I'd never pulled the sled into anything like it. The wind hit my body like a wall, forcing me, without ever consciously deciding to change anything about my posture, to lean into it, curling over slightly toward my ski tips.

I was creating a line against the wind like my tent's, I realized—streamlined with the wind's direction to minimize the impact. When I stopped to take a quick pee, I saw quickly that I'd never peed in wind like that, either. Even with my back carefully positioned to the wind after I unzipped the fly of my overalls, the pee stream sprayed wildly away from me.

As I zipped up and turned back into the wind, it struck me that I hadn't shot enough video of dramatic weather like this either. I'd been journaling with my camera in recent days, recording my thoughts in the tent before sleep and filming scenes outside of deep snow or beautiful weather. In addition to my journaling, I was capturing photos for my nightly Instagram post and videos to share later when I returned from Antarctica.

That day in the wind the idea of what to film was pretty basic: me trudging across the frame, pulling the sled into horizontal blowing snow. But complications quickly ensued.

I grabbed my GoPro, which was mounted onto a little tripod, set it up facing out across the ice, and reached down with my huge ungainly mittens to fumble with the record button. Video rolling, I left the camera in position and walked back to my sled. But just as I got halfway across my big scene, I looked over and saw that the tripod had toppled in the wind. That meant starting the entire process all over. So I retreated to my starting spot, unhitched, walked over to put the camera back upright, then tried the whole thing again. And again it fell. I felt like an actor in a low-budget movie where the sets are cardboard and the swap meet–quality props are guaranteed to fail.

The cold was starting to get to me by then, and I knew the battery would also be stressed from the frigid air, and that I needed to be making progress pushing south. When I got back to the camera after the second knockdown, I was getting frustrated with my cinematic partner.

"Okay, man," I said aloud. "I know it's windy out here, but three legs should be good enough. I'm getting around on two. You can do this."

The camera stayed upright this time, but it was a clearly ridiculous exercise all the same. The camera recorded me pulling the sled into the wind, going out of the frame, but then a few minutes later walking right back and reaching down with my big black mittens to pack it all up. I gently folded the little tripod legs, then peered into the lens one more time. "Yeah, I know," I said. "The things we do, huh?"

I was trying to bring some levity to the situation to take my mind off the bitter cold and in some small way normalize what was abnormal. After all, with this trek, I was engaged in something that demanded all my strength and will. My survival instincts naturally rebelled against taking time out to "shoot selfies." But if that picture you're creating can't be viewed, how can it inspire? How would my life have been different if I hadn't been able to *see* Pablo Morales win that butterfly gold medal in 1992?

THE WIND CONTINUED AND WORSENED through that morning, taking the windchill down to what had to have been well below minus fifty, and by noon I was really looking forward to my quick midday break and my ramen noodles. I unclipped and sat down on the sled, pulled on my extra parka, and grabbed my thermos. I poured water from the thermos into the mug with the noodles and pulled up the mask to take a slurp. But then just as I was pulling the mug to my face, I caught a glimpse of myself in the little mirror that jutted up from the front of the compass. With a flinch of panic I set down the mug and I yanked the compass toward me for a better view.

The tip of my nose was frostbitten. A white spot about the size of a pinky fingernail had formed right on the tip. I looked down into the mask, a Darth Vader–like plastic mask-and-goggles combo that covered my face completely from the top of my forehead to below my chin.

A caked layer of ice had formed inside, right where the mask touched my nose. Because of the headwind, my breath had condensed and frozen inside, instead of being blown out the side as I breathed, which happened with any kind of crosswind. And the pressure of the mask had then pressed my nose up against the wall of ice. That had been enough to do it. With the mask off, I quickly grabbed a ski pole and jammed it down into the mask, and after four or five jabs, the ice finally broke into shards and I shook the mask upside down to clear it before putting it back on, my heart pounding.

People lost parts of themselves in places like this—I couldn't help but think of Everest expedition survivor Beck Weathers. And I thought of the promise Jenna and I had made to each other, that I'd always come home in one piece even if it meant failure.

I'm being changed, I thought as I touched a mitten to my mask, now back on my face. I'm becoming someone I don't know. Frostbite felt like a symbol, the beginning of something bigger. Antarctica was taking my body and my mind somewhere far away from what I'd been before. There'd be positive pieces of that journey—I firmly believed that, even if they were mixed in with the negative elements. But might I lose sight, in obsession or error, of the promise I'd made to Jenna about my safety? What was the price I'd have to pay for my dreams?

I'D PAID PRICES BEFORE.

After falling in love in Sydney, Jenna and I continued building our relationship over the next three years. Jenna finished college in Florida, I took my job in Chicago, but over this time we never lived in the same city. We dreamed of sharing a home and, in 2010,

Jenna moved to Portland so we could be together. But on a steamy day in July 2011, when I was twenty-six years old, I stood at the curb outside an apartment building on West Burnside Street in Portland, throwing the last few bags of clothes and gear and books into my fifteen-year-old turd-brown Subaru. My triathlon bike was already secured to the rack on top, but other than that, I was traveling light—running shoes, swimming caps and suits, and enough other clothes to get me by when I wouldn't be training.

I certainly wouldn't have said at that moment that I was a jerk, or a fool, or even confused. But I stood there, sweating and impatient, full of the absolute blind certainty of every confused, foolish jerk I've ever known. I looked at my watch, thinking about summer traffic that can snarl Interstate 5 south of Portland. I thought about California and Australia, where I was going to live and train, and all the grand triumphs I'd surely have ahead. I was about to hitch a rocket ride, and if there were implications in that for my relationship with Jenna, I couldn't see them, or perhaps on some level I'd chosen to ignore them. Jenna was twenty-four that summer, dressed for work in her sharp and smart business clothes, heading off to a campaign staff meeting with my mother. Her "politics clothes," I called them. She'd just come out of our apartment and stood on the curb looking at me, arms crossed on her chest. Her eyes were red. She'd been crying. I'd done that.

I could see the balcony of our apartment over Jenna's shoulder— our first apartment, near enough to the Portland Timbers soccer stadium that we could hear the roar of the crowd on game day. I saw the tomato starts she'd put into our little terrace looking out over the city street. "Our first garden!" she'd said, her hands covered with black potting soil, as she came back inside. There'd be lots more gardens, we told each other.

But I also *didn't* see those things. I was leaving, and there was nothing much more to discuss.

"This is a once-in-a-lifetime chance and I'm taking it," I said to

Jenna. I didn't say anything about us, or ask anything about her. I declared it.

She looked me in the eyes across the sidewalk, but didn't say anything for a while.

"I moved across the country from the East Coast nine months ago to build a life with you," she finally said. Her words were a declaration, too, a statement of fact. She wasn't pleading or crying. "Left the community I knew, left everything . . ."

"I know," I said, shrugging. "I know that."

We stood there silently after that for a while. I saw her eyes well up, and she bit her lip.

"But you have to do this, I know—it's an incredible opportunity," she said. "And you should . . . it'll be . . ." She shrugged.

"Long-distance," I said.

She nodded. "And I've committed to working with your mom," she said. "I can't just walk away from that." She straightened up. "I'm just a little sad right now, that's all. It'll be lonely here without you."

In other circumstances, Jenna's comment, and her implied suggestion about my priorities and loyalties—that I was walking away from my own family and she was not—would've stung. My mom, after years of passionate grassroots political involvement, had decided earlier that year to make her first-ever run for public office, trying to become Portland's next mayor. And Jenna, my mom's first campaign hire, was using her political science degree—helping shape campaign events and organizing Mom's every minute, from her first early-morning wake-up call to the last meeting of the day twelve hours later. Mom and Jenna were dashing around the city together day after day sprinting through five-minute lunches, speeches, and neighborhood meet-and-greets, and I'd seen that Jenna was dedicated to it and was good at it.

But couldn't they both see what had fallen into *my* lap? I'd been invited to join a super-elite triathlon team. World championships, the Olympics, medals, glory, half the year in Southern California, the other half in Australia—all of that beckoned like a glittering jewel. Even getting the call from the coach who'd invited me, a former world champion herself, had been exhilarating and flattering. But she said the offer came with a condition. "You have to be all in, Colin," she said. "If you're not all in, 100 percent, then don't bother coming."

And so, pumped up with an inflated view of my own destiny, I drove off into the muggy Portland afternoon, blind to what I was leaving behind.

All in, all gone.

I'D BEEN AFRAID TO CHECK MY NOSE again through the rest of the day until I got into the tent, but I hadn't been able to stop thinking about it, reaching up periodically to feel my mask, wanting to pull it off to check, knowing that made no sense and could worsen the problem.

But then, once I was inside the tent that night, I couldn't stop looking. I stared for a long time at myself in my little hand mirror, which was definitely not a good idea. The longer I looked, the stranger and less familiar I appeared somehow, so unlike the person who'd always gazed back at me in mirrors before that. The still-white spot of frostbite on my nose created a bull's-eye target in the middle of my face and I couldn't stop staring at it, and probing with my finger.

My dot of frostbite was superficial. I knew that. White indicates the lowest level, just past the pink of frostnip, baby steps into the spectrum of horror that can lead to the blue-black of tissue damage and amputation.

I knew my nose needed extra protection now, just in case something like the ice-mask problem happened again, so I grabbed for my first-aid kit. I had blister and salve cream in there, and bandages to wrap puncture wounds, cuts, and burns. None of those things were a fit for this particular problem.

Then I found a roll of kinesio sports tape—the stuff you see on athlete's shoulders and arms, meant to help stabilize muscles and tendons. It wouldn't heal my frostbite, but it would at least cover it up, function like a little jacket that would hold in my skin's warmth, a tiny suit of armor. I cut two more strips to put across my cheeks; even though I'd seen no frostbite, it felt like insurance.

By the end I looked like a defensive lineman from the brawly, leather-helmeted days of the NFL—damaged and bandaged, but by God, going back out onto the field, ready to get clobbered all over again.

Then I looked at my fingers. The fine-dexterity work with the tape had made them hurt like hell, and I saw that if anything, they were in even worse shape than the nose—not frostbitten, but cracked wide open in the cold. Fissures ran deep into my fingertips, and as I held them up in front of my face in the pinkish light of the tent they seemed alien—Frankenstein fingers, crevasses down into the ice, not part of me, not the Colin I knew or had ever known. I'd have to do something about them, too.

I shuddered and pawed through my medical bag again, looking for my superglue, which I'd thrown in as a fix-all. I needed to close the cracks to keep them from growing, so I laid one hand down on the top of the sleeping bag, took the glue with the other hand, and ran a bead down each crack.

Gluing my cracks closed was in some ways even more disgusting than the cracks themselves—in almost any other time or place in the world I'd left behind, it would have been absolutely revolting, if not unsanitary, unsafe, and insane. But all things had changed. What was disgusting had become strangely comforting. What was only very cold, and not brutally cold, felt almost warm. What was monotonous, in food and the daily grinding rhythm of life in pulling the sled south, became an element of autopilot calm, one less thing to think about. I held up my hands before me in the diffuse red light of the tent, clenched my fingers to make a fist, felt the glistening glue beads drying stiff and tight in the cold air, then looked into my eyes one more time in the mirror, wondering what other cracks I might be gluing closed before I was done.

I WOKE UP DURING THE NIGHT feeling overwhelmed and ganged-up on, my defenses down. Things I could wrestle with rationally by day—the wind and cold, and the effects that Antarctica was having on my body in cracks and frostbite—seemed suddenly bigger in that 3 a.m. space of anxious uncertainty. I pulled off my sleep mask. Sunlight beamed through the roof. The wind still blasted outside. And I needed to pee, so I grabbed my pee bottle to bring it inside the bag, where I could relieve myself without having to leave the tent in the middle of the night. But just as I did I was seized by a wave of hunger that made me ravenous and a bit out of control. Still half-asleep, I grabbed the duffel bag with my food supplies and ripped it open, then grabbed chunks of Colin Bars and stuffed them into my mouth.

In my delirium, they were candy bars, the most delicious things I'd ever eaten. Every bite swirled into my senses. I'd never tasted anything like it. And then just as abruptly, I was horrified, realizing what I'd done.

I'd broken the rules. I'd lost control. I'd eaten tomorrow's food. I slumped into my sleeping bag, raging at myself and feeling the bars churning in my stomach. Antarctica was almost every day demanding hard choices, and in a moment of half-awake dream-scape reasoning, I'd made a choice and responded to a need deep inside me that was probably more than just hunger. That seemed clear enough to me as I lay there, unable for a long time to even close my eyes.

Consequences of that moment of blind need would unfold. But it also struck me, as I stared at the red tent roof for a long time, watching my clothesline bounce and dance with the motions of the wind, that our defeats can't be separated from our victories. Scars and triumphs both make us who we are. I reached down inside the sleeping bag and touched my thighs and calves, running my fingers along the places burned and healed.

The good and the bad couldn't be separated. What I was and how I'd come to be there, tucked into my little world on the ice, was a consequence of every event in my life. My food-raid mistake would have repercussions, and those repercussions would have consequences of their own, and the best I could do was hold on and hope that pulling one thread wouldn't unravel everything.

CHAPTER EIGHT

Ghost Town

DAY 16

woke up feeling sick and disgusted with myself, and as I leaned over to light my stove, I knew I'd be hungry for the day, and I accepted that as my fate. I'd made a mistake in the night—worse than that, I'd shown that I was weak—grabbing extra food in my half-awake, half-asleep dream state.

I bounced the remaining day's worth of Colin Bars up and down in my hand as my water heated on the stove, weighing them in my mind, trying to assess exactly how many calories I'd gobbled and so how many fewer I'd have in my pockets as fuel during the day. About half were gone, meaning I'd eaten somewhere around two thousand calories in my raid, and that would take me down to about five thousand calories total for the day when I'd still be burning ten thousand. Rudd rations, I thought as I pushed the bars into my pockets. Even less.

My stomach was gurgling as I broke camp, and I had to stop several times as I packed, straightening up with a hand pressed to my belly. I heard Dr. Troup's warning again in my head, that the high-fat, high-calorie bars he and his team had created for me were, in a way, a food on the frontier—designed for high performance in an extreme

120

environment, but also extreme in their own way. The bars had worked beautifully and burned cleanly in my body on a day-to-day rationed basis, but gorging myself last night—eating the most ever in a day and far more than anyone had ever expected in a twenty-four-hour period—had pushed me to the border of my body's tolerance.

The gurgling churn in my stomach continued as I harnessed up and began pulling south into a brilliant clear day, and I felt I could see forever across the ice even as I found myself focusing more and more on my digestion. I'd certainly been aware of my body before, in my previous fifteen days on the ice. Muscle fatigue and cold were constant companions. But things felt pulled to a new place now. When a new wave of rumbling gurgles rolled through, my gut grabbed my mind entirely, and I tried to fight back by focusing on things outside myself—on the sun and sky and ice around me— trying to absorb Antarctica as a kind of escape from my internal struggle.

But after about four hours, the wave surged to a new place. I needed to relieve myself and couldn't avoid it much longer, and at that point logistics took over. I'd been fortunately regular, going to the bathroom every morning without fail in the snow-floored vestibule sheltered by the outer layer of my tent. Now I looked down at my gear. To get out of my clothes, I'd first have to unharness and remove the compass from my chest, then take off my jacket, then my windproof overalls underneath. Only then, having arrived at the base layers, could I pull down my underwear.

The clock would be running. A glance at my thermometer said it was almost twenty-five below. I'd have a lot of skin exposed. Frostbite was possible and was definitely on my mind—even as my gut roiled, I thought about my frostbitten nose. But then the wave passed and I told myself I could make it through the day. I shrank back from the challenge and difficulty of relieving myself outside, and clung to the idea that I could wait and do it safely and securely in my sheltered little bathroom vestibule.

But I couldn't make it. At about six hours, a wave came that wouldn't stop. Instinctively, I thought that I'd get relief if I was able to pass some gas, so I tried. Unfortunately, more than gas came out. I was relieved and disgusted at the same time, and it didn't help that I knew I had another six hours left of pulling forward before I could properly clean up, and that every step would now be accompanied by sticky chafing.

To minimize the weight I would be hauling, I'd brought no change of underwear. And, of course, at the first waypoint, I'd gotten rid of all but ten wet wipes. I'd use at least one of those ten tonight when I got inside the tent, and until then I'd have to get by with a quick and partial cleanup on the ice. It was all very humiliating, the sort of thing that armchair adventurers never imagine but that likely crops up, with wide variation, on any journey where the stakes are so high and the resources are stretched thin. As my stomach settled down, I was soon starving again on my reduced post–food raid rations, and that didn't help.

THE CLEAR WEATHER CONTINUED through that night and into the next morning, my seventeenth day on the ice, and I woke up excited by the prospect of an important waypoint: My GPS told me I'd make it to Thiels Corner. Thiels felt important, as a symbol and as a geographic marker. From there, I'd be at eighty-five degrees south, three hundred miles from the South Pole and more than two hundred miles from where I'd started. It also marked a turning point on my compass. I'd navigated toward Thiels, an airplane refueling depot, from those first days on the ice at the Messner Start, skirting around known crevasse fields in the process, and now I'd adjust the heading for a straight shot south toward the Pole. A first important leg of the journey would be over, and though I'd been steadily climbing from my starting point at sea level toward the nine-thousand-foot-high polar plateau, Thiels marked the place where the climb would intensify, making my already burdensome sled feel even heavier. And Jenna had told me the previous night that I was more than nineteen miles ahead of Rudd, which felt like a solid lead. I'd planned a little celebration for myself in making it there, especially after the undignified fiasco of the previous day. Thiels would be an achievement, especially when judged against those horrid first hours and days when everything felt lost.

The visibility remained stunning as I pushed on. I could see an actual horizon—the white of the ice marking a sharp and clean horizontal break with the blue sky, which felt bracing and limitless after being locked in by the whiteout. And after only about another half an hour of pushing south, I began to see the outline of a structure emerging in the distance.

Seeing anything other than ice, snow, and sky was stark and jarring, even though I couldn't tell quite yet what I was squinting at. A dark rectangular shape, the sun glinting off a metallic surface of some kind, was all I could see, but even that was enough to make it an instant obsession. It was something different. That alone meant I couldn't take my eyes off it, and that I didn't need to use my compass. I could navigate toward it.

And it seemed so close. After first seeing it, I thought to myself—bang! Thirty minutes and I'll be there. But I pulled toward it for an hour and it looked exactly the same, and then another hour and still it seemed just as far away. I couldn't tell whether it was some trick of the light or just the vast emptiness of the landscape, but the effect was profound—as though I was on a treadmill with a photo of some desirable destination dangled in front of me, and no amount of strain or struggle would ever get me there. If I'd needed another reminder of my absurdly tiny stick-figure smallness alone on the ice in Antarctica, and the distances I still had to go, here it was.

But gradually I could see more details emerging: fuel barrels, the outline of a runway. Thiels, about halfway between Union Glacier and the South Pole, had been created for planes that couldn't make the whole seven-hundred-mile distance. And as I finally got there, I saw that the depot and its landing strip, this early in the summer expedition season, had been unused since the onset of winter and darkness the year before. Evidence of abandonment, of time standing still, waiting for something to happen, hung over everything.

Ironically, a covered porta-potty toilet sat at the runway's edge, frosted and tilted partly over, and I stopped and stood there, thinking of my grim experience the day before. Even if right in the middle of my gut-churning episode, I'd stumbled on the only working outhouse for hundreds of miles in Antarctica, I would've been afraid to use it for fear of violating the rule of taking support of any kind. I'd been doomed no matter what.

I'd also imagined in a general way that arriving at Thiels and seeing things from off the ice, things manufactured in a factory and brought here by people doing their jobs, would be welcome and comforting. But as I walked up the ice runway, unplowed and untouched by anybody for months, and then stopped to touch one of the fifty-five-gallon green barrels of jet fuel, still deep in its cocoon of winter snow, my sense of comfort and celebration started to evaporate. Thiels felt empty in its abandonment, hollowed out and ghostly.

A tractor with a plow on the front sat at the runway's edge, and I felt compelled toward it. I ran a hand down the frost-covered hood, then climbed up and looked through the window into the cab. It felt like an abandoned museum: Supplies, emergency kits, and tools were jumbled on the seat and the floor where the driver's feet would go, next to a big cardboard box labeled, "Meals, ready to eat, individual." I couldn't have taken or eaten any of the supplies, of course, even if the cab had been open, with a sign that said "Help yourself," because of the unsupported nature of my crossing attempt.

But still, it was hard to look away, and I pressed my face to the window and reached up a hand to the frosted glass, wanting somehow to touch the things inside and smell them and run my hand down the box to feel the smooth sides and sharp corners and imagine the person who'd carried it all there in closing down Thiels for the season. Just the phrase "ready to eat" was enough to make my mouth water, however frozen, locked away, and unattainable the food really was, because the food inside there was something different, something beyond my iron routine.

After so many days of isolation in my little universe of tent and sled and all the pieces of that life, it felt as if I'd wandered into a ghost town, a place of lost and lonely things. The barrels and the tractor and its frozen contents had sat there in the dark through the long Antarctic winter, and I was the first person on the planet to see them since.

I've stepped out of the world of human things, I said to myself, standing there on the tractor's steel step. I don't belong here. The jolt of that thought made me stand up straight and look around me again.

But the even weirder thing was that it was all so familiar. I'd been here before. *Exactly* here. When I'd been flying back to Union Glacier in 2016 from the South Pole after my Last Degree expedition, the A.L.E. plane had stopped for refueling. As I stood on the tractor's step, I saw everything about that landing, and how our pilot, just a few minutes before our arrival, had looked back over his shoulder. "We're picking somebody up at Thiels," he said. "So it might take a few minutes longer with all that."

Doug.

He was waiting for us at the depot, and had been there for two days. He'd been trying to make a solo, unassisted crossing to the South Pole, starting from the Hercules Inlet, and had called at Thiels to be picked up, abandoning his project. That's all the pilot knew as we came in to land.

Doug was bent over, packing things into his sled, as I walked over from the plane, and when I said hello, he stood up suddenly with a startled look. He was in his mid-forties, with a gray beard and a face that had been beaten and weathered by the wind and cold.

"Sorry," he said softly. "I've sort of forgotten what it's like being around people . . . you know, talking." He gave me a half smile and turned back to his sled.

"How long have you been on the ice?" I asked him.

He straightened slowly this time and looked out across the landscape for a second.

"Forty days," he said. "Thought I'd make it . . . a nagging foot injury." He spoke in partial, clipped sentence fragments. "It slowed me down, the foot." He fell silent again. "And weather."

That he was incredibly tough was obvious just by the look of him. But he volunteered almost nothing more about himself or his journey on the ice as I helped him wrestle the sled onto the plane. I only learned later, in reading his expedition blog, about his accomplished life—West Point graduate, former US Army infantry officer, lawyer, mountaineer. He'd rowed a boat across the Indian Ocean and been obsessed with Ernest Shackleton and Antarctica since fourth grade.

I'd never met, until that moment, anyone who'd just come through such a long time alone in Antarctica, and at the time I think I was more puzzled than anything else by Doug and his strange demeanor. But as I stood there a second time at Thiels, a new understanding swept through me. Antarctica had gotten inside him and changed him.

He seemed removed from the world, turned inward, focused on someplace that his journey had taken him, a landscape beyond words—hellish or transcendent or both, but clearly nothing that was of the regular world. I had no idea where Doug had gone, in his mind, through his forty days on the ice in 2016; my second time at the depot, I still wasn't sure.

But the deeper realization that struck me, and sent a chill through me worse than any Antarctic cold, was that I was now heading toward that same portal of challenge and change that he'd emerged from. What he'd seen, where he'd been, what haunted those eyes—that was my own future, too. I was going into the unknown, just as Doug had, the uncharted place where there really was no map or guide to say where I'd be inside at the end. And would I even make it to the end? Antarctica had broken Doug, forcing him to end a dream he'd nurtured for decades. Would the same thing happen to me?

Rudd knew that Antarctica changed you. That's what polar wisdom and experience had taught him, I suddenly understood, and what he'd been talking about on our flight together from South America. I'd looked at the devastating photo he showed me and only seen the physical transformation, the superficial one.

I suddenly needed to flee, and I hustled out past the unplowed airport to continue south. Doug had wrestled with Antarctica's demons in this place, and had been defeated and broken by them. And my glimpse of him that day told me his fight had been heroic and epic against demons that were formidable and terrifying. They were still here and I needed to get away.

PULLING THE SLED GOT HARDER and harder through that afternoon, and very soon I found I was almost unable to move forward at all without huge, sustained effort. The snow felt much deeper after Thiels, forcing me to push through thick powder, but I'd also fled the depot, hurrying out to escape the strange place it had taken my thoughts to, and it occurred to me that I was still being affected by that. After a while being in the harness felt as hard as the first day, when I'd groaned and heaved toward a waypoint on the continental edge.

The sled was definitely lighter by then—by Jenna's estimate, at least fifty pounds lighter, from the things I'd removed and buried back at the first waypoint and the sixteen days of food and fuel I'd used since then. I knew that. It couldn't possibly have become heavier. And yet it felt that way, which threw its own burden of doubt on all those difficult decisions we'd made, to remove food and potentially crucial tools and supplies. Had all of that been a mistake? Was my body breaking down? Even the question of whether the snow was in fact deeper, or just seemed that way, hammered into me as I pulled ferociously in the harness.

The line between reality and perception, what I could trust or not about myself and my conclusions and sensations, seemed tenuous, as though I were walking a tightrope between two worlds and could fall to one side or the other—toward some great new place of clarity, or into utter darkness. Doug, I think, had walked that tightrope.

And in the muffled shuffling of my feet, powdery snow brushing up over my boots to mid-calf, another thought hit me: There was no way to know which world was the true one, the real one, no way to gut-check my own perceptions. There was no one there with me to ask a second opinion of, no one who could look out and say with objectivity, "Yes, Colin, this snow is deeper today, and much harder to push through," or "No, Colin, it's all in your head. You're tired and you're blaming the snow when the answer or the flaw is inside *you*."

The deep snow and the emotional challenge of the day gradually wore on me through the afternoon, to the point where I started to search for ways to get past it. I focused on my breathing. I counted my steps, trying to fall into a rhythm. But the snow felt like quicksand that I would sink into without some more dramatic solution. Finally, I decided that I should break my silence and reach for the thing that, until then, I'd resisted: music. So I looked through the tiny list on my phone and selected Paul Simon's *Graceland*. I'm no musician, and most of the time I can't really even quite say what moves me exactly in any song or album. I either like it or I don't.

But when the first chords of the title song blasted into my head, I was a little boy again, joyously dancing with my parents and my sister around our kitchen. The album was released in 1986, when I was still in diapers, and was the soundtrack of our house from my earliest memories, always played at high volume, often before school to get some of my energy out before my teachers would ask if I could please, please just sit still in class. I associated *Graceland* with gray, gloomy mornings in Portland that would be lifted from their gloom by those glorious rhythms and the sight of my family dancing crazily around me, twirling and jumping and laughing.

I danced on the ice alone. I jumped. I remembered how it had thrilled me, but in the deep space I'd found—everything around me moving in rhythm—I heard it differently, too, as though for the first time. And the lyrics that had gone over my head as a child seemed deep and powerful, like they'd been written for that moment, for Antarctica, for me: *Everybody sees you're blown apart. Everybody sees the wind blow. I'm going to Graceland.*

THE PAUL SIMON ALBUM, which I put on repeat all afternoon, got me through the day and the deep snow, but it also brought me back again and again to thinking about my parents. As I remembered them dancing to Simon's songs, I also recalled their choices in raising me and Caitlin, and the respect for each other that had endured even through their divorce, and the integrity they'd demonstrated over and over, not through any kind of deliberate lessons, but by simply and quietly living their lives.

I was still thinking of my mom and dad after I finally got through my twelve hours, set up the tent, and climbed inside. I hadn't yet written the Instagram post that I'd been composing in my head all afternoon, gushing that Paul Simon was a transcendent genius. I hadn't begun any of the evening's chores beyond lighting my stove to begin snowmelt for my water, always the first priority.

I slumped down for a second, trying to gear myself up for the tasks ahead, exhausted by the day, and opened my inReach. A text had arrived from my dad, as if he'd known, as if he'd read my thoughts and knew I was thinking about him—knew that maybe I needed something more from him that night.

He'd sent me a quote to encourage me, as he did many days. But this one smashed into me with a power I didn't expect. It was from Des Linden, the first American woman to win the Boston Marathon in thirty-three years, in 2018. "Some days it just flows and I feel like I'm born to do this," she said. "Other days it feels like I'm trudging through hell. Every day I make the choice to show up and see what I've got, and to try and be better."

I read it again. And then again, and kept coming back to the four words in the middle, "every day . . . show up." That suddenly felt like an important key. If the arc of my journey was really taking me to someplace beyond the known world—that spot on the map Doug had touched and come back haunted by—then every day and every step was important. And it also meant that every day was its own fight. If there's deep snow or frostbite or emotional demons, you show up and see what you've got, and that's maybe how you get to the end. It was a sentiment my dad himself would say and live by, that the good fight itself was the victory and that the smallest moments of life say the most about who we are inside.

CHAPTER NINE

Getting Home

DAY 20

After nineteen days and nights of repetition and routine, time was starting to blur. The myriad tiny details and steps of my life from the first moments of the alarm until the last chore inside the tent were starting to feel like a continuum, as though I'd always been here, wandering across the ice alone. The rhythms of work—seventeen-hour days consisting of two hours of chores in the morning, twelve hours pulling the sled, and three hours of chores at night—and cold and wind had begun to swallow me, 270 miles from the start.

But this day instantly felt different, from the first moments after my 6 a.m. alarm because out there somewhere it was Thanksgiving Day. And as I broke camp to begin my day, the tent fluttering around me, exhalations of breath whitening to frost on the outside of my mask, I could picture everything about the traditions that would be unfolding back home.

Thanksgiving dinner, since I was in college, meant my mom and Brian's beach house in Manzanita on the Oregon Coast. It meant walks along the empty beach, and toasts around the outdoor firepit. It meant salad! That thought alone was enough to make my knees weak even without the family part. The idea of anything fresh and green, through the iron grind of my frozen or reconstituted rations on the ice, had become by then an obsession.

But as I broke camp and pictured the scene and glorious smells and laughter, it struck me that Thanksgiving was really only one element of the deeper force that held my family together: *ohana*. The word means "family" in Hawaiian but with a broader sense than the English-language equivalent—it means the family we choose to love and bring into our lives, not just our relatives by blood. My parents, after their divorce, had vowed that the family would continue on in a new way, and *ohana* had been their answer—introduced to us by my stepmom, Catherine, who'd raised her two daughters in Hawaii, where my dad now lives.

For one weekend a year in the summer, they made it work, bringing together a sprawling, blended family of spouses and former spouses, siblings, children, and in-laws, along now with Jenna and her family added into the mix. We were a smattering of last names, in fact. Mine was different from anyone else's in my family. At birth, my parents opted to combine my mom's last name Brady with my dad's last name O'Connor to give me my name O'Brady. It was an utterly unlikely and wondrous group, connected only through my mom and dad and the complicated journey of their lives.

Seeing my mom hugging Catherine and getting to hang out with my five older sisters—Caitlin, my full-blood sister; my stepsisters Eva and Lili from Catherine's previous marriage; and my stepsisters Sadie and Casey from Brian's previous marriage—and my half brother, Richard, felt like magic.

At an annual *ohana* weekend gathering a few years earlier, we'd played charades.

When Mom's turn came she drew a tough one. "Three words," she signaled. "Movie." Then she let us know she planned to act out the first and second words at the same time. "Okay," we nodded. She paused for a second. A sort of blissful openmouthed expression came across her face as she gazed up toward the sky. She turned to look at us all, palms up as if we should immediately get it. We stared for a few blank seconds, then broke out laughing.

"Happy!" someone shouted. "Crazy!" Mom just kept shaking her head, reverting to her openmouthed posture, which made us all laugh even harder the second time.

I glanced around the couch at the wondrously unlikely scene: Caitlin sat with her four stepsisters bundled in around her; spouses comfortably in the company of former spouses.

But Mom was struggling and we all couldn't stop laughing. She tried the third word of the title and got nowhere, then tried the blissed-out look again. Finally, in hysterics, we gave up.

"*La La Land!*" she shouted.

AT AROUND NOON THAT DAY, still wrapped up in my thoughts about family and imagining Jenna and me starting a family of our own to add to the mix, I paused to take a midday rest break. I unharnessed, took off the skis, and sat down gently on the sled, feeling it first with my mitten to avoid sitting on my tent poles and bending them. I pulled on the puffy extra parka that I always kept strapped in at the front of the sled, grabbed the ramen noodles from my day bag and mixed them with hot water from my thermos into my blue insulated mug, immediately slurping the warm noodles before they could grow cold.

Each sensation and motion was so deeply ingrained by then, through repetition, that I could've seen it and felt it all with my eyes closed. And there was a kind of comfort in that. From here, I felt I'd be sharing something of the Thanksgiving meal and the celebration thousands of miles from home. I hoisted up my mug in a toast to faraway family, then reached with my other hand into a pocket for my ChapStick—and at that moment a plastic bag left in there by accident got stuck to my mitten and fell out. It had been a food bag, then a sock-liner bag, pulled off my foot the night before and retired from duty with a hole in it.

Then, in the briefest of instants, it became a kite, blown from my hand out and across the ice, fluttering and rolling. And without thinking, or really even deciding, I jammed my food mug down and ran after it.

The bag looked like it had a mind of its own, skittering across the snow, then stopping for a few seconds before catching a draft and lifting up, puffed with air, and back to the snow to roll and tumble again. And even as I scrambled, slipping and falling and getting up, never taking my eyes off the bag for fear of losing it, I questioned what the hell I was doing. I was wasting precious energy. In running across the ice without skis, something I'd been careful to avoid, I was risking a really disastrous fall as my boots postholed down into the snow. The bag was tiny and, in the grand scheme of things, probably insignificant—its disappearance out onto a universe of ice would be no loss to me.

But I couldn't stop. I'd committed myself to catching it and putting it back into my sack of trash. I'd leaped from my sled and run for reasons that were already there inside me, baked in. I leaped partly because of my dad, Eagle Scout, worshipper of the public lands and forests of the West, and I thought of him as I scrambled and fell and chased. I saw his face looking down at me when I was little and we were hiking somewhere in the Cascade Mountains east of Portland.

"Stewardship," he'd said as he bent down to pick up a little piece of tissue that a previous hiker had dropped on the trail. He'd said the word like a conclusion, as though it summed up a philosophy or a life, which in my dad's case, it probably did. He traced his love of the land and the outdoors to my grandfather's decision in the late 1960s, when my dad was ten, to move the family from Los Angeles to the deep emerald embrace of southern Oregon. On the day Dad and I were hiking in the Cascade Mountains, I saw him jam the tissue into a backpack pocket that was already stuffed with other things people had dropped and he'd retrieved: gum wrappers, plastic bags, wet wipes. His garbage pocket, I called it. "Leave no trace, Colin," he said as we resumed our hike. "Then go further. Leave the trail in better shape than when you started."

Finally, my skittering across the Antarctic ice came to an end as I caught the bag, leaping onto it like it was a fumbled football. Feeling stupidly proud of myself and ridiculous at the same time, I rose up onto my knees, clutching it in my mitten.

And when I looked back in the direction I'd come, I felt a mix of anxiety and love that probably could only make sense after nearly three weeks alone on the Antarctic ice.

My sled.

I'd dashed off away from it on the rawest of impulses, and there it was in the distance, looking so tiny and fragile and alone. My sled had become an extension of me, and it was now out there by itself, and it felt like in a weird way that it needed me. We completed each other, bonded in a pact of survival. I would die without my sled, and my sled, like the iced-in tractor at Thiels, would disappear, it felt right then, into this vast landscape without me—another lost and ghostly piece of the continent.

Until that moment, through nearly three weeks on the ice, I'd never been this far from the sled—I'd never been more than six feet from it, day or night around the clock—and that's certainly part of what led to my anxious ideas and thoughts. The sled was dinged up and used, still hugely heavy and smelling of gas, but it also contained everything that would keep me alive, and being this far away from it made me suddenly and deeply anxious. It was totally irrational, I knew: I could see my sled as I stood there with the bag. It was, at most, fifty yards away. There was no way I'd lose it or not be able to get back to it.

But as I began to walk back—faster than I needed to in the odd and fretful mindset that running after the bag had put me in—a second thought struck me, too: that getting home is sometimes harder than it looks. The things we do, the decisions we make out of impulse or calculation, the dreams and prizes we envision beyond home that push us to abandon what we already have, can lead us deep into the wilderness, where trails leading back home are very hard to find.

SIX AND A HALF YEARS EARLIER, on a June night in 2012, over a campfire at California's Joshua Tree National Park, ten months after that disastrous summer day when I'd driven out of Portland, speeding off and away in pursuit of my triathlon dreams, I was in a desperate search to find my way home.

I'd ruined a lot of things that day of my departure, putting into motion a chain of events that had gone very wrong. And for what?

I'd gone to the dream team training camp and severely over-trained my body—testosterone levels slammed to those of an eighty-year-old by the endless days of swimming, biking, and running I'd logged while trying to keep up with some of the best athletes in the world. I'd been mostly absent through an important moment in my mom's life, her run for mayor, and worst of all I'd lost Jenna.

For a while after I disappeared—to begin training part of the year in Southern California, part in Australia—Jenna and I talked on the phone. But then days would go by, followed by weeks, until the breach I'd created in leaving, and the self-important way in which I'd done it, took on a life of its own. Slowly, the breach became a vast gulf of silence and distance, and we'd both started seeing other people.

Now I desperately wanted her back. I wanted another try at all the things that had collapsed for us, mostly due to my actions. Jenna was regrouping, too, jobless now after a year spent working on my mom's campaign, which had ended with a third-place finish in the primary election that spring—just short of the cut that sent the top two vote-getters to the general election.

I'd sent letter after letter to Jenna from Australia that she'd mostly ignored, then tried weekly bunches of flowers. When I'd come home earlier that year, after having quit the triathlon team, and took her out to a tear-filled dinner in Portland, I told her I still loved her. And from her own place of hurt, she'd spoken a brutal truth: "You care more about racing than you do about me."

I had no convincing reply because everything I'd done, in ripping myself apart from her and my family, said it was true.

But finally she agreed to accompany me on the drive back north from Southern California to Portland, camping along the way. The same triathlon gear I'd had with me as I roared away from our Burnside Street apartment the year before—bike on the roof, bags of gear stuffed into the trunk—was all in there with us, heading back home as well.

"No promises," Jenna said in agreeing to come along. She was meeting her mother in California anyway, she said.

"Okay . . . no promises," I replied, though it was the last thing I wanted to hear.

And on the way to Joshua Tree, we stopped at an REI and I bought her a new sky-blue down sleeping bag for her twenty-fifth birthday, and she picked up, on a whim, a glossy how-to book called *Climbing the Seven Summits*. It was about the highest peaks on each continent, from Everest in Nepal to Denali in Alaska—with lots of beautiful photos, route maps, equipment and training tips, and the history of first ascents. We read it aloud to each other that evening in the car on the drive east from Los Angeles, and Jenna lingered especially on the pages about Kilimanjaro in Tanzania and the wonders of the Serengeti Plain, which she'd dreamed of visiting since she was a little girl. The book was planting an important seed in both of us, one that would germinate and grow in the months and years ahead—though I didn't see that at the time.

"I haven't told you the whole story about Leanda," I said as the campfire at Joshua Tree crackled.

Jenna stirred slightly on the log she was sitting on but didn't say anything.

"I was with her in a restaurant in Noosa Heads, north of Brisbane," I said finally, staring into the fire. Jenna wrapped the blanket around her a little tighter. "We'd put in a brutal session of biking and running that day in the national park there."

I saw Jenna nod. She knew about Leanda Cave, a triathlete I'd been dating in Australia, at the team training camp there. Cave was the only woman in history to have won the Kona Ironman World Championship—2.4-mile swim, 112-mile bike ride, and a marathon—and a world championship at every other triathlon distance, including Half Ironman and draft legal Olympic distance. If there was ever a Mount Rushmore for triathletes, she'd be on it.

I stopped for a few seconds, staring at the fire, wanting to tell the story right. "Something Leanda said over that dinner changed everything for me," I continued.

I'd asked Leanda about her proudest moment or fondest memory in a life of amazing races, and I expected to hear the usual things athletes talk about—challenges overcome, world championship victories, last-minute come-from-behind sprints. But her story came out of nowhere.

"It was when I came in second at the 2002 Commonwealth Games in Manchester, England," Leanda said.

I was stunned and sat back in the restaurant booth.

"Really? Why that one?"

"Because my family was there to see it," Leanda said. "They were rarely able to travel to my international races," she added with a shrug. "But Manchester was local, and they could afford to come."

I stood up and poked the embers, sending up a cloud of sparks into the night, afraid to look at Jenna for fear I might cry. "So then

Leanda looks me in the eyes and says, 'You want to know what real loneliness feels like, Colin? It's standing on top of a world championship podium with no one out there you care about. That's the world's emptiest place.'"

It was growing chilly as the early June night settled in. A breeze had picked up from the desert to the east of us, carrying scents of sage and dust. I started to slide over the log I was sitting on, to be a few inches closer to Jenna, but then I changed my mind. She might think it was calculated.

I looked back up into her eyes. "At that moment I realized I had to come home—find you again if I could." I shrugged. "I kept imagining myself standing on the podium . . . a world championship or Olympic gold medal around my neck, and looking for you."

GETTING BACK TO THE SLED, with the runaway plastic bag zipped safely into a parka pocket, wasn't so easy, despite the relatively short distance I'd traveled in my stumbling, fumbling sprint. Without skis on, my legs sank into the snow up to my knees at times, forcing me to flail around with my arms, pulling myself up and out of the deep powder. I felt my heart pounding in my chest, partly from the fear of twisting my ankle or knee. In running after the bag, I'd been focused on catching it; now I just wanted to get back in one piece.

Finding your way home. The idea kept invading my thoughts as I remembered the journey that Jenna and I had begun on that camping trip up through California and Oregon. The whole rest of my life, it suddenly felt to me—the path leading to this moment on the ice—was a consequence of those days and nights, and I fell even deeper into the memory as I pushed south.

* * *

JENNA WAS BEHIND THE WHEEL of my Subaru as we neared Portland a week after that night over the fire in Joshua Tree. She still wasn't sure about us. She'd kept her guard up, and I couldn't blame her. She'd been badly hurt and the wounds hadn't healed.

I'd told her by then that even though I'd quit the triathlon team I'd been training with, and had no intention of going back to it, the idea of professional racing still appealed—the mental and physical discipline, the competition, the world travel.

I looked up from the *Seven Summits* book I'd been reading aloud from. "But you're more important," I said. "If there is some new path to find as a professional triathlete that puts us on that road together, then I'll do it," I said. "Or, I'll quit and we'll think of something else."

She'd said nothing in response. But now, as she drove up through the Willamette Valley, past the state capital in Salem and the mile after mile of farms that line the Interstate, she seemed to reach some new conclusion or resolution. She'd been silent for a long time, staring forward through the windshield.

Suddenly I saw her posture change, her chin going up, back stiffening in the seat. Her hands shifted their grip on the wheel.

"I don't think I've told you exactly how it went the day . . ." She faltered for a second, but kept her gaze straight out the windshield. "The day my mom told me about Brett."

Now I sat up in my seat. Brett. Jenna's first love. I resisted my desire to reach out and touch her.

"I'd thought at first, when I walked into the house that day, that it was another party, even though I was walking in the door fresh off my June birthday and high school graduation celebration," she said.

"But my aunt was there, and my best friend and her parents, too—the McCarthys, the people I'd just come back with from Bermuda." She stopped and took a breath. "Mom's big graduation gift splurge was that airline ticket," she continued, glancing over at me with a faint smile, thinking about her mom. "So I should've known it was something . . . else."

Jenna had met Brett, I knew, when she was in high school in the little town of Stockbridge in the Berkshires of western Massachusetts, where she'd grown up. Brett had come up from Florida, where he was from, to visit a friend, and he and Jenna had become instant long-distance high school sweethearts. And after a year of falling in love, she'd chosen where to go to college, in Florida, to be near him.

"So, anyway, I get back from Bermuda, and finally make it home, and when I walk into my house, everybody looks sort of sober-faced and strange. But still, I don't think anything . . . I'm eighteen, center of the world, high school graduate, in love, oblivious to the fact that it all could change in an instant."

She paused for a moment.

"In the living room—everyone was seated, looking up at me—Mom asks me to sit down, and then she takes my hand across the couch . . . I can hear the words and the exact way she said them. 'I have to tell you something,' Mom said. 'There was an accident . . . Brett was on his motorcycle.'"

Jenna turned her head and looked at me.

"My life was changed that day—there was a path, a road ahead for me, then after he died there wasn't. It was all unknowns," Jenna said. "I wasn't given a choice then . . . Brett was just gone and there was nothing I could do."

I clenched my jaw, feeling horrible all over again that I'd hurt her.

"I know," I said. "And now I'm asking you to take me back. And I know you've got lots of reasons to doubt me still." I kept talking to her as honestly as I could, telling her how much I respected her. "I'll keep your heart safe. I'll never hurt you again," I concluded, "and, if you'll just give me another chance, I'm convinced we can be extraordinary."

We drove for a while in silence, and I was afraid that my words hadn't sufficiently accounted for all I'd done. But it was sincere, and she saw it, and it made the difference.

*   *   *

LATER THAT YEAR, we moved together to Spain, then Austin, Texas, to resume the triathlon life, this time together, traveling all around the world even as the slow healing of our relationship continued. I raced, and Jenna dove into every detail of managing the business of a professional athletic life, on and off the race course—from the travel logistics and sponsorships to the profiles and race histories of the competitors I'd face.

We also made a commitment, as part of our new partnership, that we'd do more than just charge around the planet, as so many professional athletes do—another hotel room, another race, another country and passport stamp—but also have at least one adventure together in each place we visited. And, in fact, one adventure back then would stand out from the rest.

A couple of years later, Jenna had mapped out a trip after a race in Brazil. The two of us would climb Ecuador's three highest volcanic peaks—including Cayambe, a nearly nineteen-thousand-foot giant in the Cordillera Central range of the Andes—and I'd decided in advance that I would make this a trip Jenna wouldn't forget. As we were beginning the climb, I pulled aside our local guide, a short and burly Ecuadoran named Henry, and told him my plan.

"*Tú eres un hombre muy romántico!*" he said, grinning and punching me hard on the arm.

I reached into my pocket and pulled out a ring. When I told him the story of it, he hit me again, a little less hard. "*La familia,*" he said, nodding.

Grandma Sue's ring. Holding it there in my palm, sun glinting off the diamonds, I thought of the afternoon she'd given it to me, in her bed at home—end-stage cancer, just skin and bones by then, eyes far away.

"You and Jenna will marry one day?" she'd said, reaching for my hand.

"Yes, G-Sue," I said. "I hope so." She smiled at the shorthand nickname I'd been calling her since I was little. "This should be hers then," she said, reaching over to her nightstand, which was cluttered with bottles of pills and wadded tissues. "I may not be here to see her wear it, but it makes me happy to know that the story goes on," she whispered. She pressed the ring into my palm and closed my fingers around it with her own.

The climb up Cayambe's slopes, just north of the equator, was mostly chilly and gray, alternating with moments of intense equatorial sun, but I could think of little else but G-Sue's heirloom ring, and what I'd say to Jenna, and where and when I might say it. As we climbed, I kept reaching down to touch the ring in my pocket, fearful somehow that it would slip away or fall out. And I thought of the road Jenna and I had been down together since meeting on that beach in Fiji seven years earlier, all the waypoints: falling in love, breaking up, reuniting, sharing what felt like a lifetime of experience on the professional racing circuit through twenty-five countries and six continents. After about eight hours, as Jenna and I and Henry reached the summit, the skies cleared and the rugged spine of the Andes scratched out a line for hundreds of miles, marching south into Peru.

I looked over at Henry, who was watching me—waiting for his cue. With my left hand I threw him my camera. With my right I took Jenna's hand and went down on one knee in the snow. Henry started snapping pictures.

Jenna seemed confused at first. Around us, the thin air at just below nineteen thousand feet seemed crystalline and pure. Brilliant sunlight filled every space around us.

"I liked seeing you there, tied into the rope ahead of me as we climbed up here today," I said. "I loved that we were *connected*, working together toward the same goal. It felt right."

She saw now where I was going and wiped the corner of her eye. "I want more of that," I said. "I want that as the anchor of my life, having you by my side, building an incredible life together. Jenna, will you marry me?"

She reached down to touch my cheek. "I want more of that, too. Yes!"

She threw open her arms, as though she were trying to capture the whole world with a single gesture—the mountain, us, the moment of me kneeling on the snow.

"What we do next . . . I don't know," I said. "But it'll be as big and as great as that horizon out there if you're there with me."

THAT DAY ON THE ANTARCTIC ICE, after almost losing my plastic bag, I went twelve miles.

My mind wandered far into memory through those hours in the harness, reliving my proposal to Jenna, and the sometimes crazy arc of our lives in the years before and after. But when I looked down at my GPS, I was jerked abruptly back to reality and to the present. Twelve miles, only one mile per hour, was terribly slow, and three miles less than what Jenna's mileage plan said I needed to go.

That night, I slumped into the sleeping bag after the rounds of chores, exhausted and dispirited.

"Hi baby, how are you doing? How was the day?" Jenna asked when I called in. It was always her way of saying hello, and it always lifted me.

The connection sputtered with a sudden bark of static and I thought I'd lost her, but she came back, mid-sentence. ". . . struggled today" was all I heard.

"What? Can you repeat?"

"Lou struggled today," she said. "Barely made two and a half miles."

I was jolted by the number. Two and a half miles could only mean severe trouble, and I pictured him, now in his tent, too, just like me, maybe checking in as well with his team on the sat phone.

"Really struggled," Jenna finally added after a pause. "He posted to his blog that he made a mistake . . . almost could have been . . . really bad."

I breathed in sharply, felt the cold air penetrate deep inside my chest. Jenna didn't say "really bad" unless it really was, and usually that meant worse than really bad. She understated things as a rule.

"What happened?" I said, not sure I wanted to hear the answer.

"He thought the deep snow was just concentrated in one place, a flukey thing that couldn't possibly go on and on—he'd never seen conditions like that in his other expeditions, and he'd been in this exact part of the continent before just two years ago on a previous expedition. He figured he could sort of shuttle around it," Jenna said. She paused for a second and I thought we'd lost the connection, then she came back. "So he broke down his camp and his sled load into two lighter piles, leaving one pile on the ice, then going ahead a couple of miles with his lighter load, dumping that and circling back to get the first load." There was a burst of static then and I only caught the end of her next sentence. ". . . left his tent and sleeping gear in the snow and went ahead."

My stomach was already tightening. Jenna's story was going somewhere bad, I could tell. Rudd had somehow hit the wall despite his bravery and experience, despite a knowledge about Antarctica that was so far beyond my own.

My head spun with the numbers, too. I'd been so disappointed with only twelve miles that day, pushing through deep snow, but now everything had changed. Twelve miles to his two-and-a-half put nine more miles between us in one day. That put me farther ahead of Rudd than at any point since I'd passed him on the sixth day. But two and a half miles! It was a number that could only mean crisis.

I felt immediately, horribly conflicted. It didn't seem right that I could be happy and excited about expanding my lead, but also gripped by empathy and fear over what might've happened to him out there. Rudd and I were competitors, unquestionably, but also brothers of a sort—bonded by this thing we were each attempting.

"He went back and couldn't find the place he'd left the gear, the sleeping bag and tent," Jenna said.

"Oh my God," I said, feeling as if every muscle were clenching down inside my bag. Losing his tent and his sleeping bag wasn't something Rudd or anyone else could survive, and I could imagine it too easily. My separation anxiety from my own sled earlier that day, barely fifty yards away, felt utterly insignificant as I pictured how it would feel to really be disconnected, in a whiteout.

"Deep blowing snow covered his tracks back to his stash and covered up his stuff at the same time," Jenna said. "I just read about it on his blog."

"Oh my God," I said again, a wave of empathy pouring through me.

Static barked across the line. "You there?" Jenna finally asked.

"Yes," I said, trying to breathe normally. Rudd's moment of crisis had come out of nowhere, and worst of all it had come as a result of his deep knowledge. He believed, based on experience, that he knew what to do, and that made what happened all the more terrifying. I later learned that the much deeper than average snow caused several experienced polar veterans to cancel or abandon their high-profile Antarctic expeditions that season.

And Rudd's belief that he knew what to expect—that he knew what Antarctica's averages were, in having walked across that very section of ice before, was the very thing that had tricked and betrayed him. He hadn't seen the curveball coming, and neither would I.

My mom, Eileen Brady, introducing my sister, Caitlin (age four), and me (age two) to the beauty of the Cascades near Portland.

On the starting block at one of my first swim meets. I began swimming competitively when I was six years old. Swimming was the through line of my athletic life, from childhood to Yale University.

With my dad, Tim O'Connor, at a swim meet. His wise pre-race mantra was always the same: "Colin, remember the most important thing . . . have fun!"

Jenna and me falling in love in Australia shortly after our chance meeting in Fiji. This was taken just weeks before my accident in Thailand.

This photo with my childhood best friend, David Boyer, was taken on a scuba dive boat on January 14, 2008, the morning of the Thailand fire accident. He stayed by my side as disaster unfolded.

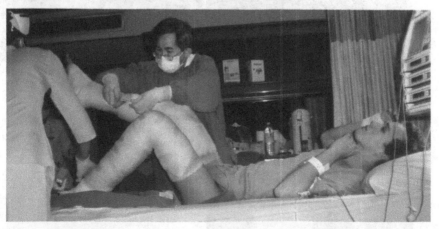

"Colin, you may never walk again normally"—devastating words to hear from the doctor just days after my burn injury.

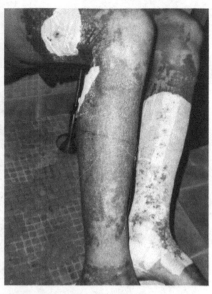

In my Thai hospital room every day, Mom always made sure to smile and encourage me to dream about the future.

My legs six weeks after the accident—a big improvement compared to what they'd looked like in the accident's immediate aftermath.

Beating the odds to make a full recovery, I went on to race professional triathlons between 2009 and 2015 in twenty-five countries on six continents. *Credits, from left to right: Wayne Jones-Nevrilk, David Lacey, Jenna Besaw*

In 2014 on the summit of Cayambe, Ecuador's third-tallest peak, I asked Jenna to marry me.
Credit: Henry Moya

From an altitude of nineteen thousand feet, I stared up to the left at Mount Everest. Directly in front was Lhotse, the fourth-tallest mountain in the world, still dwarfed by Everest's magnitude.

Stepping into the "Death Zone" on Everest at twenty-six thousand feet, moments before a sudden storm forced Pasang Bhote and me to hunker down overnight at Camp 4 and abandon our first summit attempt.

May 27, 2016. After 139 days of nonstop climbing, I took my last steps to reach the summit of Denali in Alaska, breaking the world record for the Explorers Grand Slam and the Seven Summits. *Credit: Tucker Cunningham*

Ohana Weekend, 2016. My blended family's unique way of coming together every year, even after my parents' divorce.

In July 2018, my dad, always my greatest inspiration for outdoor adventure, joined me on his sixtieth birthday to climb Arizona's highest peak—part of my Fifty High Points world-record project. *Credit: Ryan Kao*

Jenna and I paused on my descent from Mount Rainier during the Fifty High Points project. Fifty states in twenty-one days was an exercise in collaboration and preparation—more training for Antarctica. *Credit: Berty Mandagie*

My strength coach, Mike McCastle, designed creative and often brutal workouts like this: a wall sit with my feet in ice buckets, trying to solve a Lego puzzle with frozen hands. *Credit: Mike McCastle*

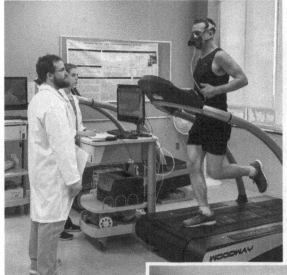

Testing my body at the Standard Process Nutrition Innovation Center. More than a dozen doctors, scientists, and nutrition experts collaborated to create a custom food I'd eat day after day in Antarctica. *Credit: Mike McCastle*

Food prep in our Airbnb in Punta Arenas, Chile, days before departing for the ice. *Credit: Tamara Merino*

Standard Process dubbed the special food they created the "Colin Bar." I cut the bars into chunks, which were easier to eat when frozen solid. *Credit: Tamara Merino*

Most of my crucial equipment is pictured here. Sled, boots, skis, harness, stove, GPS and satellite phones, along with the historic Explorers Club flag, which I was deeply honored to carry. *Credit: Tamara Merino*

Captain Louis Rudd, one of the world's most experienced polar explorers, sitting next to me on the Ilyushin flight to Antarctica. We were forced to sit shoulder to shoulder for the four-and-a-half-hour ride prior to our race across the frozen continent. *Credit: Tamara Merino*

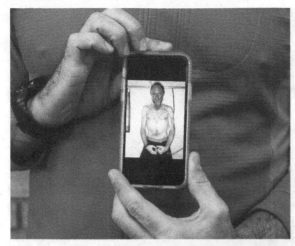

This is the image Captain Rudd showed me on the plane from one of his previous expeditions in Antarctica. I spent the entire crossing haunted by the thought that my fate might be this same extreme weight loss and suffering. *Credit: Tamara Merino*

After twelve hours of pulling my sled, there was always the nightly ritual of setting up camp, which included anchoring the tent and shoveling snow around the perimeter for additional protection from the nearly constant wind.

My view in a whiteout. The only way to navigate was to focus on the compass strapped to my chest.

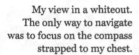

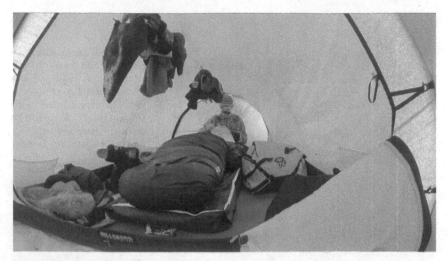

Inside my tent, the twenty-four-hour sunlight cast a red hue through the tent's fabric. I laid out my minus-forty-degree sleeping bag and hung my frozen mask and gloves on a bouncing clothesline.

I took this photo a few weeks into my crossing. Dry bags contained my daily food rations, while the orange duffel bag held my personal gear, repair kit, and first-aid supplies. The long blue sack beside my sled is arctic bedding, which held my sleeping bag and pad so that I didn't have to restuff and pack everything each day. The metal containers and bottles hold white gas fuel for the stove. Short skins are pictured on the bottom of my skis.

Melting enough snow for water each day was an arduous process. With all the exertion from pulling my sled twelve hours per day in the bone-dry air, I had to drink at least six liters of water daily to stay hydrated.

The harsh and nearly constant winds of the frozen continent carved endless fields of sastrugi—speed bumps of ice and snow—which made pulling my sled, 375 pounds at the journey's start, extremely difficult.

Long days were spent pulling the sled through deep snow, one step at a time. Note the footprints on the right side. I was my own photographer, so I had to set up a tripod and use a self-timer to capture the images.

Setting up my tent amid Antarctica's brutal winds produced some of the expedition's most challenging and frightening moments.

On the polar plateau at nine thousand feet, all you can see is endless white. Here the air is thin and extra cold, making for even harder work.

The ice sheet moves several feet every year at the Pole, so the true geographic South Pole marker is moved annually to the correct spot. The buildings in the background are the Amundsen-Scott South Pole Station. *Credit: Samuel A. Harrison*

A rare moment of stillness after passing the South Pole. These circular rainbows, which are created by light refracting off ice crystals, are called sundogs.

The bitter cold and strain began to weigh hard on me toward the expedition's end. In a makeshift solution to prevent further frostbite, I put tape on my face.

Navigating through fields of sastrugi—a terrain of endless bumps and holes—made me constantly anxious about falling and possibly sustaining a serious injury.

Setting up and taking down my tent on massive storm days, where the windchill could—and *did* on this day—plummet to seventy-five degrees below, was perilous. If I lost my grip during setup, sixty-mile-per-hour gusts could send the tent beyond my reach, leaving me without shelter.

I arrived at the top of the Leverett Glacier, viewing the Transantarctic Mountains and my pathway to the finish after seeing nothing but endless white for nearly two months.

At the edge of the Antarctica landmass where the Ross Ice Shelf meets the continent, there was nobody cheering or waiting—just a simple wooden post in the ice that meant I'd finally made it. I called home to Jenna and my family, who were gathered for Christmas, to tell them the news.

Lou finished his crossing two and a half days after me. We exchanged stories of our respective journeys before a plane picked us up to take us home.

Before and after: I put on twenty pounds of muscle and fat ahead of my crossing to give me a buffer for the inevitable weight loss. At the end, I'd lost about twenty-five pounds.

Far different emotions than during our tense plane ride to Antarctica. Lou and I shared a laugh on our way home after completing our crossings. *Credit: Tamara Merino*

My true finish line. One of the happiest moments of my life was seeing Jenna for the first time in two months when I returned to Punta Arenas, Chile. *Credit: Tamara Merino*

In the taxi from the airport to our hotel, I collapsed into Jenna's arms, knowing I could never have achieved this crossing without her strength, commitment, and organizational genius. *Credit: Tamara Merino*

I love speaking to students and, as a way to get them to dream about what they can accomplish, asking them, "What's *your* Everest? What's *your* Impossible First?" *Credit: Marianna Brady*

CHAPTER TEN

The Whiteboard

DAY 27

The solar panel above my head, tucked into its little pouch, swung like a chandelier in an earthquake. Roars and squeaks filled the air from stressed tent poles and stretched-out nylon tent fabric. But the tent itself was the attention grabber: it thrashed and rolled around me, looking like it was being wrung out like a rag—the frame torquing, twisting, and shuddering as it leaned to my left or right, before coming back briefly into shape, all the while being slammed from the side with ice and snow flung at high speed by ferocious winds.

The storm woke me long before my alarm that morning, my twenty-seventh day, 353 miles from the start, and my first impulse was to reach up and somehow stabilize the tent that was so violently thrashing around me. I wanted to grab the tent poles and hold them in place as a way of telling myself things were under control. But then almost instantly I second-guessed that thought and shrank back—tent poles held in place might be stressed even more, and if they broke, the storm would become a crisis.

I'd been braced for a change in the weather, or at least I thought I was. After I'd crawled into my tent earlier that night, feeling an almost luxuriant soreness after twelve hours of pulling the sled—my muscles ached, but I was satisfied with what I'd done through a brilliantly blue, cold, and sunny day—I pulled out my inReach and saw an alert from A.L.E. that was unusual if only because it used lots of new words: "WARNING!" it said. "A Low Pressure Zone has formed on the edge of the polar plateau."

Through all my previous weeks on the ice, A.L.E.'s daily weather advisories had been both dull and short: the forecast temperature and prevailing wind speed and direction. Sometimes the forecast said it would be a little colder or a little windier, but that was basically it. Antarctica's atmospheric pattern, it had begun to seem, had a brutal consistency that changed only at the margins. Shockingly cold and harsh weather—minus twenty-five degrees, with minus-fifty-degree windchill—was the standard stuff. So as I sat in my tent that night before sleep, hearing behind me the hiss of the stove, wiggling my toes inside the bag, feeling even a little warmth radiating through the tent's roof from the sun, I read the words again, trying to guess what might lie ahead, and wondering especially what level of severity merited the capitalized word "WARNING!"

I did know by then that I was approaching a zone where trouble of various sorts, especially strong winds, could be expected. Dixie, the Belgian explorer who'd become my mentor—and who lived, by great coincidence, part of the year in Oregon—had warned me about that, and pushed me in my training to prepare for it.

"The polar plateau spills wind, like this!" he'd yelled into my ear, standing at my elbow on a blustery day at the Oregon Coast and gesturing out toward the water, where winds were blasting off the Pacific Ocean. We'd hauled my sled there in the back of my Subaru and shoveled hundreds of pounds of sand into it, which Dixie now wanted me to pull down the beach. Back at his house a few hours later, my muscles quivering from the workout, he pulled out a map of Antarctica and spread it across the table. "The great plateau, at nine thousand feet, sits square in the center of the continent," he said, holding his hands in the shape of a ball, one above the other. Antarctica's famous katabatic winds, he told me—KAT-a-ba-TEEK in his Flemish-accented pronunciation—are essentially high-density air masses that come down from the continent's heights, often violently, driven by gravity. "The katabatics flow off downhill. You will hit a headwind in this place." He reached down and stabbed the map with a finger. "Right . . . here."

And here I was, I thought as I looked at the weather warning again. Katabatic winds and a low pressure system as well. Okay, I thought with a shrug as I pulled up the sleep mask. I'm prepared. The confidence that had been building in me through those previous days was still bubbling along. Tomorrow would be a tougher day, probably the first of a string of tougher days until I finally completed the climb up to the plateau itself, but I'd known it was coming. "I'm strong and I'm capable," I said. I'm prepared.

I *wasn't*.

BY THE TIME the 6 a.m. alarm went off—the tent still heaving around me—I was already starting to bargain with myself as to what I should do. Jenna and I, in planning the project, had talked about the idea of rest days. I'd need them now and then, we'd decided, for my body to recover. And there'd certainly be days of severe weather, we knew, where a decision to stay in and rest up could be driven by safety concerns.

But all that planning and discussion had happened in what I now thought of as the era of Before Rudd. We'd planned my crossing of Antarctica around the goal of trying to complete a thing that had never been done. How long it took was more about how much food and gear I could carry with me and whether we could solve the math problem of supply and time and weight—whether I'd have enough food, how much I could pull, and how long it might take, given all the unknowns of weather.

When it became a head-to-head race back at Union Glacier, everything changed. With Rudd there behind me—relentless and experienced, strong and clearly capable—my competitive instincts had surged, and I knew Rudd's had as well. I'd gone to twelve-hour days of pulling the sled, from the nine or ten hours I'd imagined, because of Rudd. I'd cached and left behind food, narrowing my margins of safety, partly because of Rudd and the pace Jenna had calculated I needed to maintain and how much I could pull to sustain that pace. Rudd was pushing longer days than he had on his previous expeditions, too, because of me, and every night adding his famous eleven steps.

But there were limits, in theory. There were days, again in theory, that were simply too severe or dangerous, when staying in the tent marked a line of wisdom. Was this one of those days? Without much thought, I decided that it wasn't, because it seemed clear to me that Rudd would say it wasn't one of those days either. Rudd was Rudd. He would definitely go out, I told myself, and so I had to as well, and do the best I could to go twelve hours into the storm.

But I had to admit I wasn't entirely confident. I'd never seen weather like this. I didn't have Rudd's experience. I didn't know for certain what he'd do, how he'd reckon his chances, sitting in his own little tent-universe, hearing the storm rage outside. And every minute it felt like the storm was probing my defenses, seeking weakness: When I zipped open my kitchen space to light the stove, I jerked back in shock at the blast of frigid air and the face full of spindrift snow that hit me, blown in through the vestibule vents during the night.

But the voice inside me was also speaking loudly by then, and it said that I'd committed to this thing—I'd committed to Jenna's and my shaping of what the project could be. As much as I wanted to beat Rudd across the continent, I wanted even more to fulfill the promises I'd made to her and to myself.

As I shoveled the protein-powdered oatmeal into my mouth, that word—"promise"—kept repeating in my head, and it conjured up an image.

The whiteboard.

Jenna and I bought a two-by-three-foot whiteboard after coming back from Ecuador. We figured we'd chart out our future. As I sat in my tent eating, I could smell in my memory the sweet chemical aroma of the colored markers, and see the board on its easel in the living room of our Portland apartment. It sat empty and blank at first, challenging us with its blankness. Then one day Jenna walked over, picked up the bag taped to the back, and reached into it.

"There's an eraser," she said, holding it up. I nodded, getting her point immediately. No idea was so crazy we shouldn't write it, or dream it.

So we dreamt and wrote and erased, and we did it together—that was the crucial thing. Inspired by our now tattered book from REI, we decided we'd attempt to break the world speed record for the Explorers Grand Slam—climbing the tallest peak on every continent, the "Seven Summits," plus trekking to the North and South Poles across the last degree of latitude. We wrote "The Explorers Grand Slam" on the top of the whiteboard.

Jenna would run the project and I'd climb the mountains. We kept scribbling and erasing ideas beneath, but one word remained through all of our brainstorming: "Impact." We'd build the project around a nonprofit aimed at inspiring young people to develop healthy habits and chase their dreams, which we named Beyond 7/2, a nod to the larger mission beyond the seven peaks and two poles.

We'd possessed boundless enthusiasm but no money, and barely a clue what we were doing. And yet the whiteboard connected it all, as I only understood gradually over time. More than just a place to jot ideas, it became a spaceship, our transport to destinations that we dreamt about.

Empty white space defined my world that morning in Antarctica, and as I pulled my things from the clothesline, zipped my bags closed, and climbed out into the gale, I reached out and back to those days of planning in our little apartment, and the idea that blank spaces are sometimes just spots on the board, waiting to be filled.

But the memories only went so far in helping me through the start of a brutal day. When I stood up outside the tent entrance, I felt smothered by the cold and wind. The sun overhead was tiny and vague, a pale dot peering through a white blur. The tent and the sled were all but buried. The whiteout closed in like a blanket.

And my head wasn't in the game. That was the first bad sign. The weather warning had spooked me, made me nervous. However much I'd tried to shrug it off, I'd started to bargain with myself again within the first hour of pulling south—wondering if perhaps there was a reason to cut the day short, get out of this weather, back into the tent. I began to look for reasons that would justify a half day, or a three-quarter day, and in my distracted state I stopped for a moment and leaned over to unzip the sled to get my even larger mittens out due to the extreme cold—and in one quick moment of stupidity, things began to go wrong.

I'd trained myself by then, in a routine of muscle memory, that whenever I needed to bend over, I had to pull the mask off my face because the heat from my breath would rise up to fog my goggles. But for the briefest of seconds that morning, I forgot, and as I leaned into the sled, pawing through my bag for the mittens, I let out a big, nervous breath, and it happened: the air filled my goggles, the goggles fogged, and in the minus-fifty- or minus-sixty-degree windchill of the storm, the fog almost instantly froze into a layer of ice on the lenses. The goggles were ruined for the day, with no way, until I could get into the tent that night, to thaw them out and fix what five seconds of cold and distraction had done.

I stood up with the goggles still on, ferociously angry at myself, and realized I had to pee. But since I couldn't see anything but a frosty blur, and had almost no manual dexterity through the extra heavy mittens, feel and muscle memory were all I had to go on. I turned away from the wind, pulled up the snow skirt, unzipped my pants, and began to pee—staring blankly out into space as people do while they pee, or at least as men do. A sudden sharp sting of pain that felt almost like an electric shock reeled me back into the moment. *Craaap!* Shouting and jumping, I ripped off the mask and looked down.

My thermometer, frozen as cold as the temperature it was measuring, just past twenty-five below, and attached to the bottom of my jacket, had swung down and its icy metal tip had touched my privates just long enough for frostnip. A white spot the size of a pencil eraser had already appeared, not bad enough to scar or worry about long-term—I peered down and let out a puff of air with relief—but enough to enrage me all over again. An absurd chain of events—unfortunate and only by luck not completely disastrous— had unfolded from the simple act of leaning over, one of the most normal things you can do. People bend over to tie their shoes, pick up a piece of trash on a hiking trail, or pet a dog. As I found the spare goggles, swapping them out as quickly as I could to minimize the number of seconds that my skin would be exposed to the open air, it struck me how far from normal I'd traveled—that bending over for a few seconds in the storm would have such outsized effects. Maybe, I thought, this was the sign I'd been secretly hoping for, that things were too crazy to continue and that I should cut my losses with a partial day.

But of course I didn't, and I couldn't.

*   *   *

AS I SLIPPED BACK INTO THE HARNESS, everything felt alien. The sastrugi would've been hard to deal with even without the storm. The katabatic winds would likely have been formidable even without the storm, I thought, recalling Dixie yelling over the wind on the beach. But this storm was a stew of everything—tough terrain, intense headwinds, and cold, all folded together and compounded into something way worse than its individual components.

And as I started slowly to move forward, I felt a change in my posture, too. I leaned in, leaned down, strained forward to see, as my muscles clenched to hold in my body heat. I was curved over like an ancient wanderer, ski poles for canes, a hook-shaped man clawing forward on the ice. I focused entirely on my compass, which became the center of my universe. All things beyond the compass were impossible to see anyway, and even the compass, a foot and a half from my face, was sometimes hard to see as snow and ice blew down onto it, coating its face.

The combination made every step a test of unknowns. Would three feet ahead of me be a slope up, or down, or sideways? And how strong would the next blasting headwind be? I jammed ski tips into sastrugi I couldn't see in front of me. I slipped sideways and fell on sastrugi I didn't realize I was on top of, and felt my anxiety growing almost by the minute—a fear loop that fed on itself.

And then on another sastruga I couldn't see, I slipped and slammed down, and as I started to get up, I saw that one of the skins on the bottoms of my skis had peeled off. It hung down, flaccid and useless, and I knew I couldn't go forward another step without fixing it.

Skins are the traction tires of cross-country skis. With the weight I was pulling, their absence would mean standing in one place and just sliding back and forth going nowhere, or worse, sliding backward. So I'd brought two kinds of skins with me—one pair of each, a short and a long. Short skins were good for moving across flat or moderate terrain, in allowing me a tiny bit more glide in each stride, while long ones were for days like this, when gripping the snow was the key thing.

So the detached skin, a long one, had to be fixed, and it struck me that I'd never remotely trained for a job like this, at least under these conditions. Even my hands-and-feet-in-the-ice-bucket training with Mike back at the gym in Portland couldn't fully prepare me for this. I certainly knew how to change a skin—clean off the ski, unfold the skin to expose the sticky side, and press down the changed skin—but I'd always done it in what now felt like perfect conditions—in a tent, or outside in weather that was just cold or just snowy. The storm had now changed all the variables of that equation.

As I stood there holding the ski, I watched in dismay as the bottom surface, where the skin had just been pulled off, became almost instantly coated with frozen snow. A replacement skin wouldn't stick if it were too cold, or if the ski wasn't clean enough. And the brutal cold meant that the job had to be rushed. Even with my big puffy parka on, I could feel my body temperature falling.

So I quickly peeled off the long skin that had partly detached, and stuffed it inside my pants near my body, hoping that the warmth would thaw it enough for use later in the day. Then I unharnessed myself and got my replacement short skins from the sled and stuffed them into my jacket, too, hoping to warm them up, if only a little, in preparation for the repair.

I knew that the window would be short for trying to make the fix—the new skin would stick or not and I'd know immediately. And I knew I had to get out of the wind, or at least find some way of blocking it long enough to have any hope. So I tried hunching over, curling myself around the ski, making my body a windbreak. Then as quickly as I could, I brushed the snow from the ski and reached for the replacement skin inside my coat.

But the snow was too much. Even as I tried to press the skin into place, I saw that it was useless—the adhesive surface was completely caked with white.

That left me only one usable skin remaining—the second short one—and so only one hope left to make the repair. And I had to get a better windbreak. So I lay down, nestled against the sled's edge, hoping that being on the downwind side would be enough protection, and as I curled in with the ski beside me, I remembered the little sheet of instructions that came with every skin set. "In severe cold, you may have trouble mounting the skins," the sheet had said. "Make sure the skis and skins are clean and free from ice and snow."

Hah. I grimaced inside my mask at the absurd impossibility of that. I looked down at my hands, bound up inside my thickest, clumsiest mittens. If I could just take my hands out, I thought, I could get the task done correctly. I could press my fingers down on the ski skin, forcing out the bubbles and gaps, and push the sticky surface into place. It would be so easy, and the images of doing it—the step-by-step simplicity of a simple task—rolled through my head as I nestled against the edge of the sled with the storm raging around me. But using my bare hands wasn't a choice. If I took out my hands, the exposed skin would be at severe risk for frostbite. Clumsy and awkward were all I had, but I had to try.

So I knelt over the ski and sheltered it the best I could from the gale. I scraped the ski with my mitten, trying to clean it. Then at the last second, I pulled the short skin from inside my coat, hoping it had caught a little warmth from my body, and as fast as I could I pressed it into place.

It wasn't a great job, not even a particularly good one. There was no way to get all the ice completely off the ski, so there was no hard adhesive bond. In the real world, in a comfortable place like a ski lodge, it would be an obvious do-over. But the cold and the wind and snow made for a hard running clock. Good enough would have to do.

As I struggled back to my feet, feeling like the wind might knock me over, I thought of the morning back at Union Glacier, before our flight to the Messner Start, when Rudd had offered a lesson about skins. He'd been whipping around on the edge of the ice runway on his skis, no sled behind him, looking so completely natural and powerful that I just stood there and watched. It was a thing of beauty.

He saw me and swung across the ice, coming to a stop and stepping out of his skis in a quick and efficient motion.

"Beautiful morning," he declared.

"Absolutely," I agreed.

He turned the bottom of one ski toward me and ran a mitten up and down it. Snow fluttered off in a rainbow cloud of crystals, glistening in the sun as they floated and slowly fell to the ice.

"What's your plan for short skins and long?" he said as he ran a hand down the other ski.

"I've got a set of each and can switch out for different conditions," I said.

"But just one set of skis?" He leaned in toward me, sounding surprised.

"Skis are heavy," I said. I looked back at him and straightened up my spine. Rudd had left me feeling insecure over and over since we'd met. It was a grim and repetitive cycle, but now I felt a sudden wave of confidence. This was an issue I'd thought a lot about. I knew what I was doing. "One set of skis cuts my weight a lot and I can then carry more food and gas."

"True. All too true," Rudd said, nodding.

He stretched and looked out over the ice for a second.

"But changing a skin can be a bastard of a task. I'm a glue man now," he said. "Two sets of skis, one with a short skin, one with a long, both superglued down permanently. And the spare set of skis can be used as tent stakes."

Okay, I guess we'll see who's right, I said to myself, supremely confident that it would be me.

* * *

AS I CLIMBED BACK INTO THE HARNESS, having completed my repair, I tried to summon back the self-assurance I'd felt that morning with Rudd. I'd fallen. I'd fogged my goggles. I'd been frostnipped. And I'd definitely have some further repair work in the tent that night on the skis, to get a correct set of skins on. One short skin and one long felt strange—I had more traction with my left ski than my right.

But things wouldn't get worse, I figured. My progress forward was hard and brutal and cold, but I was finding my rhythm, and starting to feel even proud of myself for pushing on through such conditions. I am one with the storm, I told myself. I'm embedded. I'm surrounded. I'm a blue dot in a sea of endless invisibility. Because of the weather and terrain, I'm in a place without possible rescue, where no plane can land. But I'm going on, and I'm strong.

In any horror story or suspense thriller, the hero's moment of greatest coolheaded calm, or arrogance, is always where the killer jumps up with a knife out of nowhere, or a door suddenly springs open to reveal the rotting corpse of the murder victim.

And so, in thinking about it later, I probably should've seen it coming.

As I climbed a huge sastruga, there was a hole I couldn't see in the whirling sea of white. I came over the top and plummeted, falling four or five feet, skis twisted around me in a tangle. My body slammed on the hard ice of the sastruga on the way down and my leg was twisted sideways.

But then as I lay there at the bottom looking up, I saw that the sled, pulled forward and still connected to me by my harness, was now at the top as well, teetering and leaning. One move too quickly on the harness and it would crash down onto my splayed-out legs, breaking bones, or skis, or both.

Moving carefully, so as not to disrupt the sled from its precarious perch above me, I assessed the damage, reaching first, out of instinct, to the parts that hurt worst. My right elbow had smashed on the way down, on the ice or on a ski, and my hip and ribs had clearly banged on something as well. But when I reached down to touch my leg and over to my ankles, I found I could move them, which was the crucial thing. They weren't broken. I wiggled my toes again just to make sure.

All the outcomes screamed with potential disaster. If I broke a leg and couldn't put up my tent I'd die in the storm. If I was injured but able to get into the tent and reach A.L.E. for rescue, they surely couldn't come anytime soon or land an aircraft anywhere near me.

And the fall had ripped off the skin I'd just put on, which meant that the very thing I'd spent the day trying to avoid—losing a day in the tent—was now the best possible scenario. I had no choice but to regroup and see how bad things were, so I eased up out of the hole, made it back up to the sastruga's top, and spotted a place nearby that looked flat enough to pitch the tent. The storm had won.

For a moment after I'd climbed out, skis now off and jammed vertically down into the snow, I just blinked inside my goggles. It was mid-morning. I was terrified, brutalized, and bruised. I couldn't go on with unusable skis and I had never put up the tent in such conditions. Every step forward or back was a place I'd never been. And then I checked my GPS and saw that I'd gone barely three miles. Three miles. Three miles of damage, wounds, and failure.

What is this place? And why am I out here? It all seemed unreal. The only certainty was that I needed to get my shelter up quickly. But at that moment, even the rituals of the tent seemed new and frightening. I knew I had to clutch the tent with every ounce of my grip and my strength, but I also knew that my strength had probably been compromised already by the cold and the struggles of the morning. I was afraid, I decided, for very good reasons. If there was a day when the tent could escape me and blow off into the white, it would be a day exactly like this.

So my defensive posture, curling up against the wind and the cold, extended into tent assembly as I clutched and clenched, holding everything so tightly it hurt, anchoring the tent's edge down to the front end of the sled and then creeping slowly around to the back to anchor it there and pull the poles into position.

But everything still felt completely inadequate in the face of that wind and cold. An anchor into the ice? What was that? It seemed like nothing. What was holding down anything really, from just flying off into the storm? My little circle of possessions there on the ice was nothing, and I could so easily picture all of it—the sled, the tent, and me with it—just lifting up and away, disappearing into the void. Everything now was uncertain except the need to get inside as quickly as I could.

I shoveled my snow barrier around the edge, a hunched-over man of gritted teeth. I pushed anchors into the snow with clenched leg muscles. I shivered and I counted shovelfuls, and I brought over my kitchen and cinched the sled cover, and I knew I'd forgotten nothing. But I still had to stop and check it all again in my anxious uncertainty. But finally I convinced myself that all was done, and I unzipped the tent flap to climb in.

And then the pieces of the storm, or the consequences of my actions in dealing with it, chased me right inside—including my skis. I shoved them in alongside my sleeping bag and then clamored over and reached to pull off my mask, realizing as I did that my usual routine there was shattered, too. My clothesline, dangling there before me, would be useless in trying to dry or thaw or defog anything as long as the storm raged. The sun was barely penetrating through the cloud cover and onto the tent's roof, casting everything inside into a red-hued gloom.

Body heat would have to do the job. So I pulled off my boots, took the damp, steaming socks out of the plastic bag liners, and stuffed them down into my pants against my thighs. I took my frozen mask and pulled it up against my body under my parka.

Without the clothesline, my gloves would have to go up against my body to dry, too.

Then came the even worse part: the skis. The only way to make the adhesive stick was to get both the skin and the ski relatively warm and dry. I could use the stove to melt snow off the skin to make it sticky again, but keeping it, and the ski, warm after that was another question. With hardly any radiant heat from the sun penetrating through the storm, the tent was freezing. That left me dependent on my body, the closest thing to a heater for hundreds of miles. So I brushed the ice off the ski as best I could, shoved it into my sleeping bag, and climbed in.

Behind my head in the kitchen vestibule my stove made its familiar white-noise hiss in a faint counterpoint to the roar and flap of the tent. The water finally boiled, and I poured it into my Nalgene bottle, which I immediately pulled inside my bag with me, too, to help warm my body and dry the clothes. And the flood of warmth up through my body made me feel just a little less alone.

THROUGH MY DAYS ON THE ICE, in the daily and nightly rhythms of pulling the sled and the clockwork chores in making and breaking camp, I'd fallen into a rhythm of work that became almost like the ticking of a clock. The constant motion, never really stopping but for the five or six hours of sleep I tried to get each night, was crucial and necessary—every day was filled from start to end with things I had to do to move forward and stay alive. But routine also chased away, or at least kept at bay, the reality of isolation.

Being inside the tent when I should be outside working stripped away all those protections. I no longer had a routine to cling to and hide behind, which made everything way more terrifying. On a typical night when I might wake up and check my watch, hours before my alarm, I was still embedded in the rhythm of what had happened during the previous day and what might happen on the next—still bobbing along in the river of tasks and schedules. It was night, though still daylight. Sleep time. I could chase away crazy thoughts by calling them nightmares. Close your eyes, Colin, and go back to sleep.

But today at 1 p.m., when I finally settled myself inside the tent, my insecurity felt almost overwhelming because everything, at that hour, felt new. The rhythm was broken and the doubts and the fears could surge in to fill the empty spaces. Normal for me had been my daily grind of chores and hours in the harness.

Normal was now gone, and I felt suddenly even more aware of my profound isolation. If I went out there now, I thought, I'd die and no one would know, and even if Rudd, who was the closest human being to me on the planet, was by some unlikely turn of events exactly on my path, he could walk directly by me in the storm—in zero visibility, tent and sled all but buried—and never even know I was there. Rudd was the closest thing I had to a first responder, and even he could never respond.

I tried for a while to tell myself that a rest day had been imposed on me and that I should use it, grab onto it and try to actually recover—not just from the horrific morning, but from the days of hard work before that. My crash and fall was perhaps a gift after all, I said. The blizzard outside, however much it was still rattling and twisting the tent, would not get me today, would not kill me or break my leg. I'd made it safely inside; I should close my eyes and sleep. But it didn't really work.

Had I earned my food rations? I lay there for a while thinking I hadn't, and that reduced calories for reduced work was the hard math of how the world worked. But then I second-guessed that. I should eat regular rations. A recovery day, I decided, meant healing, and healing needed calories. Still, as I shivered in my bag, I was glad I'd brought no extra food inside the tent with me. I might feel weak again later, vulnerable and in need of comfort, and my next day's supplies were freezing solid outside, safe from a desperate raid.

And then I rationalized and bargained again. Being finally driven inside to shelter by mid-morning after only three miles was in fact the best thing that could've happened, I told myself. Rudd had taken rest days and storm days in his *past* expeditions. Given the brutality of the day, it just might be possible that the polar giant in his wisdom had taken a look outside and stayed zipped in.

But when the text from Jenna arrived late in the day on my inReach, my defenses collapsed entirely. Rudd hadn't stopped, or sheltered in.

"Rudd did fifteen miles," Jenna wrote.

"Fifteen miles," I said, letting out a sad exhalation. In one day, he'd gained back more than twelve miles. I'd been about twenty-six miles ahead the day before, and in a single day, my lead had almost been cut in half.

Things were a mess. I was a mess.

I was physically uncomfortable, with all my wet, cold, and hard possessions there with me inside my pants and against my body in my parka, with the ski dominating everything—sticking down to the bag's bottom and up over my head right to the tent's edge. The tent spot that had seemed flat enough was not, with big round bulges of ice that poked up into my back through the bag and the bottom of the tent. And the psychological blow from the Rudd report made the discomfort even worse.

After I said good night to Jenna, eyes wide open and sleepless, I reached for my camera, popped out the little tripod legs, and hit record. The red light of its eye just then seemed so comforting and warm, almost alive, and I felt as soon as I saw it that I wasn't quite as alone as I'd been.

"Hi," I said. "We're here in the storm, as you can probably hear. Things got screwy with the skins, and then Rudd—"

I stopped myself. There was, unquestionably, no "we" there in the tent—just me and my stuff, and I realized with a little start that I wasn't just talking into my camera, I was talking directly to it. Through night after night of journaling my experience, the camera had become almost like a confidant and a friend—part of the story, not just the device for helping me remember. So what? I thought with a shrug. I needed a friend, that night especially.

I reached over and swiveled the tripod to show my sleeping bag and the ski jutting out the top, then leaned over to be back in the picture. "As you can see, it's pretty cozy in here," I said. "No people, but a nice sharp ski to cuddle up with."

I tapped off the record button, pulled out the camera battery, and stowed it in my inner jacket pocket, against my chest, then carefully folded up the tripod and laid it down next to me. "See you tomorrow, Cam," I said without even thinking.

RUDD, SOMEWHERE OUT THERE in the storm right now in his own tent, had probably gained new strength and resolve from the day he'd had, even as my own confidence had crumbled. Because my GPS signal, unlike his, was globally public, posted continually for anyone to see exactly where I was, he knew exactly how far I'd gone and how much he'd advanced on me. My open information decision had given him an advantage in knowing my progress, and that night he would benefit from it. He'd soldiered on and I hadn't.

Rudd had clearly believed from the beginning that in my inexperience there lurked the potential for a mistake—a moment of overconfidence, underplanning, or ignorance. And now, I felt, it had happened.

It was unquestionably a race again. One bad day and everything had changed. That was the great truth of it. I'd been gaining almost a mile a day or more on Rudd for two weeks running, and was almost to the point of thinking that the gradually growing numbers would soon reach a tipping point, a place beyond which he couldn't catch up no matter what. My confidence had been growing—more than it should have, I now saw. And as I'd seen that morning in stepping over the edge of the sastruga and going down, Antarctica preys on exactly those moments. It's when you think you've got it all nailed down that Antarctica roars out to get you.

CHAPTER ELEVEN

The Ripple Effect

DAY 28

I became a machine after that, a stoked steam engine, propelled by needs that were deep inside me. Rudd had closed much of the gap between us in a single day—that was a big part of what changed. It was a race again. But the even bigger impetus was that I felt I had to rebuild my rhythm, strength, and confidence—not because of Rudd, but for my own sake.

Through the next eight days, my twelve hours in the harness stretched sometimes to thirteen, and my rest breaks grew shorter. Even stopping during the day for a drink of water and a two-hundred-calorie chunk of Colin Bar, which had felt in the past like a little reward for all my hard work, came to carry a deadline. "Eat it and go," the clock said.

But by my thirty-fifth night on the ice, 495 miles from the start, eight days since the broken ski skin had stopped me in the storm, the days of harder effort had taken a toll, and I lay exhausted in my sleeping bag, another night when I'd been barely able to get my evening chores done. I cooked, chewed the food I'd cooked, and melted snow for the next day's water, and every motion felt one step too far. Even talking to Jenna that night, in her regular checkup on my physical, mental, and emotional state, was almost too much.

"Look, I know you're tired," she said, when I'd slurred some response to a question, or just lapsed into silence in the middle of a sentence. "But there's one more thing you need to do tonight—I need you to call this number."

"What? No, no . . ." Our connection faded out for a few seconds. "I can't talk . . . I'm just too—"

"Trust me, call this number," she said. Then she repeated the number again for about the fourth time, through static, until I got it down.

"Okay, fine," I said, sighing. We hung up and I fumbled with the phone, aggravated all over again by my glue-crusted fingers. In my exhaustion, even the ringing when the call finally went through sounded annoying and I started hoping for voicemail. But then a man's voice came on the line.

"Hello," he said.

"Um, hi," I said. "This is Colin from . . . um . . . Antarctica."

"Hey! I've been expecting your call. This is Paul."

"Paul?"

"Paul Simon."

I immediately decided that I'd lost my mind. There was no possible way that I could be in the middle of Antarctica on the phone with my musical hero Paul Simon. That it was a strange and vivid hallucination made much more sense.

Okay, I thought, and went silent, waiting for the next weird thing to happen.

"I heard you were listening to *Graceland*," the voice said.

Graceland. It all flooded back. Listening over and over as I'd pushed through the deep snow. The memories of dancing in the kitchen with my family. The Instagram post I'd written on the seventeenth day and forgotten about.

"Yeah! Wow!" I stammered, coming back into the moment, but still reeling, wondering how Jenna had gotten Paul Simon's number.

"It was so great to think about you down there listening to those songs," Simon said. "I liked imagining them playing out there on the ice, having a new kind of life in that incredible place. . . . It's ice everywhere, right? And how cold is it, anyway?"

Now my imagination played out, picturing Paul Simon thinking about me listening to his music in the middle of Antarctica. That was almost as surreal as hearing his voice. But I was also struck by the thought that I hadn't really talked to anyone other than Jenna and strictly business Tim from the A.L.E. Comms Box for weeks. Paul Simon would expect real sentences, and I wasn't sure I still knew how to do that.

"Yeah. The ice is more than a mile thick under me right now where I am in my tent," I said. "Average is about twenty-five below."

"Wow and wow," he said. "Wait, I've got to ask you something else, just because . . ." The line went white with static for a few seconds. "You know how musicians are."

"Sorry, say again?" I said.

"What else have you been listening to down there?" he said.

"Hmm. Well, actually a lot of nothing . . . silence mostly, trying to find a place in my head where . . . um . . . it's hard to describe, but—"

"I totally get it," he said. "Sounds of Silence," he added, and we both laughed.

"No, yeah, really," I stumbled, feeling like my tongue was thick in my mouth. "I actually deleted almost all my music files except for six albums before I got down here."

"Then I'm really honored," he said.

"So, what I kept was *Graceland*, the Grateful Dead's *American Beauty*, Bob Marley's *Legend*, Counting Crows' *August and Everything After*, Sublime's self-titled album, and Blind Pilot's *Three Rounds and a Sound*."

"Very cool," he said. "But I want to hear more about the silence. You know, it's an old songwriter's cliché, but it's true—the spaces between the notes are the most important parts of any song. So what's that like? Are you finding it, that place in your head?"

I paused, thinking of the times when I'd felt so completely present in the moment that I melted into it. Simon's phrase rattled into my head, and I knew I'd keep it and use it: the spaces between the notes, the place of power. "Sometimes," I said. "I find it sometimes for a while. The silence can open a door . . . and then there's a whole world beyond that, especially down here where the empty ice goes on forever." It sounded cryptic and impenetrable in talking about it, but he seemed to have immediately understood.

"Yes," he said. "That's a place definitely worth going to. All art is about seeking something you're not sure you'll ever find, but trying to get there anyway."

OUR CONVERSATION, and the unlikely wonder of it, was still replaying in my head the next morning over my oatmeal and my chores in breaking down camp, and as I got out onto the ice. A whiteout had thickened during the night, and as I rolled up my tent, I looked down at my boots, dusted white with snow, and another of Simon's lyrics came to mind, from a song played on the stereo over and over in my house growing up.

"Ta na na na na!" I croaked out into the emptiness in my terrible singing voice as I cinched the straps of the sled. "She's got diamonds on the soles of her shoes!"

Simon's vision, that making art is a process and a journey, and that you should push toward it in hope, even if you're not sure where you might end up, felt suddenly somehow even truer than his lyrics. My journey into Antarctica was itself a work in progress—a block of stone that might become a sculpture if I could complete the goal, or might never be completed despite all my efforts at chipping away, and I wouldn't know until the end.

I'd glimpsed that place of wonder before, and as I pulled into the harness, I thought of the morning just before sunrise at Burning Man, the annual gathering of nearly seventy thousand people who, for a week in August every year, build a temporary city in the middle of the blazing Nevada desert in celebration of community and unbound, radical self-expression.

Light and darkness are intertwined at Burning Man, as days of dazzling, hard desert sun give way to star-strewn nights of deepest black. And the sunrises and sunsets—the great transitional moments of the day—seemed to me most magical of all in illuminating or casting into shadow the whole, mystically created city of giant art installations, music, and dance. The *playa*, as Burners call it, is more than two miles across. It rises from an ancient salt-pan lake bed, explodes into life for a single week, and then is packed away and cleaned up, down to the last scrap of paper. Stewardship of the land, like the rule that bars the buying or selling of anything at Burning Man, is baked into the culture.

Jenna and I, after our first day at the festival, had danced all night, then jumped on our bikes somewhere around 4 a.m. We were riding out toward the *playa*'s edge, through a world of swirling dust and pulsing music and light—from brilliantly lit two-story-tall art installations, to fur-and-feather-wrapped bikes and people out walking with their headlamps—when something in the distance caught my eye and I felt compelled toward it.

It was a tree. The Tree of Ténéré. In a place where there were no trees for as far as the eye could see, artists had created a huge, stunningly lifelike tree with shade and branches that could be climbed. And then as we stood there, our eyes wide with wonder, we saw that the tree itself seemed to be almost dancing. Thousands of tiny LED lights on the tree's leaves flickered and fluttered with the music that was being performed down below.

"They're climbing the tree," I whispered to Jenna.

She glanced up at me, looking puzzled, cloaked in her Burner costume of faux fur, fishnet stockings, and dark-tinted goggles.

I thought for a few moments about what I was *really* trying to say, and as I did I pulled off the formal but tattered top hat I was wearing as part of my own Burner costume, and ran a hand through my hair, which was thick with fine *playa* dust.

"The artists who built this tree knew people would climb it. They didn't just create it to sit in the middle of the desert by itself. They made it with a greater purpose. The tree is a vehicle for the real art. The people in the tree, under the tree, the two of us here, dancing, being inspired by it—that experience is the real masterpiece."

I stopped and fell even deeper into the spell as the pulsing echo of music from one of our favorite DJs, Tycho, rippled through the tree's electric leaves. The great glow of the desert sunrise was exploding from over our shoulders, too, lighting up the tree in a new way.

"Our adventure projects . . . they're a vehicle, too. Our expeditions are like the tree. I love sharing them with the world—not so people can passively observe them as entertainment, but so they can experience them alongside us and be inspired to act on their dreams. I'm certain that everyone has a masterpiece inside them. Inspiring even one person to unlock their potential creates a ripple effect of positivity."

Jenna turned sharply to face me, beaming. "Yes, our projects aren't about world records or athletic feats, they're about the ripple effect." She turned back toward the tree for a moment, then looked at me. "From the whiteboard into reality," she said.

IN MANY WAYS, the real floodgates of possibility—what might be or could be—had opened with our engagement on the summit of

Cayambe. A new chapter had begun for me and for Jenna, just waiting to be written, and in late 2014 I flew to Chicago to see Mr. Gelber, the commodities firm owner who for years had supported my dream to race as a pro triathlete and maybe one day make the Olympics. I was terrified, mainly because of the debt of gratitude and respect I felt I owed him, which had grown like compound interest ever since he'd changed my life at that backyard barbecue just after I'd won the Chicago Triathlon five years earlier. Now I had to tell him that I was walking away from the very thing he'd been so supportive of for so long, my triathlon career, and ask him instead to sponsor me for the Explorers Grand Slam project, a commitment of several hundred thousand dollars.

He met me in his downtown office, and after a few minutes of exchanging news about our families, I confessed my ambition to start a new chapter, leave the triathlon world and break the speed record for the Explorers Grand Slam. Then I paused, afraid to take the next step and mention the cost, even though Jenna and I had mapped it out exactly. So I described our goal of building a platform that would inspire young people and the passion we felt. But finally I couldn't drag my feet any longer. Jenna's and my grand vision, I said, would cost $500,000.

"Wow, that's a lot of money," Mr. Gelber said. He was silent for a few seconds. "But it sounds like you're becoming an entrepreneur, and I respect that, of course. That's where I come from, too. I have to say, though, that I'm a little disappointed that you're leaving triathlon and your dreams of the Olympics. I've supported you for a long time in those dreams, Colin."

"I know that, and I hope you know how grateful I am," I said instantly. I could feel my heart pounding in my chest as a long bead of sweat ran down my neck into my shirt. The last thing I wanted was to disappoint this man sitting across from me, who'd been so generous and believed in me.

"As you know, this year I've had my career-best results racing triathlon on the world stage. But the truth is that the Olympic dream"—I paused, looking for the right words—"I don't think it's going to happen, and this world-record project can be just as meaningful as the Olympics. Jenna and I have a vision for something we can build that can have more impact than any success or failure on a triathlon race course. Mr. Gelber, I always imagined you being there for that moment at the Olympics—you and your family in the stands cheering me on. But it would be just as meaningful to have you as part of our new dream."

I stopped and let that sit for a second. "So would you be interested in coming in as a title sponsor now, for this new venture?"

He paused for a long time, and I felt I saw his expression harden.

"Here's the thing on this new venture, Colin," he said, his eyes boring into me. "I'm not going to be your bank. I'm not going to just write you a check."

I lurched forward instinctively with my mouth open, afraid I'd pushed too far, afraid I appeared ungrateful.

"I didn't expect that, Mr. Gelber—"

"My point is this. Entrepreneurship is hard. The *hardest* thing. Mostly it fails." He stopped and looked kindly at me across his desk. "Show me something. Colin. Don't talk plans and dreams. Come back to me with some poured concrete, something real, money committed from legitimate corporate sponsors, your own skin in the game, and maybe then I'll match whatever money you're able to raise."

And when I got home to Portland, we wrote another item on the whiteboard and underlined it: "The Gelber Match."

A FEW WEEKS LATER, on a gloomy Pacific Northwest winter Sunday, Jenna and I decided to go for a hike in Forest Park, the great greenbelt across Portland's northwest corner, partly just to escape for a while the deeper gloom that we were falling into in our apartment. The Explorers Grand Slam project had taken vivid shape by then, but only in our own minds and no place else. We'd made no progress at all toward the "poured concrete" that Mr. Gelber expected.

As we headed into the park, the drizzle turned into a cold rain, and we pulled up our rain jacket hoods. Drips rolled down off the top in front of my face.

"Okay," Jenna said out of nowhere. With her face covered up by a big green hood, she was just a voice. I couldn't see her expression. "We've got some money saved, right?" she said.

"Sure, we've got about $10,000 between us," I said.

"I'm thinking we should put it all on the line, every dime," she said firmly.

I paused. I'd heard that tone in Jenna's voice before, that firm resolve. She'd been thinking a long time about this, I could tell, before ever opening her mouth.

"What are you saying, Jenna?"

She pulled aside her hood with a swift motion, getting a face full of rain. It ran down over her eyelashes onto her cheeks.

"We gotta go all in," she said. "If we're really going to do this project, we need a website and a cohesive message. . . . If you're really going to change the world, you have to look the part. *We* have to look the part, and have a fully built-out brand and a one-sentence idea that a sponsor can instantly grasp—something that says what the Explorers Grand Slam is, and what larger impact we will have, and why it's something the world should care about."

"It's pretty much our life savings. . . . Are you sure?"

"I'm sure," she said, then smiled up at me. "And if in the end our idea doesn't come to life, well at least we'll have a cool website."

* * *

THE SCARIEST THING about creating a website that says you're going to do something is that then it becomes real. And Jenna's website, built over the next few months with our savings, not only declared to the world that I'd go climb some of the world's tallest mountains and trek to the North and South Poles, but do it faster than anyone in history—and begin it all in December of that year, 2015, only six months after the website's launch. I'd certainly climbed some mountains growing up, and I was strong and fit from my years of triathlon racing, but I'd never been to the Himalayas, never been on any mountain above twenty-one thousand feet.

What was even scarier was we still had no real support or funding to make it actually happen. We'd spent our last penny on the website, not knowing how the vision would become a reality.

So then desperation really set in. The faintest whiff of a lead on someone who might know someone who might possibly be able to help us became the stuff of instant obsession. There's a cocktail party and someone who worked a few years at Intel's Oregon office might be there? Great, who do we call? She retired five years ago from Intel? So what? You never know.

The doors slammed over and over in our faces, and the message— sometimes veiled, sometimes flatly stated—became a drumbeat that however enthusiastic and earnest we were, we were still young and naïve.

I became acquainted with every possible variation of the word "no," and learned to hear the cues as well for false, veiled enthusiasm, and all the horrible variations of the word "maybe," which were so often just polite ways of saying no while keeping false hopes alive. But the dismissal that never lost its power was "good luck, kid," which conveyed both rejection and doubt at the same time. It said no, and then suggested that everyone else with a lick of sense would say the same.

We made cold calls and left messages and wrote fawning, suck-up emails to corporations and high-net-worth individuals, month after month, often with no reply in return. We rehearsed, over and over, what we'd say if and when we could get our foot in the door of a big sponsor. Jenna had calculated costs and logistics, researched potential sponsors, and established a partnership between our new nonprofit, Beyond 7/2, and the Alliance for a Healthier Generation, an organization that was at the time impacting more than 20 million American schoolkids in twenty-nine thousand schools nationwide, working to combat childhood obesity and encourage lifelong healthy habits.

We became hyperaware of any potential opportunity to bring our idea to life, no matter how slim the chances. We talked to everyone. Whether through a chance encounter, a random introduction, or a meeting with someone we already knew, every conversation was like another bread crumb on the trail.

But the estimated $500,000 of bare-bones costs—the tab for getting around the world to the Seven Summits and two poles with an expedition at each location—seemed completely beyond reach. Chartering helicopters to and from remote locations, and rushed last-minute changes in getting flights, permits, and supplies would make for soaring logistical costs. We'd make no money doing it even if we could pull it off, but that didn't matter. Blinded and fueled by our passion and the impact we dreamed of creating, the whiteboard filled up, got erased, and filled up again.

And then one day I ran into a friend who mentioned that a friend of his worked at Columbia Sportswear, the big Oregon-based outdoor clothing and gear company. Jenna and I immediately took the unsuspecting Columbia employee to coffee, cornering him in a booth in downtown Portland as we poured out our dreams and plied him with lattes. Might the company be enlisted as a sponsor? Who would we need to pitch to? He promised to talk to a colleague higher up in the company's leadership, and then we cornered her with caffeine and enthusiasm until she said she'd talk to someone else. We bought a lot of coffee. We were desperate.

Finally, the fourth or fifth person in the chain of connections we'd made inside Columbia called and said he'd gotten us a meeting with the CEO himself, Tim Boyle.

"After that you're on your own," our connection said, sounding happy to be finally rid of us.

So then we started really studying the company—not just its historical successes and mistakes, but also its advertising and marketing strategies. Jenna read everything she could get her hands on about the Boyle family—refugees from Nazi Germany who'd come to America, bought a little hat company in Portland in 1938, and renamed it for the great river of the Pacific Northwest. She learned that Mr. Boyle favored casual button-downs over formal work attire, and she also learned about the legend of Tim's mom Gert Boyle—the daughter of the company's founder and still, in her nineties, Columbia's hard-charging chairwoman. Gert's blunt, "get things done" approach ran deep in the corporate culture. And as we drove to the suburban office park where the company had its headquarters, we felt ready.

Jenna had intended to wear her politics clothes that morning but changed her mind at the last minute and opted for Portland casual, a simple top and slacks. I put on a sport jacket. I'd considered getting even more dressed up until Jenna said my image, as the athlete who'd be out on mountaintops and polar caps doing the project, should be a little scruffier. "Clean but rugged," she said. "That's the Columbia sweet spot." For good measure, I added to my not-so-scruffy ensemble a Columbia shirt and pair of shoes. We couldn't know what little touch might turn the decision in our favor.

We parked, found our way into the office building, and an assistant took us down the hall into a windowless executive boardroom. Mr. Boyle was already there, sitting at the head of a long wooden table that was lined with water pitchers and glasses from a previous meeting. We'd expected a group of marketing, advertising, or sponsorship people, but he was it. For better or worse we'd be pitching in the major leagues, trying to sell our idea to one of the wealthiest and most powerful businessmen in the state. We glanced at each other and I felt my jaw tighten. My heart pounded in my chest as we took seats adjacent to Mr. Boyle at the table's end.

Jenna had prepared for weeks what she'd say and went through it flawlessly, how Columbia's image around the nation and the world was tied to the outdoor spirit of the Pacific Northwest, and how our project was in many ways trying to tell that same inspiring story, about a local Oregon boy heading out to some of the world's most challenging places, living the Oregon dream.

"Your current campaign is 'Tested Tough.' What better way to test Columbia's gear and showcase it than to have Colin wearing it in some of the world's harshest places?"

Then, on her laptop, we pulled up our project's launch video from the life savings–funded website we were so proud of, watching every muscle on Mr. Boyle's face for a reaction.

Unfortunately, the expression we saw wasn't good. He looked ready to yawn as the video played. Then he glanced at his watch and stood up, clearly already gone, thinking about his next, more important meeting. After barely five minutes, the pitch meeting we'd agonized over for weeks was sputtering to a close.

"Nice meeting you both," he said cordially. "Good luck with this."

I kept talking as we scrambled to our feet, trying to spark something, anything, that could keep us all in the room, but Mr. Boyle shut me down with a stern glance and a little downward tilt of his head. "Good luck, Mr. O'Brady," he said, emphasizing the word "luck" in a way that sounded like a thousand slamming doors.

Then Jenna charged. It was the same stiffening of posture I'd seen in the car driving back that day into Portland. She'd resolved something.

"I think you're missing something here," she said, taking a half step closer to Mr. Boyle and looking him in the eyes. "This isn't just a feat, or a stunt—we're building toward something larger." For the next minute she talked about how the Explorers Grand Slam project would be a brick in the wall of a much bigger vision, how we wanted to use it and projects like it to inspire people, especially kids. She stressed how Columbia Sportswear would be a great partner with us, that there'd be "mission alignment."

Mr. Boyle stopped and ran a hand across his jaw. For the first time, he seemed to be listening. This assertive twenty-seven-year-old woman had stepped up and impressed him.

"Talk more about mission alignment, please," he said, gesturing to the seats we'd just jumped up from. The meeting wasn't over.

The tables had turned, and Jenna eventually had him smiling, then laughing. I knew to keep quiet. Jenna was leading the way, making her play, and my role was to be the smiling, supportive partner—clean but rugged.

"This is all about the idea that really difficult challenges and dreams can be at the edges of the globe and on mountaintops around the world but also right there in front of you, too, ready to be taken on," Jenna said. "And the goal, in getting Colin's story out into the world as much as possible, is to drive home that message—that whoever you are or wherever you're from, audacious goals can be accomplished with grit, purpose, and a growth mindset. Maybe your goal isn't Everest or the North Pole, we're certainly not assuming that's for everyone. But what's *your* Everest? The main thing is, all of us can do more than we think because we all have reservoirs of untapped potential to achieve our dreams."

Mr. Boyle leaned back in his chair and looked up at the ceiling. It felt like time had stopped—that the fate of everything we'd been working on would be decided in the next few seconds.

"I think we can do something here," he said with a warm smile, standing up and glancing at his watch again. The meeting was now really, truly over, but we had our first sponsor, our anchor, the cornerstone on which all else might be built. I wanted to scream as I leaped up to shake Mr. Boyle's hand, and as he turned back to Jenna, my mouth widened into a huge, silent expression of joy, which Jenna saw and acknowledged. I could see in her eyes that she was trying her best to contain her excitement. "Someone on the team will be back in touch," he said as he left the room.

The company didn't grant us the full sponsorship we'd hoped for, but Mr. Boyle generously signed on to contribute the gear I'd use while shuttling around the world through the months of the project. The crucial thing, though, was that, because of Jenna's charge, we'd landed our first sponsor, a respected, high-profile name that we planned to drop in every pitch yet to come. Jenna had picked up the pieces of a failure in free fall and turned it into a victory.

BUT AFTER MONTHS OF MEETINGS with the same optimism, and the clock ticking down to my departure date, we hadn't made a lot more progress on the sponsorship front. Columbia's highly respected tents, jackets, and gear—mostly from their Mountain Hardware subsidiary—had reduced our total cost by about $50,000, and we'd cobbled together another $50,000 from friends and family and a few other smaller sponsorships. That still left us woefully short of the $500,000 that it would take to make the project a reality.

Despite the gap that had to be closed, just about every week we were going into local schools, talking to students, and also to their teachers—about how they might incorporate the project into different curriculum subjects, from geography to history, global politics, and climate change, while at the same time instilling the health and fitness message in conjunction with the Alliance for a Healthier Generation.

I was beginning to feel like a fraud, though—fearful that being unable to get the money together would make me look like the guy who'd told all his friends he'd jump into the ocean from the very highest cliff, only to chicken out at the last second. I'd forever be the guy who *hadn't done it.*

By October, two months before I was supposed to depart for the first expedition, the $400,000 shortfall was impossible to ignore. We sat on the couch looking at the number on the whiteboard. We wrote it on sticky notes that we put on the fridge just to remind us again. It filled our waking moments and our dreams.

But one day at a coffee shop near our house, I ran into a friend named Angelo, who said there was somebody I should meet. Angelo, who knew the troubles Jenna and I were having launching our project, attended Sunday morning spin classes, and this person, he said, was also a regular.

"She was a big-time runner in the past—a world-record holder. Might lift your spirits. Anyway, you should come and meet her," he said.

I almost didn't.

Even though I'd raced my last professional triathlon by then, Ironman Japan that summer, I was still a professional athlete. It was my identity. I was training to break a world record. Even worse, I still had a bit of the foolish and full-of-himself guy inside me, the one who'd driven away from everything that was important in leaving Jenna in order to chase the dream of professional sports. Come on, I thought in my pompousness, a Sunday group fitness class at a local gym? It felt beneath me.

But at this point I had nothing to lose, so I said yes and went to the class. Still, I had to sigh a little bit when I walked into the spin room and saw the neatly lined up rows of stationary bikes, all facing forward toward a wall of mirrors behind the instructor. I'd be going nowhere fast, and I'd see myself doing it.

Angelo walked over as I was raising the seat on my bike, and pulled me toward the side of the room where a woman was already riding hard even though the class hadn't started. She looked to be in her mid-fifties and was lean and amazingly fit. Sweat glistened on her arms and neck, and I had the sudden realization that spin classes had real athletes in them.

"Colin, this is Kathy. Kathy, Colin."

Kathy paused from her workout and we shook hands.

"Kathy broke the world record for the 5K in the 1970s," Angelo said. "Kathy Mills then, collegiate legend."

"Million years ago," Kathy immediately said, grabbing a towel and shaking her head as though it wasn't that important. "So what's this project Angelo has told me about?"

I took a breath. I'd told the story hundreds of times by then in meetings, coffee shops, bars, schools, even in the street when I'd meet some old acquaintances, and though I knew I'd probably gotten better at it, the lack of success had started to nag at me. Maybe I wasn't doing it right.

But as I opened my mouth that morning, it all came together and flowed out, both the passion and the clarity. I already instantly admired Kathy, but I wasn't *pitching* her, wasn't *asking* anything of her, and that was probably the difference. I was just a guy in a Sunday morning spin class talking about his dreams and goals.

And then for the next ninety minutes I spun. It was a fine workout, better than I'd expected, and when it was over, I wiped off my bike and walked over to say goodbye to Kathy. A guy was toweling off next to her.

"This is my husband, Mark," Kathy said. He was about her age, with salt-and-pepper hair, a lightly stubbled chin, and the look of a former athlete. "Tell Mark the thing you're working on, Colin," she said, as he and I shook hands.

So the story poured out again, distilled down and simplified. Around us, people laughed and wiped off their bikes as they chatted and packed up their stuff. And it felt like the story—the dream that Jenna and I had crafted so carefully—had in a strange way become bigger than us. In all the other more formal meetings and presentations, I realized, even as I stood there talking, that I'd been trying to force it, make something happen. Now I just conveyed my passion with no expectations whatsoever.

When I was done, Mark immediately nodded. "I like this," he said. "And I think it fits in really well with some things we've been doing at the company I work for."

"Great," I said, happy to hear any kind of welcome response, but expecting nothing to come of it. I'd heard too many people say similar things and then add "good luck, kid" at the end.

"Here, let me get you a card," Mark said, bending over and rustling through his gym bag. "Send me an email and a link to your website if you have one and we'll talk."

I held it in my sweaty hand, staring down at it.

"Mark Parker," the card said. "Chief Executive Officer, Nike, Inc."

ON ANOTHER GLOOMY PORTLAND SUNDAY, in mid-November, a month after I'd met Mr. Parker, and only a few weeks before I was scheduled to board a plane to Antarctica to begin the first step of the Explorers Grand Slam—crossing the last degree of latitude to reach the South Pole—no Nike money had come. We'd had meetings and conversations at the corporate headquarters, but the great shoe company giant of Oregon, an organization we'd dreamed of being involved with, looked like it would be another dead end. The $400,000 we still had to raise stared at me from the whiteboard, now underlined numerous times in emphatic, bleak black lines from our markers.

Jenna was upstairs in the shower. I sat down at the computer. There was an email from my mom discussing plans for Thanksgiving, a save-the-date for my upcoming ten-year college reunion, and a note from my dad, who said it had been too long since we'd come to see him in Hawaii. I sighed.

But then, as I sat there, another email dropped. Nike was in the subject line. I held my breath, afraid for a long time to open it. I looked out the window at the gray day and listened for a few seconds to the sound of Jenna up in the shower. Finally, I clicked the mouse.

"We're in for $150k," the message said. "What you're doing is inspiring and has the potential to shift people's minds on what's possible. This is a perfect alignment with our global community impact initiative to help our nation's youth lead more active and healthy lives."

I leaped up, knocking over the whiteboard easel. Our math problem was solved—$150,000 plus the other $100,000 we'd cobbled together, and the Gelber Match, would get us over the threshold.

I ran up the stairs screaming. Jenna pulled back the shower curtain as I burst into the bathroom, her eyes wide.

Then I stopped. Time stopped. I wanted to scream it again, but I also wanted to wait just another beat, to stretch the moment out for both of us. Then as calmly as I could, I said the words: "Nike committed."

Jenna screamed. And with all my clothes on I climbed into the shower with her and we jumped up and down over and over, crying and holding each other as the hot water steamed up the bathroom.

CHAPTER TWELVE

Farthest South

DAY 39

Civilization was out there, just in front of me—people working, living their lives through a season on the ice. I knew that, but I couldn't see it. A deep whiteout had gripped the sky and folded itself around me during my thirty-ninth day on the ice. My GPS, after twelve hours in the harness, told me that the buildings of the Amundsen-Scott Station at the South Pole were there just ahead of me, somewhere in the blankness. But, for all I could tell, they could've been a million miles away.

I'd been here before, on my sixty-nine-mile trek across the last degree of latitude when the South Pole was my finish line for the first expedition of the Explorers Grand Slam in 2016. I remembered visiting the station. I could smell the pine-scented clean of the tiled hallways and could hear in my memory how the station's foot-thick insulated metal front door clanked and squealed as it closed. And I knew that I could, with only a few more hours of pulling the sled, perhaps even less, actually get there. I could pitch my tent in a place where the smells of coffee and bacon wafted out from the cook tent that A.L.E. maintained at the base for its tours and expeditions, and be in human company for the first time in more than a month since the day I'd passed Rudd.

But all those same things—the warm buildings, hot food, wonderful smells, and people who might with the best of intentions try to assist me in some way—were also red lines of danger because under the rules of an unsupported, unassisted crossing, I could accept no help, as the Pole wasn't my finish line this time. Even stepping into a heated building for five minutes would negate everything I was trying to do, and I'd have to quit, surrendering the race to Rudd.

The strict environmental rules governing Antarctica itself had gotten more complicated, too, in the three days since I'd crossed over the 89th degree of latitude. I'd been required to start bagging and carrying my human waste with me on the sled instead of burying it in the ice as was allowed before that point. Though I was happy to comply, it also meant my sled hadn't been getting any lighter, and wouldn't until I got all the way across to the far side of the last degree, sixty-nine miles past the Pole.

In my most rational place, I knew I wouldn't be seduced into an error at the Pole. My resolve was firm. And yet, even with all of that resolve I still couldn't face the idea of going the last three miles to the Pole that night. I wanted to be fresh and fed when I walked up there, not hungry and tired as I was at that moment after a full day of work. And I wanted to be ready to keep going past the Pole to make my next camp. Treating the Pole as just another waypoint— important and symbolic, but also a place to check off and pass by quickly—would minimize the risks of getting tempted.

I stood there for a long time, still in my skis, hitched to the sled, staring south. It felt strange to be so close to a place that generations of explorers had sacrificed so much to reach and not want to go the rest of the way. As I retrieved the tent and started to make camp, I found myself stopping over and over and turning back to look. I desperately wanted to see a hint, a shape, a shadow—something, anything signifying human presence—but the thick, cold white sky was impenetrable, and sealed me out.

THE NEXT MORNING, as I pushed through those last three miles, still in the thick of the whiteout, a phrase came to me that I'd first encountered in reading about the early efforts to get nearer and nearer to the Pole, before any human being had actually ever set foot there.

Farthest south.

Captain James Cook, the great Pacific Ocean explorer, had established a farthest south in sailing past the Antarctic Circle in 1773. Captain Scott, years before his famed polar expedition, got three hundred miles closer to the South Pole than anyone before him. An expedition led by Shackleton then got even closer, reaching a point just ninety-seven miles from the Pole, a new farthest south.

Achieving a farthest south meant you'd inched closer to the great prize of the Pole itself, but also that you'd surpassed a previous farthest south achieved by yourself or someone else. Every farthest south was a tiptoe to the edge of the map, the edge of the possible, a challenge for others to follow, and it echoed everything about the world of sports that I loved and had steeped myself in for so many years, since childhood. All records were pieces of a farthest south. The pole vault bar could always be notched a millimeter higher, the marathon run a fraction of a second faster, and there was wonderful drama and humility in that.

As the South Pole station buildings began to emerge, looking like ghosts in the white, blank light, I realized that this approach to the station was far harder earned than the last time I was here. Every step now marked my own personal farthest south. Only twenty-seven people before me had ever completed a solo coast-to-Pole crossing, unsupported and unassisted—only two on the route that Rudd and I were following. I would keep going after that, of course, and if I could become the first person ever to cross the continent alone without assistance or support, well, that, too, would be a farthest south in its own way. And the great drama would surely continue from there as future explorers aimed to surpass me in their ambition or the difficulty of their goals, which is exactly how it should be. Records are meant to be broken.

Finally, the hard, straight lines of actual architecture began to emerge—something I hadn't seen since boarding the Ilyushin in Chile to fly to the continent. I'd certainly felt a human imprint in the supply tents and hangars at the Union Glacier base, and at the Thiels fuel depot, but the polar station, in its cluster of structures and their obvious importance, felt like a giant, teeming city. It had corners and walls, even real buildings with doors and roofs, and it felt stunning and strangely shocking after so many days of seeing nothing but emptiness and white, or the scruffy and cramped little world inside my tent.

I also knew as I drew closer that South Pole station managers were precise and picky about how people on expeditions were expected to enter the area, so that scientific study zones on the ice wouldn't be disturbed. And that roundabout route took me right past the A.L.E. camp, where a short, burly, and bearded Canadian named Devon, the camp manager, stepped out to greet me. He'd known from my nightly calls to the Comms Box that I was due at the Pole that morning, and knew that under the rules of an unassisted, unsupported crossing he could offer me nothing except congratulations in making it this far.

"Well done, Colin," Devon said simply. He saw me looking at the rows of small tents that had been set up in the camp and what was obviously a kind of heating system running into each one from what looked like a central propane burner. My mouth fell open. Heated tents.

"Rich tourists," Devon said with a smile and shrug. "Fly in to the Pole but want it toasty in the sack as well—and I totally get it. A warm tent is . . ." He looked back at me sharply. "Sorry, didn't mean to rub it in—warm isn't something you've had much of, I know."

"It's okay," I said, still shaking my head at the sight and feeling, as Devon had known I would, a pang of envy at even the idea of heat.

We could see the actual South Pole marker from there, surrounded by the twelve flags of the original Antarctic Treaty–signing nations, all fluttering together in the same direction, which felt somehow powerful itself as a symbol of unity and purpose. But as Devon and I walked closer, I could see no other people, which I was very happy about. Fewer people meant fewer potential complications and risks.

When I actually stepped up to the marker—a silver orb about the size of a basketball, perched atop a candy-cane pole—the unquestionable power of the place hit me again. The Pole was far more than a waypoint. It resonated and shimmered. The station science building suddenly seemed more astonishing and beautiful, too, stacked on its pylons driven down into the ice, all aligned lengthwise to the wind's prevailing direction, just like my tent every night—as streamlined as possible in a place where the winds rarely stop.

As I stepped out of my skis, and unhitched from the harness, I walked up and saw a piece of yellow tape on the silver globe, and thought for a second that perhaps the orb had cracked or been damaged and was being repaired. South Pole temporarily out of service, I thought with a laugh. But as I got close enough to read, I was stunned. The tape had my name on it. "Go Colin, Go!" it read, and was signed, "South Pole Station," along with a little drawing of a heart. I glanced around nervously, as though the message's authors might be hiding and would leap out and yell, "Surprise!"

I touched the tape with my mitten, then shifted my head in closer to the orb and peered into its reflective surface, and saw my distorted image looking back at me, my red-and-black jacket and pants making my legs look ten feet long, my oversized head filling the orb's surface.

When I pulled up my mask, I got another jolt. My face looked so thin. I brought a mittened hand to touch the black sports tape across my cheeks and nose. For a gasping, shocking second, it didn't look like me at all, and I pulled back. Better not to look.

Then I saw two men emerge from the main station building, and I immediately tensed up again. I knew I wasn't breaking any rules or doing anything remotely wrong, but this was where it could get weird.

As they got closer, I saw that one was carrying what looked like a tripod, with a camera mounted on top. And they kept coming.

"You must be Colin!" one man shouted. "I've been following your Impossible First expedition and race against Captain Rudd in the *New York Times*. Amazing!"

They were walking faster toward me now, and I shrank back in retreat, suddenly feeling the orb of the pole bulging into my back. I wanted to run away.

They stopped about ten feet away, one holding the tripod upright, the other standing with mittened hands hanging to his sides. I think they could already tell that something wasn't quite right with me, my backing away making little sense. In the normal world, at least.

I nodded. I knew from Jenna that the *Times* was extensively covering the race between Rudd and me—but the coverage had seemed, out on the ice, like something so far away as to be barely real. It shocked me that people here could get up every morning and read the news.

"Sorry there aren't more of us out here to greet you," one of the men said with a faint accent I couldn't quite place. "It's kind of the middle of the night for us here."

"Oh." I stood up straight, taking my back off the pole. "What time is it?" I said, glancing down at the Rolex that I'd become so attached to since borrowing it.

"Two-sixteen a.m.," one of the men said after glancing at his own watch. Then he shrugged, looking a little embarrassed. "I'm a scientist," he said.

His friend laughed. "Yeah, it'll never be quarter after two for him."

"Well, it's 10:16 a.m. for me . . . uh, and I guess that would be yesterday—your yesterday, anyway. It's still today for me . . . I think."

"Yeah, we're on Christchurch time," the man with the accent said, lifting up the ski goggles he'd worn in stepping out of the building.

We were all silent for a minute after that, digesting the strangeness of it. The four of us were standing ten feet from one another in one of the most remote corners of the planet—a spot where no one can ever just pop in or drop by—and we were all functioning in sharply different time zones, and even days. My Rolex was set to coordinate with A.L.E., which was based out of Chile, sixteen hours different from the New Zealand time that the station ran on.

It got weirder. I suddenly realized that I recognized the man with the accent who'd just pulled up his goggles. I stopped and questioned myself before saying anything. It felt about as likely as talking to Paul Simon. In all of Antarctica, in my own little time zone, I'd run into someone I knew. Reality felt as distorted as the world seen through a reflective silver orb.

"Uh, actually I think we've met," I said.

He looked blankly back at me. "Um . . . I'm not sure I—"

His hesitance gave me a flicker of doubt. "You're . . . French, right? You work on the telescope? We met here in 2016. . . . I toured the station—"

"That's right! Now that you mention it, of course I remember. Of course!" he shouted with a radiant, toothy smile, which reminded me again how much I'd liked him the first time. "Welcome back and good to see you again, Colin! I hope it hasn't been too terrible for you out there," he said, waving his hand toward the rest of the continent. "I assume we'll get to see Captain Rudd as well, but congratulations on getting here first."

I mumbled a thank-you and fidgeted, feeling anxious to be off.

"Well, I really can't stay," I blurted. I'm sure that sounded crazy as well. I'd just arrived. People struggled for years to stand where I was standing. I'd put in forty exhausting days to get there. But it was too much, too alien, and too threatening. I needed to be on my way. Sure thing, my 2:16 a.m. camp greeters said, though I'm not sure they did, or could ever remotely, understand.

"But one thing," I said. "Can you please take a picture of me with the Explorers Club flag?"

This was a moment I'd looked forward to from my first days on the ice, from the first planning of the expedition, and I'd already dug into my sled and retrieved it—carefully folded in a plastic bag in the bottom of my big orange duffel: "Explorers Club flag number 109."

Almost every well-known explorer, from Neil Armstrong, the first person to walk on the moon, to Sir Edmund Hillary and Tenzing Norgay, the first men atop Everest, has been a member of the Explorers Club. The club, founded in 1904, had allowed me to carry one of its 220 flags across Antarctica on my project, flag number 109. The flags all have rich histories, linking to the places around the world, and even on the moon, where they've been carried. Flag 109 had journeyed, since its creation in 1941, from the Lyngen Alps of Norway, to the waters of Hudson Bay in search of the wreckage of the HMS *Hampshire*, sunk in battle in 1697. Its fabric had tiny, proud scars from those many expeditions, in the holes and carefully stitched patches, and as I held it there in my hands, I felt I could burst all over again with pride and awe. Number 109 had a new story to tell whether I finished the crossing or not.

I carefully climbed on top of my sled, skis laid on the snow, and held the flag gently in my mittens as the still-smiling scientist took my photo. Standing there, I couldn't help but think of the sweep of history and movement and change.

Even the silver orb of the Pole itself and its twelve flags, which looked so majestic and permanent in their installation, were always changing, always moving—along with the polar station buildings—as the great continental ice sheet they sat on slowly slid and shifted beneath.

But here, the constant, imperceptible movement of the ice meant that the ceremonial spot where I was standing was not technically the true geographic South Pole, where all the latitude lines of the planet actually hit their bull's-eye. The true geographic pole was about a five-minute walk away. Each year, with the ice having moved about ten meters, the true Pole was measured and a simple metal stake in the ground was moved slightly to its new location.

I felt I had to honor that place, too, with a brief stop, just to touch it, running my mitten down the stake, trying in a way to absorb its power. And the scientists, perhaps curious about me by then in my probably pretty strange behavior, followed me over.

"Could you please take one more photo?" I asked as I got to the geographic pole. When they were ready, I flipped over to do a handstand, my red-and-black legs rising up into the sky. "I'm at the bottom of the world, holding it up!" I shouted, just before falling over onto the ice.

It was mind-bending, that technically in that moment all directions from that place were north. Only when I'd gone a few steps farther would east or west even exist. And as I headed out past the station's airstrip—the exit route from the camp as strictly mandated as its entry points—the power of that brought Steve Jones to mind. Jones is a warm and enthusiastic Brit in his fifties—but even more than that he's an astonishing historian, a living encyclopedia of Antarctic history and lore. As A.L.E.'s expeditions manager, he's also the great connector of all the dots in how independent expeditions on the ice are accomplished, or not.

Jones, who had worked in Antarctica for decades for A.L.E., had an aura I'd come to love about so many people who had been touched and affected by this harsh and astonishing place, where ferocity and extreme conditions can turn people inward, to reflection. He carried the spirit of Scott, who wrote glorious prose in his tent as he lay dying, and Shackleton, who journaled his thoughts in trying to survive shipwreck. Jones, in his years of study, had become a master of the arcane details of Antarctic dreams—the follies, disasters, and triumphs. He knew every nuance of everything that had ever gone right or wrong on the continent.

I'd called him in early 2018, after the trip to Whistler when Jenna and I first began planning The Impossible First project, and told him I was interested in trying a solo, unsupported, unassisted crossing.

"Well, you should know, things have changed, Colin," Jones said.

Henry Worsley's death, beyond the news it made around the world, had sent a fierce ripple through A.L.E., as people all over the globe second-guessed what had happened and why. Though the company had done exactly what it was supposed to do—sending out a rescue expedition when Worsley finally, too late as it turned out, called for it—the storm of publicity had hurt. The company's owners had ordered an internal review of how expeditions were approved and what routes would be allowed, Jones told me.

"We've gotten much more restrictive about what expeditions we'll support," Jones said. "Any solo expedition now needs approval of all four owners of the company, so that's your first step." Jones didn't have to say the rest—A.L.E. didn't want any more people to die, and wasn't going to put anybody on the ice that the owners weren't comfortable with.

So I got two letters of recommendation—one from Dixie, and the other from Guy Cotter, a mountaineering legend I'd met in the Himalayas, whose help had been crucial during my Explorers Grand Slam project. I also told Jones that I planned to do a Greenland crossing in preparation, which reassured the company. Finally, Jones called with the green light.

"But I have to tell you, Colin, that the route you can take through the Transantarctic Mountains is nonnegotiable," Jones said. "Leverett Glacier to the Ross Ice Shelf is the only solo expedition option. If you're going to do this, that's it. All the aerial mapping of the crevasse fields, the ground penetrating radar, everything supports this." He paused for a second. "Lots of that work is thanks to you Yanks, since the US government uses the route to send a large load of gear from McMurdo, their coastal base, to resupply the South Pole station every summer. The South Pole Overland Traverse will have already come through for the year by the time you get there, so as a result the route won't be completely pristine. You'll see some flags and rutted tracks from their vehicles, but it's the safest for soloing."

I was silent for a minute. My research into the routes through the Transantarctic Mountains was preliminary, but I'd read accounts of expedition teams on other routes navigating through crevasse fields there and, while roped together, falling through the ice daily. The thought of being alone, unroped, with no one to pull me out of a bottomless crevasse was terrifying.

"Just so you know, others have inquired about making the solo crossing next season," Jones said. "And if more than one of you go ahead with your plans . . . well, it'll be a race for the ages, that's for sure." I could hear the excitement in his voice, probably thinking about the race that still echoed down through everything on the continent, between Scott and Amundsen. He continued: "But regardless, A.L.E. will only support soloists on the Leverett on that side of the continent. You will all be in the same boat out there."

I was silent again and I think Steve took my pause for disappointment.

"I've been around for a while, Colin, a lot longer than you, and let me tell you, safe is good in Antarctica," he said. "And the second thing is that any route, whatever it is, if it can be completed solo, unsupported, and unassisted, it will be a world first—no one has ever manhauled the landmass of the continent in that way."

"No, no," I said. "I'm happy to take the safest route that qualifies under the rules—and the route has historic precedent anyway, right? Felicity Aston went across on the Leverett in the opposite direction if I remember correctly, and she really inspired me." Aston, a climate scientist, became in 2012 the first woman to ski solo and unassisted across the continent, although she was supported by two resupplies along the way. But her grit and commitment had impressed me even before that—in her early twenties, she'd spent more than two years through two Antarctic winters at a remote research station, gathering data on how climate change is affecting the world's coldest places.

"Yes! Felicity is amazing!" Jones shouted over the phone. "She's another Brit, too, you know, so watch out, Colin! We're after you!"

THE WHITEOUT THAT HAD SOCKED IN the Pole began to clear as I left, walking along the side of the station runway. I stopped and turned around for one last look at the station's buildings, watching the light change, sunlight reflected back from glass and steel. And as I turned back and fell into a rhythm going north, other clouds felt like they were lifting inside me as well. The elements that defined my life on the ice—the sound of my skis, the pull of the harness into my shoulders, the puff of my breath into the mask—all seemed in sync in their sweet familiarity, and a slow wave of joy started building.

I'd been so guarded and wary and careful getting in and out of the Pole, and I'd tightly managed so much else in my expenditures of energy in the days and weeks since the start. Even my mistakes and patchwork, in stealing food from myself, spilling gas, falling, and figuring out how to fix what needed fixing, had reinforced the sense that relentless focus and a disciplined mindset were the answers to almost every challenge.

Now it almost seemed as if I were being untied and released from those pressures, as though I'd passed through something, broken free. I felt, rising inside me, a strong current of energy-boosting emotions. And the clearing skies intensified the feeling, spiking the temperature to the warmest I'd seen since coming onto the ice—only fifteen below, my clip-on jacket thermometer said. The winds had calmed, too, almost to a point of stillness, making fifteen below feel almost balmy. I pulled off my mask and jutted my chin up toward the sun, fear of frostbite entirely faded for the moment. That I'd made it to the South Pole—the finish line for almost every Antarctic expedition—and was now ten miles beyond it was part of that release. I'd feared the Pole in a strange way because the rules about what defined an unsupported and unassisted crossing were so specific, and now I felt a palpable sense of having moved beyond the threat.

I turned my face away from the sun and opened my eyes, looking out through my goggles onto the icescape. It was as stark and empty as always, but also suddenly full. With the lifting of the whiteout, I could see vast distances in what felt like absolute clarity of vision and thought—even the far edge of the horizon seemed like something I could grab onto and pull into my embrace. And then colors started swirling before my eyes as airborne ice crystals refracting through the bright light formed a complete circular rainbow around the sun, a full sundog.

I grabbed my camera to capture the astonishing image, then turned the lens back to my face. I wanted to tell someone the depth of what I was feeling.

I smiled at Cam. "I don't know that I've ever felt this happy in my life," I said, squinting into the lens. Even as I said it, and waved Cam's eye around to capture the scene, I wasn't sure I could ever make anyone understand, because there really weren't any words for it. But as I kept talking, it came out like a prayer.

"I just feel this deep gratitude," I said, snot running down into my pathetically thin little mustache, all I had to show after forty days of not shaving. "Gratitude for all the amazing people in my life, for being alive, for the privilege of being able to attempt something like this and experience this beautiful moment."

Cam's unblinking eye stared back at me. "What a gift to be out here all alone in Antarctica," I said, my voice going quieter. "I'll probably never do this again, but these are the moments that I'm going to remember."

The winds stayed calm through the rest of that day, enabling me to make nearly fifteen miles, which only added to my surging confidence, now 578 miles from the start. And the calm made setting up camp different as well. In pulling my tent and my arctic bedding from the sled and laying them on the ice, I felt for the first time in many days almost worry free. Wind had been a constant nagging tension through almost every morning and night in getting things to and from the sled. In the deep calm I could lay almost anything onto the ice and know that, when I looked back, it would be just where I'd left it.

Like the glorious wheel of the sundog, life had spun to a new place, it seemed. Maybe, I thought, as I crawled into the tent, what had unfolded in these hours was some new permanent state. And as I listened to the stove, feeling almost warm from the radiant sun blazing through the red roof, I wanted to believe it. The high was too good, too vivid and too real, and I didn't want to come down.

CHAPTER THIRTEEN

An Inch from Failure

DAY 41

I saw sundog circles with my eyes closed that night after the Pole, as though the image had been burned into my retinas from staring at it too long. It actually felt a bit like a hangover, like I'd flown too close to the sun in my euphoria. But the idea of a circle looping back onto itself, ends and beginnings reaching a shared point, also somehow seemed like an appropriate image. Balance and equilibrium were back in my life with a vengeance that next morning, my forty-first day on the ice.

My breakfast said it all.

Surrounded by all that was so profoundly familiar—the hissing stove behind me in the kitchen, the dank smells of my lived-in clothes, the flutter of my tent in the wind—I'd stirred the oatmeal into my mug and added my protein powder, and then I just couldn't take my eyes off it because the portion looked so small. I even looked around me, on the sleeping bag and to the sides of it, to see if perhaps I'd spilled some, though I knew with absolute certainty that I hadn't. I wanted to gobble the oatmeal in two bites. I wanted to savor it. I wanted to save it for later. I wanted to do all three things at the same time.

The question of food had clawed its way back and would have to be faced. I'd eaten forty days' worth of rations in reaching the South Pole, and now only had fifteen days of rations left from the fifty-five I'd started with at the first waypoint, after Jenna and I had pared down my load. I almost certainly had more than fifteen days left to my finish line at the continent's other edge, on the Ross Ice Shelf. But beyond that essential fact, I had no clue what the balance point really was of food supply and miles left, or even how to estimate it.

Though expeditions before me had gone by foot up the Leverett Glacier—Felicity Aston in particular, in her amazing 2012 trek—descending the Leverett all the way to the Ross Ice Shelf solo, unsupported, and unassisted, had never been done. There was no historical data I could check; I was truly stepping into the unknown.

Ben Saunders had intended to complete the same route last year, descending the Leverett after reaching the Pole. He'd arrived at the South Pole with fifteen days of food supplies left, the exact amount I had on my sled as well, when I'd walked up and touched the great silver orb the day before and unpacked my Explorers Club flag. But then Saunders, with vast experience on the Antarctic ice under his belt, had decided that the math problem of food and miles in going the Leverett route was too uncertain, and he'd ended his project, rather than risk running out of food.

"Standing here with less food for the remainder of my journey than I'd planned, with a safety margin that I feel is too slim, I have decided to end my expedition at the Pole," he wrote in a blogpost announcing his decision to stop. "In some ways it was an easy, logical decision to make, and in others it was extraordinarily hard, particularly as I'm not currently in trouble." I had a tiny fraction of Saunders's experience, but I'd made the choice to continue on, and now as I stared down at my breakfast, the implications of that decision felt deep and uncertain.

Crossing the Pole had distracted me in some ways from the food math. I'd thrown up my armor and my defenses in going past the

Amundsen-Scott Station. And then I'd been swept up in that wave of euphoric invincibility after the Pole. And all of it, I now saw—the anxiety, the wonder, the glorious post-Pole moment in the shadow of the sundog—had diverted my attention from the nagging, serious issues that had to be resolved. But now reality was back. Food was reality. Oatmeal was reality. The 350 miles ahead of me to the finish was reality.

I had to reduce my food intake or risk running out completely if I continued to eat regular rations. That was the reality that stared back at me from my mug of oatmeal. The amount left on the sled wouldn't last, if I continued to eat my allotted seven thousand daily calories. My only choice now was to stretch out the food I had left, pushing on every day with less in my already constantly hungry belly. Less now each day, as bad as that sounded, would also be way better than none at all at some grim future date if I got injured or sick on the Leverett and couldn't be quickly rescued.

The math looked bad: It had taken me forty days to cross the 566 miles to the Pole, averaging fourteen miles per day. That left me with roughly 350 miles to go on the morning of my forty-first day. If I went the same pace for the miles left—fourteen miles per day—it would take twenty-five days to reach the Ross Ice Shelf. The only answer was to reorganize again, find a new plan, divide up the food that was left.

And that night, I knew, I'd have to have a conversation with Jenna, which I'd been resisting and she'd been gently suggesting had to happen, about how exactly to do that, specifically how much less food I could have in the days I had left. I'd dreaded the conversation and its implications, but as I pushed through that forty-first day, making eighteen miles by the end, I could think of little else. I even planned out, as I shoveled the snow and drove in my tent anchors, what I'd say to Jenna. "Let's work the problem. We can solve this." But when I heard her voice, the dam broke.

"I'm looking down at my body and I don't recognize it," I said, halfway to tears with my first words. I pressed the sat phone so hard to the side of my face that it hurt, and stared up, watching my mittens, mask, and thermometer bobbing on the clothesline. "I'm experiencing rapid weight loss, baby, my wristwatch is sliding around on my arm." I held it up over my head and saw the watch slide down toward my elbow as though it were on a greased pole. "I'm starting to get scared."

"Oh babe, it's going to be okay," Jenna said. Her voice cracked with emotion through the harsh static of our phone connection, pouring into my head, and I tried to pull it deeper into me, seeing her at our long, dark wooden kitchen table and smelling sautéed mushrooms and onions on the stove. The puppy she'd brought home while I was on the ice, a soft-coated wheaten terrier named Jack, whined in the background, and I tried to see him, too, and pull him into the phone, into my tent. "Colin, just remember. We've got a team of doctors, and they're going to put you all back together when you get home. Just remember that," Jenna said. Something about how she said the word "remember" told me she was trying to convince herself, too.

"I don't mean to sound alarmist—really," I said, trying to recapture the rational, let's-work-the-problem mindset I'd aimed for. "I just need to keep telling myself I'm fine, that's all," I said. "It's not like I'm falling apart . . . but it's scary when you look down," I faltered for another second, "and your legs are so small."

"It will all come back, Colin, just remember that," she said, speaking slowly, as though to a child.

"Yeah, okay," I mumbled, wanting her to think that I wasn't in as bad a place as I really was.

Our specific task that night was fairly straightforward: Fifteen days' worth of Colin Bars and daily rations had to stretch to twenty days at least, and even that was a guess. Since I didn't know how long it would take to get to the end, I couldn't be sure that any amount of stretching out the supplies would be good enough.

And every calorie calculation came with repercussions. At full rations, I'd been eating seven thousand calories a day, which in the real world was a huge amount, a surefire formula for piling on the pounds. Out here, pulling the sled twelve hours a day in brutal cold, it had the opposite effect. Because I was burning through at least ten thousand calories a day, seven thousand was a starvation diet, forcing my body to seek out and use up any fat reserves it could find inside me. And when the fat was used up, the muscles were next.

Now I'd go to less than six thousand, which I knew would leave me hungry almost every minute through the day and accelerate my weight loss. And just bringing all the food into the tent to sort through made me uneasy. I'd been so strict and careful since my nighttime food raid to never bring any extra supplies into the tent, and now here it all was in front of me—all my food in the world— and it didn't look like much. Ten daily ration bags, each in their own Ziploc, fit into one larger dry bag. The thirty-five-thousand-calorie stash of Colin Bars, which I'd pulled aside on that morning at the first waypoint when I cached food and supplies, sat in their own separate bag, frozen solid as bricks.

So my first step, as I held the sat phone with one hand, was to pull out the individual daily ration bags and lay them out on the sleeping bag. Then I'd count up the component parts and start rebagging—oatmeal stretching out into smaller portions, ramen rations going to every other day, and on down through a process of a scoop here and a scoop there that was making me anxious and hungry even before I started.

I got the daily bags in a row. I got the spare bags all set in a pile. And then I went down the row of rations, counting it all up.

"Hmm," I said when I finished, shaking my head. There should be ten food bags and somehow I'd counted eleven.

Just then the phone line popped and buzzed for a second.

"What did you say?" Jenna said when she came back.

"Nothing, nothing," I muttered. I was counting again by then, going down the row, tapping each bag with a finger. Somehow I got to eleven again. I flopped back and stared up at the tent roof for a second.

"You okay?" Jenna said. "You ready to start rebagging?"

"Um . . . almost," I said. "Just having a little trouble."

Mental trouble is what I thought but didn't say. There had to be ten bags. I knew there were ten. It struck me, and frightened me, that maybe I wanted so badly to have eleven bags that I simply saw the number I wanted.

So I counted again, tapping the bags with a crusty finger and mouthing the numbers silently to myself as I went down the line . . . six, seven, eight . . . thinking that this time I'd get the number that made sense. Then another time. I stopped, feeling a wave of growing panic. This is how it starts, I thought. If a simple thing like counting small numbers was now beyond me, the big things could unravel very quickly.

Finally, I heard a little sigh followed by a wave of static at the other end of the phone.

"What?" I said. "Hello? Are you still there? Hello?"

I felt suddenly desperate and alone. If the line was dead and it was just me in my tent with confusion and my uncountable food bags, I feared I might just really go crazy.

But Jenna was back on the line.

"There's an extra day, right?" she said softly.

I froze and blinked, staring at my food.

She knew.

And I finally got it out of her. Based on her own count, she knew I probably had eleven full days of food left, plus the extra Colin Bars. But she'd been afraid to say it. She'd been protecting me, just in case she was wrong. She knew that if she'd told me I had eleven and it really somehow turned out to be ten, the disappointment could've been devastating. Of course she'd known the correct number; she'd organized every detail of this expedition and meticulously tracked every choice along the way. She also knew what a brittle, fragile place I'd come to.

I lay back in the bag when the re-sorting was done, feeling relieved, but in some ways even more freaked out than before. The extra seven-thousand-calorie food bag meant that I'd been given a brief reprieve—I could eat a full day's rations tomorrow before starting on the new reduced food regimen. But the fact that I'd been so confused in figuring it all out, and that Jenna had been so concerned about my mental state, meant that I was also really hitting some new place of jeopardy. Food supply fears were coming at me from one side, mental confusion and weight loss from the other, and it was all related. I felt surrounded, ganged up on and overwhelmed, and I wasn't sure how, or if, I could fight back.

And though I couldn't see it, the worst was only beginning.

SOMETIMES DURING THOSE NEXT FEW DAYS it almost felt like time had screeched to a stop or ceased to have meaning.

The blank emptiness and numbing monotony of a landscape without features, and the ferocity of effort required to move across that landscape while never seeing much evidence that I was actually getting anywhere, had come to feel like a vast and perverse treadmill.

People I loved were out there somewhere—my family, my wife, my friends—along with strangers from around the world who were following my progress. I knew that, and I tried to draw strength from it. I thought of the French scientist, reading the *New York Times* on his computer in the South Pole station. I thought of Tim in the Comms Box dreaming of Christmas Day on Bondi Beach. But it all felt shallow and incomplete, like a cartoon, a reflection of reality and not the real world itself.

I tried telling myself my reduced rations didn't matter and

weren't having an effect. And for the next five strange days, I pushed ahead on them, pulling the sled for twelve hours each day, trying to pretend that everything was the same, that I was strong and that fifteen hundred fewer calories per day didn't matter.

But it did matter. Just as it was that night when I'd been unable to count food bags laid out in front of me, I found that many little things were becoming different and harder—harder to physically accomplish or sometimes even to understand. Sometimes in pulling the sled, and staring down intently at my compass, I'd start to lose the sense that it was separate from me, and I'd feel like I might fall down into it, spiraling into its depths as though it were a black hole. One night, in building the snow-wall embankment around my tent, I stopped in the middle of the task, frozen in place, shovel in hand, not quite sure what I was doing or why, as though my mind had just sort of walked off the field.

And the cold seemed to be tightening its grip like the slow turning of a screw. The human body burns calories to stay warm, to heal, to stay alive. Heat is life. But through those days after the food redistribution, the temperature also seemed to go into slow free fall, down to thirty below or often worse. And my thermometer was only easily readable down to about that temperature—after that the little red mercury line got harder and harder to see—so I found myself tapping it with the thumb of my glove sometimes when I'd check it during the day, wondering whether it had, like so many other things around me, gone slightly off-kilter. And I began to think I was actually chilling down deeper inside than I had before. A defensive perimeter had been penetrated. The cold had found a chink in my armor.

I was sitting on the sled, eating my reduced portion of ramen, when I thought of Henry Worsley's descent into peril. I certainly didn't know what his final days had been like, or the exact symptoms of his decline, but he'd clearly hit some dark corner of his mind and body, a place where something of Antarctica had confronted him or changed him. And that night, when I froze again in place, suddenly confused about lighting my stove, it struck me that perhaps Worsley, a giant of Antarctic wisdom and experience, had not known what to do when he hit that inflection point. Maybe he'd become locked in place, unable to choose or see the correct path ahead, and that's what had turned a problem into a crisis.

And that was perhaps the single most terrifying thought I'd had in forty-six days on the ice—maybe in my entire life—that Antarctica's cruelest, hardest force wasn't its weather or its brutal cold, but the quiet erosion of judgment and reason and sanity, and that it was also the one thing you couldn't possibly defend yourself against.

I'D SEEN THE GREAT STORM gradually coming toward me through my forty-sixth day on the ice. It didn't roar in suddenly, or surge. It crept in with slow, almost imperceptible changes of light and wind, and then with the first light drifts of blowing snow. No sign or signal was ever in itself abrupt or alarming. It all just built and built, until the pace became part of the experience, deepening my dread about what was to come. The growing cold, along with the chill I increasingly felt inside, in my bones, through the day, was another signal that a low-pressure front was grinding toward me across the flat, featureless expanse of ice, with nothing to block it or divert it or change its path.

I'd learned by then to trust my skis, too, in gauging the weather outlook, and they told me to brace myself. How much snow was blowing across them at any one moment—whether they were fully or only slightly covered as I went forward—told me how much snow was actually in the air, something that was otherwise very hard to tell with no contrast of white on white. And the skis, through the day, were increasingly buried.

Then, through that night as I tried to sleep, the storm fully unfolded in its fury, until by the time I climbed out of my tent the next morning, I was in the thick of it.

And it was the worst possible time. My compass and GPS told me that I was approaching a place in my journey that I'd dreaded even in good weather—a one-hundred-mile stretch of ice where the sastrugi, which I'd managed to deal with through the miles and weeks when they were one or two feet high, became monsters. They'd now be three to five feet high, each with potentially huge holes on any side—a hellish stretch that previous explorers had nicknamed with wonderfully deadpan irony Sastrugi National Park.

The name said a lot about Antarctic explorers themselves, that their idea of levity was to dub one of the hardest places on the continent to get across a "park." And yet there definitely was a kind of grandeur to the awfulness of it.

I stopped, straining to see ahead of me in what was gradually becoming an all-out blizzard. The wind smashed into me, gusting to what I estimated to be fifty or even sixty miles per hour, which would produce windchills in the range of eighty below or worse. But the real terror of Sastrugi National Park was also the most ironic. This park was in a real way "off the map"—unreachable and inaccessible. On a continent with thousands of square miles where a rescue plane equipped with skis could come in for a skid landing, weather permitting, the great sastrugi zone made landing impossible.

I thought of Simon, A.L.E.'s travel safety manager. His office in Punta Arenas was lined with maps, and the day we conferred we had my route map displayed on a wall-mounted TV.

"Okay, right here's where you definitely don't want to get into trouble, Colin," he said, drawing what seemed like a huge circle with a laser pointer and looking up at me. "If you call for help in here, you won't get it," he said. "You'll be on your own."

On your own. I'd nodded and shrugged and thanked Simon, but until that moment, standing at the edge of the sastrugi zone—though I couldn't see even a hint of it yet in the storm—I hadn't really understood. With my next steps I'd be on my own in a way I'd never been before.

I started falling almost immediately, and with each fall Simon's words kept coming back to me because I saw how easily and quickly trouble could happen. In the blowing snow, I couldn't see a sastruga, however big it was, until I was directly on it, and by then my forward momentum made it hard, if not impossible, to react. And the uncountable years of wind that had made the sastrugi had also polished them into fierce and icy hardness. So any fall was a fall onto hard ice, and the deeply uneven surfaces meant that the impact of that fall could hit me anywhere. Elbows, hips, knees, and shoulders were all bruised and hurting within the first hour. I started wishing after one particularly bad fall that I'd brought a helmet. Getting knocked unconscious out here, in the storm, without hope of rescue, would unquestionably be fatal.

I began to bargain with myself. Had I learned anything from that disastrous day when I'd been forced to stop, when I'd curled up at the edge of the sled seeking shelter from the wind and still been unable to repair my ski skin? Maybe I should stop, I said. Maybe I should seek shelter from the storm, after so many days without a day off.

Finally I decided, only a few hours into the day, that if I really wanted to keep going I needed to change from my short skins to my long ones. And that set up a whole new series of bargains and trade-offs. Longer skins, with more surface touching on the ice, would make for slower progress, but give me a better grip on the uneven sastrugi surfaces. I'd have to change my skins. But changing the skins, as I'd learned the hard way, couldn't be done in a blizzard, which meant I'd need to put the tent back up, only hours after taking it down, and I'd be doing it in a storm. Stopping my big-muscle movements of pulling the sled, even if I could do the switchover quickly, would also give the cold an opportunity to penetrate as I sat inside and worked. Every option I could think of was frustrating or frightening, or both.

But struggling on finally just seemed impossible, and that forced the decision. I'd have to put up the tent. So I unharnessed, looked for a spot that was more or less flat, and uncinched the sled cover, pausing for a moment as I did to stare down at the bungee cord that had held on and done its job through all the miles since the first day when I'd broken the buckle. The cord had been an improvisation that worked, I thought as I stowed it in my bag. The tent fluttered and flapped in the wind as I carried it over, and the work of putting it up—anchoring to the sled, and then on the other side—felt slow and labored. I was frustrated and cold, and the bruises from my falls made every step, however crucial, feel tedious, annoying, and painful. My patience was frayed.

Finally, I got my kitchen box with my stove, which I'd need to heat the skins, into the vestibule and then stood there looking at the sled with my arctic bedding and bags and food all still packed away. No, I decided. I'd leave them outside. It felt like one little piece of the bargaining process I could control. No bedding or food in the tent meant that however much I'd be sheltered once I got inside, I'd be unable to stay there, even if the storm worsened, even if, once I got inside, I had second thoughts. I'd have to go back out to gather my supplies if I decided that I really wanted or needed to hide from the blizzard.

But the bargain didn't work very well. I got myself and my skis and skins inside, lit the stove, and made the repair. The muscle memory of doing that, like the clenching of my hands on the tent, was almost automatic. But then, with the skis laid out on the tent floor beside me ready to go, the stove turned off and ready to pack, I froze in place.

The tent was fluttering and rolling around me, and I was shivering, and I couldn't decide what to do.

Uncertainty defined the world. If I unzipped my tent and went back out to continue the day, I risked falling, even worse than I had already, in a place where no help would be coming and in weather that could kill me if things went wrong. If I stayed inside, the great problem of food would circle back to bite me. Going nowhere for another day meant that my food supplies, already stretched, would have to stretch even further. And then there was Rudd, currently thirty-five miles behind me. I'd seen what could happen in a single day, what he could do in a single day in catching up to me if he was out there still and I wasn't.

So I closed my eyes and tried to calm my mind. I needed to find the place that Vipassana meditation had taken me, starting with that first time when Brian had dropped me off for a ten-day silent retreat near Mount St. Helens, and through the years of practice since.

Staring at the tent floor, I began by focusing on my breathing—but trying to be free of thoughts had the exact opposite effect; my mind was racing. It was like there was a party in my head, and all my angels and demons had been invited. Pieces of me that felt tossed by the storm were competing for attention and dominance—hope wrestling doubt, calm battling anxiety, confidence holding back fear—and couldn't be denied, any more than I could ignore the tent thrashing around me. I had to take control.

If I can find a way to quiet my mind, get back out into the storm, and continue to make forward progress, I thought to myself, *eventually the storm will end; it can't last forever*. No matter how bad the storm was, it was temporary.

A phrase came to me that Jenna and I had seized on and made part of our vocabulary from the meditation practice we'd begun to share—our little reminder that change is the only constant, and that success requires endurance. The words were ordinary, a common phrase, but the deep emotional connections they carried felt like a lifeline.

"This too shall pass," I repeated, "this too shall pass," eyes still closed, focusing my full attention on believing it. Then I sucked in a deep breath, unzipped the door, and went back out into the storm.

227

*   *   *

AS I STRUGGLED through the sastrugi that day, falling again and again, hunched over in the wind, I found myself thinking more and more about Rudd. He'd never completely left my thoughts, of course, but in the strange mental space I'd entered, the no-rescue zone of Sastrugi National Park, he roared back.

We'd known exactly where Rudd was—though he didn't know we knew—since the first week, thanks to my mom and her feat of trial-and-error detective work. But since the sixth day, when I passed Rudd, and we had our surreal little encounter—hey there, just two guys trying to cross the continent, bumping into each other—we hadn't seen each other.

We were unquestionably bound together on the Antarctic ice in a powerful way—each of us separately and in different ways trying to achieve something that no one had ever accomplished, that was, in fact, regarded by many as impossible. But at the same time we were also both profoundly isolated, from morning until night, through every moment of every day and every step we took on the ice. He was out there somewhere in the white, invisible, and yet always there inside me, too, in a way, just as he'd been from those first moments flying on the Ilyushin.

And the public interest in this race had begun to increase, prompting the *New York Times* to ask Rudd's team if they could have access to his GPS tracker information to post daily updates of our respective locations. To my surprise, Rudd had obliged and the race was now broadcast live for the world to see. My little tactical advantage of secretly knowing exactly where he was had disappeared.

He made me push harder. At the end of almost every day, almost no matter how long or tough it had been, I'd think of him and convince myself I had an extra half hour in the tank, or maybe even an hour, and could keep going. If he could do eleven extra steps, or eleven extra minutes, I could do twelve. He made me look over my shoulder, even when I could see nothing, thinking somehow he might be there. I thought of him when my alarm went off in the morning, and when I turned off my tent stove at night and the final little hiss of compressed white-gas jets escaped in a sigh.

AS I WALKED into the still raging storm, I started thinking about my weird plane ride with Rudd and those hours across Drake Passage, which now seemed, after all the miles and weeks, like a lifetime ago.

Distracted, I misjudged a step. Hitting the edge of a huge sastruga, I slid sideways, smashing my head. And as I climbed back up, feeling dizzy and rubbing my left temple where I'd come down, I had a strange and startling thought: I needed Rudd.

I stood there for a while, processing that idea and checking myself for other bruises, trying to regain my calm. But it was true: I needed him. As a foil to my always competitive nature, he was convenient to have around, if only for the effect he had on me. And the more I thought about it, the weirder it seemed. Rudd's existence was almost too convenient. Maybe I'd needed a Rudd, and so—I gasped to myself even as the thought crystallized—I'd created him in my mind.

And I couldn't shake it, however hard I tried. It was ridiculous. It couldn't be true. It was absurd beyond measure. I had vivid memories of being with him—how he talked and laughed and even smelled.

But like the Antarctic cold, which also came with me into the tent and couldn't be banished some nights, for all my layers of clothes, the Rudd question burrowed inside. And though I knew it was halfway to crazy, I decided that I had to ask Jenna that night. I tried to be casual about it. She was going through the medical checklist we did almost nightly, on a scale of zero to four—pain to sleep to bowels. The wind outside was still howling, pale light from the 11 p.m. sun creating a dull glow through the red fabric of the tent. And in a pause, I just sort of dropped the question as though I was asking about nothing in particular, the way you might ask about our beloved NBA team back home, the Trailblazers, and whether she thought Damian Lillard would have a good year and the Blazers might have a shot at the championship.

"Is Lou real?" I said. As I spoke, the wind, which had been blasting and shaking the tent, suddenly dropped, falling almost to calm. The tent was still, just the gentle sway of the clothesline. I held my breath.

And she answered exactly as I'd asked, with a laugh and a completely casual tone, as if my question was the sort you'd ask over food in a noisy restaurant.

"Oh yeah, he's real, no doubt about it," she said, quickly moving on to another item on the checklist.

I heard in her tone that same thing she'd done with my food supplies—the withheld beat of worry. That she didn't stop and say "What the hell are you talking about?" was an unspoken signal that said, "Hang on, just hang on. I'll be strong and you will, too."

And when she did actually speak again, her words came through just as clearly, that she knew I did need something more, some added little psychological life preserver that told me I was okay, however close to the edge I felt.

"Colin, you're doing an incredible job out there, I love you," she said simply.

And "love" was the word I held in my head that night. It felt solid and real. I could cling to it and hang on.

BUT HANGING ON WAS GETTING HARDER to do as the storm continued and seemed to worsen through the next day, my forty-eighth on the ice.

And my hands were the signal. I'd gotten used to the regular throbbing ache after twelve hours of gripping the poles, from the cold and muscle strain. But some days brought added elements into the mix and, by the 8 p.m. stopping point, I often felt as if my hands were either being slowly crushed or burned inside the mittens by penetrating cold that had come to seem like fire. They froze by day and thawed by night, day after day. When I had to pull off the mittens for even a few seconds to accomplish a task requiring fine motor skills, the stinging deep freeze in my knuckles could last for hours. I was beginning to fear permanent damage.

That day, for whatever combination of reasons, it was way worse, and by the time I stopped I could hardly bear it. I wanted so badly to get my hands inside the tent. I pictured myself curled up with my hands under my armpits. I pictured holding my hands against the aluminum water pot as it warmed on the stove.

Setting up my tent after that long day, I was distracted by my hands. That was my first mistake.

Consequences rippled out from there.

In my distraction, I rushed it. That was my second mistake.

I didn't attach one end of the tent to the sled, as I always had before that night, but simply drove an anchor into the ice, and then, before I could put in a second anchor at the other end, a ferocious gust of wind pulled out the first anchor and lofted the tent into the air. Instantly, I dove forward and grabbed the edge of the tent—the aching hands I'd wanted to baby and soothe now suddenly more crucial than ever.

If I lost my grip, everything that kept me alive would be gone in seconds, fluttering up and out into the white. With no backup shelter and no hope of rescue, the end would come relatively soon. I was an inch from failure.

My compromised hands were now everything. They gripped the tent poles as the whole structure yanked and jerked over my head like a flag, caught in the wind. In a split second, I envisioned my fate if I lost the grip on the tent. I saw my shelter blow away and disappear into the white forever . . . My life now depended on my grip, and on what would happen, or not, in the next few seconds.

Those seconds felt like hours. The tent became the center of gravity and the center of my universe. In a way, it was the only thing that existed. The tent was home, shelter, life itself.

I stared down at my hands, clenched around the tent's edge. Immediately, my mittens were coated with fine spindrift that felt as if it was burying me alive and freezing me in place.

I had to get on top of the tent to solve my crisis, but, in doing so, avoid being so much on the top that I bent or broke the tent poles beyond repair, in which case I'd be in almost as much trouble as if I'd lost the tent entirely. The margin of error felt razor-thin, and as I lay there in a panic with the wind blasting into my face, I thought of my left-behind spare poles, buried in the snow at that first waypoint marker. They'd represented a few ounces saved, but also, perhaps, one more bad choice in a cascading chain of errors that would decide everything.

And my hands were shaking. I knew I had very little time before my muscles would start to cramp. Determination wouldn't matter much after that.

But then there was a lull in the wind. At first it seemed to be nothing, only a tiny pause, but it lingered another second longer, and another. And my breath stopped. I knew at any moment the wind would roar back, and that this lull might be the only chance I'd get. Finally, as the seconds of the lull ticked on, my instinct to survive took hold and I yanked the tent toward my body and wrestled it to the ground. Desperately, I held it in place under my knees, my body shaking from head to toe in the overload of adrenaline. After one of the most intense and fearful moments of my life, I had the tent back under control and had somehow managed not to break a single tent pole. I had my home back. Security had been regained. I *knew* that, but still, as I tried to catch my breath, feeling the thunder of my heart, I couldn't unclench my hands. Their grip had saved me and now they wouldn't let go.

The shaking didn't stop as the wind kicked back up. Through every task as I began to make camp—bringing in the kitchen box, carrying over my arctic bedding, shoveling the snow barrier—I felt as if I could collapse at any moment from the tension and the post-adrenaline shock. And by the time I finally zipped in, it seemed like everything that had been chasing me through those days of storm and hunger had followed. There was no escape. The tent felt crowded with ghosts and demons and shadows.

I reached for my camera and held the tripod out in front of me, the red record light on like a little eye gazing into mine.

"I'm not doing very good, Cam . . ." My voice trailed off as I stared into the lens, replaying in my mind the last hour. I came to the brink of saying it—almost lost the tent, almost faced the crisis of my life—but I couldn't form the words. The world shuddered around me, swaying and swinging and whipping. I could feel my tailbone against the frozen ground, less cushioned from the weight loss. I could feel the deep strain in my arms as I held the tripod. Mostly I felt nothing, emptied and drained of everything—beyond tears, beyond, for the first time, even hope.

"I'm feeling like I . . . like I just want to quit," I said quietly. The camera lens suddenly looked like a hole, a bottomless swirling whirlpool that was part of the storm, part of something that was pulling me in. Cam had come to feel like a friend I could confide in. Now I almost felt he was judging me, and I needed to explain myself.

"It's just that I . . . I feel like I've failed," I said. "I mean, I managed twenty miles today . . . and I know, I know, that's pretty good, right? Right?" I said. "But the storm just keeps raging and it looks like I've got another couple of days at least, and it's just like it's all sort of swallowed me and I . . ."

I reached out and touched the camera's little red recording light, which looked so fragile and small, like a candle in the wind, then up to my clothesline, where I gave my swaying thermometer a tap.

"I'm trying to hold it together," I said, turning back to Cam, just as another blast of wind rammed into the tent, making me flinch. I straightened up and pulled the lens closer to my face. "But it's so . . ."

I sat silently for a long time after that, my shoulders slumped, biting my lip, staring into the lens without finding any more words to say. Then I slowly reached over and turned off the recording. The little red light blinked out into darkness.

CHAPTER FOURTEEN

Put Your Boots Back On

DAY 49

Failure and defeat come to all of us at one time or another. I'd known that, and accepted it in going onto the ice. To try something that might in the end be unachievable is to take a risk, and I'd told myself over and over through my weeks in Antarctica that I was up to that risk—that failure, if it came, would be accepted with as much poise and honor as I could muster.

And even as I lay in my tent through that long night of the storm, thinking of quitting, thinking of how I might say the words in telling Jenna and students around the world and others who were following my journey, I clung to the idea that defeat, if I really decided I couldn't go on, would be better than not having tried at all. I thought of Teddy Roosevelt's famous lines that I'd always loved, about the value of struggle—that the person who steps into the arena to try is victorious from the start, because, if success comes, he knows "the triumph of high achievement," but if he falls short of his goal, he "fails while daring greatly, so that his place shall never be with those cold and timid souls who neither know victory nor defeat."

Fear is different. It's slippery and dark and uncertain, and that's what I really wrestled with through that long and mostly sleepless night. Fear can freeze you in place or make you quit, or not start at all, for reasons that are real and rational or false and flimsy, and once they've wound their way inside you, twisting and coiling, it's hard to tell the difference. I wasn't sure if the fear that grew and gripped me after my near catastrophe with the tent was fear that I should listen to and respect—because continuing on had become genuinely more dangerous—or rather, fear that I should ignore—because it was simply a shadow, a product of exhaustion, shock, and loneliness.

But then toward morning, a particularly vicious blast of wind hit the tent with a force that felt as if it could bend everything over sideways, and I thought of the place where the question of fear— when to listen and when to reject its clamoring call—was most clear in my life: Mount Everest, in a storm like this, in a tent like this, on a night that marked the beginning of what would be one of the most challenging and transformative weeks of my life.

"Some things we cannot choose!" Pasang Bhote yelled in his musical, Nepalese-accented English as the wind howled outside. He was in his mid-thirties, short and intensely strong, with a huge smile and a sinewy mountain toughness that was in many ways as awesome as the Himalayan terrain in which he'd grown up. And now as he sat in the tent, hugging his knees and looking utterly calm, I tried to understand him and his strength and the hard-earned wisdom he'd gained in summiting Everest six times before. "There will be other days in this life to climb!" he said.

It was May 2016. We were at twenty-six thousand feet on the mountain at Camp 4, above the oxygen-deprived line called the Death Zone—a bleak place of ice and snow on Everest's shoulder, at the altitude of a commercial airliner's flight path—and I was seeing in front of me what looked like the end of a dream. The great craggy black rock of the summit, much of it so steep and wind-scoured that even snow couldn't stick, seemed close enough almost to touch and, at that moment, as distant as the moon.

With Pasang Bhote as my Sherpa climbing partner, I'd reached this final camp before Everest's summit, aiming to push on to the top of the world's tallest mountain that night—an emotional and literal high point of my Explorers Grand Slam project. But then a huge windstorm had swept down onto us. We'd fought together for two hours just to get the tent up as the fabric whipped in our hands and we struggled to move in the extremely thin air, and now inside, the news had only gotten worse. I'd called down on the radio, and the base camp manager had said the winds were going to get more severe.

"You need to abort, Colin!" she'd shouted through the roar of the storm. "The mountain is shut, and the winds up there will kill you if you go tonight."

Pasang Bhote's stoic calm eluded me. I'd been climbing for 120 days by that moment, through four extraordinary and intense months of physical effort in trying to break the world record for the Explorers Grand Slam. I was thinned out, exhausted, and sleep deprived after climbing the tallest peaks in Antarctica, South America, Africa, Oceania, and Europe and crossing the last degree to the North and South Poles. Just getting here to twenty-six thousand feet on the mountain—higher than I'd ever been in my life—had required me to dig deeply into every reserve of strength and determination I could muster.

And now, on the second-to-last of the project's Seven Summits—just three thousand feet below the highest point in the world, with only Denali in Alaska left to climb after that—it was all unraveling. Going up to the summit was out of the question. Going down at night from here was equally dangerous. Camp 4, in the Death Zone, had a reputation of its own that I'd grown up reading about. The 1996 disaster that Jon Krakauer wrote about in *Into Thin Air* had mostly unfolded on the mountain around Camp 4, killing eight climbers. The human body literally begins dying at that altitude, consuming itself. Strong and fit climbers trapped there sometimes went to sleep and never woke. Pasang Bhote and I dug in and waited for morning, which felt to me as if it would never come.

*　*　*

AS WE CLIMBED OUT of the tent the next morning, I looked up instantly, without choice, as though there were only one thing in the universe to look at—Everest's summit. Spindrift was blowing off the top with a long horizontal trail of white that told me immediately that the base camp manager's warning the night before had probably saved our lives. It looked like the mountain was being scoured and scraped, or almost as though it were a volcano, spewing snow instead of lava or smoke. The windchill would be lethal up there even if you could climb up to experience it.

There was only one choice: to retreat and head down to lower elevation. That was clear from the first glimpse. But it was bitter stuff, and I had to keep telling myself to focus on the dangers right there before me and remember that most accidents on Everest happened not when people were climbing up, but when they were heading down—exhausted, dispirited, or distracted in thinking of where they'd been, or might've been. They fell into the trap of believing the challenge was over and let their guard down.

"The mountain says when it can be climbed," Pasang Bhote said, looking over at me with a little shrug that morning, as though he could read my mind and the frustrated place I'd mentally traveled to.

"I know," I said, zipping up my jacket. "I'm trying to accept that."

If yesterday had been my one shot and the mountain would allow nothing more, I thought as I turned back to look one more time—if I'd stepped into the arena Teddy Roosevelt wrote about and fallen short—I'd have to find a way to live with that. But there also seemed to me a big gap, almost a chasm, between fatalistic acceptance and Rooseveltian grit. Whether I could tell the difference, if and when I did get a second shot at the mountain, was the question.

But as we descended the Lhotse face, inching our way slowly down the steep ice wall, and I focused on each footfall, dazzled by the astonishing beauty around me, I also knew that my clock

238

was ticking loudly. It was getting later in the season day by day, the calendar was inching ever toward the June monsoon season, when moisture flowing up into the Himalayas can make for the most violent snowstorms of the year. And every boot step into the snow, going the wrong direction down the mountain, narrowed the range of possibilities. Typically, the mountain was only able to be summited during a very narrow window, at the most two weeks when weather conditions perfectly aligned.

Everest was also now crowded with other climbers—most of whom, like me, had been dreaming of this mountain all their lives. They'd been acclimatizing for weeks, building up their tolerance for the altitude in staggered ascents and descents—going from base camp at 17,600 feet to the four higher camps and then back down in preparing for a push to the summit. A pent-up demand in the climbing community had made that year even more intense, because no one had made it to the summit via the Nepalese side of the mountain in two full seasons. A disastrous ice avalanche killed sixteen Sherpas in 2014, followed by Nepal's worst earthquake in more than eighty years in 2015, which devastated the country and again shut down the mountain for climbing.

Pasang Bhote and I had tried to beat that rush, climbing fast up the mountain and skipping Camp 3 entirely before being forced to head back down. But now we'd be faces in the crowd, stuck in a pack of climbers if a second chance came at all.

As we neared Camp 2 on our descent, at about twenty-one thousand feet, a thought and an image flashed before my eyes: dominoes.

That was the word and the metaphor that Jenna had used when we'd been talking about the risks and unknowns, the potential points of failure and what we might do at those moments when, not if, they arose in the Explorers Grand Slam.

"When one domino falls, everything changes down the line, and the best we can do is be ready with a new plan, a new adaptation," she'd said one day in Portland as we were going through lists and logistics. For reasons that are cooked somewhere deep inside me, I've always resisted thinking like that, about what-ifs and worst cases. Listing things that could go wrong in pursuing a goal somehow makes it feel more likely that those things *will* go wrong. But Jenna's idea was simpler—that *every* change, even if it looks like a setback, creates new options.

Everything on Everest was now different. A domino had definitely fallen. I'd been weakened by the huge effort to get up to Camp 4. But I'd learned that coming back when you're told you can't—a second chance—can in fact happen, and that life's blows and the recovery from those blows are paired phenomena. I thought of Pasang Bhote's stoical, knee-hugging posture of stillness in the middle of the storm's insanity. Maybe, I thought, the game wasn't over. Things were still in motion. As Jenna had pointed out, they always are.

FOR THREE DAYS AT CAMP 2, with five-thousand-foot walls of ice and snow towering around me on three sides, I waited. In air so thin just walking around the camp required huge effort, I tried to find the calm of acceptance, while at the same time holding on to hope that a second attempt might be possible.

I hadn't given up, but I knew that I might soon need to accept defeat. The base camp manager had even said as much to me, in congratulating me on making it that far in the Explorers Grand Slam, with the suggestion that I was done and finished and that Everest wouldn't give me a second chance. Her congratulations stung bitterly, sounding to me like the expressions of "good luck, kid" that I'd heard so many times in trying to find sponsors for this project.

"I'm afraid time is running out," I said to Pasang Bhote one day, staring up toward the mountain, which through most of those days was shrouded in clouds. He shook his head and shrugged his shoulders in reply, conveying the tough realism that people born and raised in one of the world's harshest climates understand from childhood.

But on the third day of waiting, as I was inching closer to having to say the word "surrender," I called the base camp manager on the radio just as the new weather forecast was coming in.

"Hold on, Colin," she said. I heard her talking to someone else for a minute, then she was back on the line.

"There may be a window," she said, then paused for a second. "The question, as always, is how long it holds, and this one seems as sketchy as ever. Could last a few days, or could slam back down—and when it does it'll probably really suck up there again."

But it felt like a chance, and I scrambled back out looking for Pasang Bhote. If we were going to go back up, this was it.

CAMP 4 FELT RADICALLY DIFFERENT than it had five days earlier in that grim night in the tent. It was jammed with anxious, frustrated climbers, a sea of puffy jackets and oxygen tanks—people gasping and coughing and cursing when they tried to breathe even for a moment without supplemental oxygen, then taking a few breaths from their tanks and doing it all over again.

But the weather window, at least for the moment, was holding. That meant that most of those two hundred–odd climbers would be heading up the mountain that night, proceeding through a narrow passage that led from the last camp. The route began with a steep climb up a snow slope, with precipitous drop-offs farther up. A fixed rope—put in place by an elite team of Sherpas each season to aid climbers on the route—ran up the center of the slope, and climbers would clip into it, one after the other in single file, climbing in darkness, aiming to get to the summit somewhere around dawn.

But the updated forecast said that winds were likely to pick up through the night, which meant that a slow-moving fixed rope line could be, that night, one of the most dangerous places on the mountain, if not the earth. If the window slammed as that line was creeping up, there might be no way to stay warm as the line trudged on. And although Pasang Bhote and I were climbing independently, not a part of a big guided group, being in the line would still mean that any inexperienced or unprepared climber ahead of me—the weak link in the chain—would affect everyone.

Frostbite from being locked in place, unable to heat my body with forward motion, was one of the scariest things I could imagine—claustrophobia and cold in combination—and my fears were rippling like an electric current when I finally got through to Jenna that evening. She answered, but before I could even speak I had a severe coughing fit, trying to catch my breath.

"Baby, put your oxygen mask back on. Take a breath. I'll still be here," Jenna said. She waited as I got my breathing back under control.

"You okay?" she finally asked.

"I'm really scared, Jenna," I said, staring out at the sea of jostling climbers swirling around me. "I think people might die up on the mountain tonight. There will definitely be a lot of frostbite, at least. And if the winds really come back like they were a few days ago when we had to turn around, but instead we're up on the summit . . ."

There was a long silence, as I bit my lip and pictured the horror of being caught up there, exposed in those winds. Then a coughing fit grabbed me again, which turned into a choking spasm.

"You still there?" Jenna said when I got through it.

"Yeah," I gasped, keeping my words short. "The rib."

"You think it's cracked?" she said.

"I think so," I replied.

I pressed a hand onto my left side, feeling a sharp twinge in my chest, and seeing all over again in my mind the brutal coughing fit that had hit me on the way up after Pasang Bhote and I had been forced to stop overnight at Camp 3. The coughing started as I was shoveling snow from around our tent, which was precariously perched on the Lhotse Face, a five-thousand-foot wall of ice and snow. One particular spasm left me gasping, clutching the sudden sharp pain on my side, barely able to move when it was over.

Jenna was silent for a few seconds and I could hear her breathing, loving the sound of it. I heard in it the breathing of Portland—wonderful, oxygen-rich, sea-level Portland.

"I know the rib is painful, but people are going to summit tonight and there's no reason you can't be one of them," she said. She paused for a second. "Do me a favor, go inside your body and your mind and listen, Colin. Face your fears."

I tried to breathe, to think of what I did or didn't have inside, and how clearly I'd be able to judge one way or another. And I knew the astonishing reserve of strength—the power and confidence and will that it had taken for Jenna to say those words—"no reason you can't be one of them." She hadn't urged me to be safe and take no chances, to go down the mountain and home to her, but rather, to see what was inside me and trust it was the stuff I needed.

"Go out there and achieve your dreams, Colin. I know you can do this," she finally said.

AT ABOUT 11 P.M., when I climbed out of my tent to begin, the long line of climbers had already formed. They looked like a chain gang, trudging slowly up the mountain, roped together in the subzero cold, the beams of their headlamps all uniformly tilted down toward their feet. I could barely make out the silhouette of the mountain at all, only the flickering line of lights, snaking up like a jagged scar.

But after Pasang Bhote and I clipped to the rope and joined them, I almost immediately began wondering whether being in the line really made sense on a night like that, when a killing wind might roar back at any time. Being clipped in meant you were far less likely to fall off the mountain, but it also meant that you were trapped, able to go no faster than the slowest person ahead. Unclipping and going outside the line meant risking a possibly fatal fall, but on the other hand it was a better chance to get ahead on the mountain, stay warm, and fend off frostbite before the weather turned.

The uncertainty and risk of unclipping through that section meant that it was rarely done, and too risky for guided teams. But as scary as it felt, it finally also came to seem like the lesser of the two evils. We'd be moving, I thought, and movement—from my earliest memories of life—had always seemed more natural to me than standing still.

I glanced at Pasang Bhote and he nodded that he was ready, too, and without another word we both unclipped and stepped over to the right of the line. I looked down at the carabiner in my gloved hand that I'd just opened up in disconnecting from the line. My headlamp illuminated its rounded steel curves, and it felt heavy and solid, and for the briefest of seconds I had second thoughts, but Pasang Bhote was already moving, and I heard Jenna's voice in my head as well. Go deep, she'd said. Listen to your body. Calm mind, steady feet.

We went forward like that for hours through the night, slowly trudging up the steep slope unroped. It seemed, and *was*, incredibly slow—every step requiring a pause to suck in two or three breaths before taking another step. And every breath sent a stab of pain into my injured rib as well.

But the roped line of climbers to our left was moving even more slowly, and as we began passing people, I felt more assurance that what we were doing, risky as it was, was the right choice. Pasang Bhote and I were climbing much faster than the roped climbers, our muscles moving harder, creating more heat, and yet the bitter cold was still reaching up inside to grab me. Life on the rope line, I thought, had to be even colder.

Headlamps of the cinched-in climbers swiveled toward us as we approached and went by, then swiveled back without a word, down toward the snow. People were locked into their struggles, it seemed, or in battles with their demons, as much as they were bound by the rope.

TOWARD DAWN, as brilliant pink light began filtering across the bluish black of the sky, Pasang Bhote and I reached a place where sheer drop-offs lined either side of the rope—a mile or more to the rocks and ice below and too risky to stay unclipped. The wind was beginning to pick up by then, which meant that the cold on the rope line would be even worse, but the added safety was worth it. As we clipped back in, feeling optimistic from the progress we'd made through the night, I reached for my extra heavy parka.

But as I put on my parka, I had to pull off my right glove for a second—and, looking down, I felt every muscle of my body go absolutely rigid with horror.

My hand was completely black—the black of severe frostbite that meant death of the tissue, the black of gangrene and amputation. The cold, I immediately concluded, was worse than I'd thought. I hadn't been paying attention. I'd been so focused on the pain of the rib that I hadn't felt the cold clamping its grip on my extremities. I felt the brief irrational impulse to look at my other body parts—to check my other hand and my feet, my nose and cheeks, which would of course have been the stupidest possible thing to do, in exposing more of me to the cold. So even as I shuddered with the terror, I pulled the glove back on.

And then without thinking, almost through the force of momentum, I resumed climbing, trying to figure out what to do next, stiff with fear and unable to focus on anything but my hand. The sights and sounds around me were exactly the same as before—the growing, gorgeous pink of the sky, the crunch of my boots, the hissing of my breath through the oxygen tank, Pasang Bhote there ahead of me—but none of it got through. I was a shell, moving but feeling somehow as though I'd already died. I'd promised Jenna and myself that no risk on any mountain or any expedition was worth not coming home in one piece with all my fingers and toes, and I'd violated that without even knowing where it was all going wrong.

After a few minutes, even though I knew I probably shouldn't, I had to look again. Maybe, I thought, there was something I could do . . . though I had no idea what. So I stopped and pulled off the glove again. If it was as bad as it had looked the first time, I knew I'd have to turn back. But this time it seemed different. I saw a streak in the black, a place where darker and lighter areas looked almost smeared, and when I pawed it with the glove on my left hand, the smear changed shape. I rubbed harder and saw pieces of the black actually fall off onto the snow, revealing flesh underneath that was pink and alive.

I breathed as though I'd been holding my breath forever, an exhalation that even my wounded rib didn't complain about. The black was activated carbon. The chemical hand-warmer inside my glove had ruptured. I pulled the glove back on, flexing my fingers, feeling whole again, feeling as though my body might be able to unclench.

Throwing my arms up in the air, I screamed—a howl of release and relief and joy that made even the most exhausted climbers around me perk up for a second. Pasang Bhote, just ahead of me in the line, didn't jump or flinch. He was utterly unflappable. But then he slowly swiveled back to look at me.

"We are not yet at the summit," he said, completely deadpan.

"Right," I said, resuming the climb but unable to stop smiling.

*　　*　　*

AND FINALLY, JUST AFTER 7:30 A.M., the top came into view, and as Pasang Bhote and I stepped up to the mound of brightly colored prayer flags laid down in the snow at the summit by previous climbers, I was completely overcome by emotion. Snapshot images flickered through my head as I thought of how impossible this moment had seemed through that long night in the Death Zone when the first attempt had failed, and then through the long, dispiriting climb back down and those days of watching and waiting for another chance. And now here I was.

"Top of the world! No words can describe . . ." I shouted, my voice choked by the thin air and the emotion as I smiled at Pasang Bhote in admiration of his seventh successful summit. The morning was perfectly clear, with a view out over the vast horizon of Himalayan peaks that seemed to go on forever; a panorama that felt limitless.

SHORTLY AFTER NOON that day of the summit and what turned out to be a long, bone-wearying descent, I called Jenna exhausted from my tent. "I made it to the summit, baby—back down at Camp 4 now!" I gasped and went into a coughing fit. "Only one mountain to go," I spluttered when I could catch my breath. The last stop on my Explorers Grand Slam itinerary, Denali, was feeling pretty abstract at that moment.

"Amazing!" she screamed back. "I'm so happy for you, and so proud. How are you feeling?"

"Completely wiped. Took me an hour just to get my boots off," I said.

"How's the rib?"

"It's painful, but compared to the high of making it up there, seeing that sky, that feeling of limitlessness—it's nothing," I said.

"Hands, fingers, toes, and nose all good?"

"Perfect and pink," I said, deciding I'd tell her about the black-hand scare later and lower down the mountain, when I had more breath.

"Great, great, in that case . . ." she said, then paused a second. "There's one more thing . . ."

She then said something I'll never forget.

"I need you to put your boots back on."

"What? Why?"

"I've been doing some calculations"—there was a pause—"and if you can get down from Everest today and we can get you to Denali quickly, you might be able to set not one but two world records. The Seven Summits speed record is in play."

We were both silent for a minute. Images fluttered through my memory as I thought of Joshua Tree, and the *Seven Summits* book, and those long miles of reading aloud to each other through California and into Oregon. I saw the book's pictures and route maps and Jenna's face as she listened to me intently behind the wheel as she drove.

We'd never thought, in planning the Explorers Grand Slam project, that I'd have any chance of breaking a speed record for climbing the Seven Summits, because of the time involved in reaching the North and South Poles. But even with the delay in my needing two tries to get to the top of Everest, Jenna had glimpsed a new possibility and improvised.

She didn't wait for a response. "So I've arranged for a helicopter to come pick you up at base camp," she said. "The helicopter will take you to Kathmandu, but you won't have any time to rest there or get a hotel. An evening flight will take you to Dubai, then Seattle, and then Anchorage. Then to Denali's base camp."

Finally, she stopped and I could hear her take a breath. "And here's the other thing—you know how it usually takes three weeks at best to climb Denali? Well, you'll only have three days to summit." She let that sink in for a second. "So what do you think?"

Right then, I thought that Jenna's plan seemed impossible and halfway to absurd. I was still in Everest's Death Zone, twenty-six thousand feet on the mountain. Denali seemed a universe away. But denying the possibility of it, I knew, would definitely make it impossible, and I thought as I lay there, phone pressed to my head, of one of my favorite quotes from Henry Ford: "He who says he can and he who says he can't are both usually right."

I sighed, but mainly for effect, and the expression of love it conveyed, and the admission that she was so right and knew me so well.

"Okay," I said, sitting up. "I can at least put my boots back on."

I WOKE UP OFTEN through that bleak night on the Antarctic ice, thinking about Everest and brooding about whether it was time to say "I can" or time to say "I can't."

And then sometime toward dawn, I found myself thinking of a visit I'd made to an elementary school in Denver shortly after the Grand Slam project was finished. The classes had gathered in the gym.

"I'd just climbed to the top of the tallest mountain in the world, I was so so tired," I told them. But then as I gestured at photos on a screen behind me, I explained that I wouldn't have realized my full potential in that moment if I hadn't pursued that second world record.

"I had one more mountain to climb, the tallest in North America," I said, excited to see the audience lean forward in their seats. "It was a really challenging mountain called Denali, in Alaska. But instead of having the normal three or four weeks to climb it, I'd have only three days. So I put my boots back on, and climbed down Everest as fast as I could." I then took them through the plan Jenna had devised for me to fly around the world to arrive at the base of Denali just one hundred hours after standing on the summit of Everest. The students' eyes were really wide now as I wound up the Denali story.

"And when a bad storm struck halfway to the summit—one hundred and thirty-nine days after this all began at the South Pole—I felt like quitting. But I kept going, and with twenty-four hours to spare, I reached the top. In the same moment, I broke the world record for climbing the Seven Summits and completing the Explorers Grand Slam faster than anyone before."

I love the curiosity of young students. I hadn't asked for questions yet, but a boy in the front row had had his hand raised for the past few minutes.

"What's your question, buddy?"

"Do you think I can climb Mount Everest one day?"

"Absolutely! It all starts with believing in yourself. Believing that something is possible is the first step to making it really happen. That said, I don't expect that all of you will want to climb mountains—that might not be your thing at all, which is totally fine. All of us have a dream, something we might one day hope to do or become. All of us have an *Everest*. The question I want to ask you all is: What's *your* Everest?"

Hands launched upward all around the gym. I called on a freckled redheaded girl in the second row. "My Everest is to be the first person in my family to graduate college," she said proudly.

"That's a wonderful goal!" I replied.

Next, I called on a rambunctious boy near the back whom I'd noticed earlier, partly because he couldn't sit still. "My Everest is to be an astronaut who explores space!" he proclaimed.

Hearing students reveal all of their awe-inspiring dreams warmed my heart. Ironically, I'd been trying to inspire them, but the students, with all of their boundless hope and excitement for the future, got me thinking. That "What's *your* Everest?" question, I realized, wasn't just for them. I needed to answer it for myself. Crossing Antarctica was my next Everest. I'd pursued it with absolute commitment, and now here I was in my tent, alone, searching for the courage to go on.

* * *

BY THE TIME MORNING CAME, my forty-ninth day on the Antarctic ice, I felt as though I'd been through a kind of trial—a test of my grit and determination, all in the course of one night. Thoughts of quitting were banished. As I pulled my boots on in the tent, I felt a renewed sense of resolve.

The storm was still raging, and through another twelve-hour day in the harness, it never let up. But I was in a different place inside my head. I'd found something in that bleak night of bottoming out, in the power of memory and inspiration, and it gave me a new fuel.

The next day brought still another gift, as it became clear that the worst of the storm had finally passed. The winds began to diminish, and gradually the long days of whiteout parted. I could see a horizon, which further lifted my spirits. I could see beyond my own skis and my compass. The world around me, after so many days of storm, felt vaster than ever.

And then on the following morning after that, December 23, I glimpsed for the first time the Transantarctic Mountains.

I couldn't quite believe it at first. After so many weeks of flat and featureless terrain, of hunger for anything different on the horizon, of emptiness that felt like it could swallow me, the idea that the great mountains of Antarctica were finally there before me seemed almost unreal. Like my one-night trial of the spirit in reliving Everest— which reminded me right then of Ebenezer Scrooge's one-night examination of his life in *A Christmas Carol*—the mountains felt like a Christmas miracle come early.

I pulled off my mask to rub my eyes. I blinked and squinted and closed and reopened my eyes again, but the peaks were definitely there, looking deep and mysterious. They shimmered in the distance, hinting of a finish line that was somewhere beyond them, and they made me think of home, and of Oregon.

Looking east from Portland toward the majesty of Mount Hood

always comforted me somehow, as if the mountain were a shelter or sanctuary, a kind of guardian, and I felt a wave of that now. Hood had felt like family to me because of my frequent trips there when I was a child. The Transantarctic Mountains were my pathway home. Seeing them meant that the Leverett Glacier, the great ice river through the mountains that my route would take me on, was straight ahead. For the early polar explorers, the Transantarctic Mountains had been a great and daunting barrier cutting off the sea ice of the Ross Ice Shelf from the interior—it wasn't until 1902 that a route was found all the way through them—but for me now, it felt like the exact opposite, as though the mountains were a great beacon of hope, drawing me on with every step as they grew clearer and sharper on the horizon.

But that thought also scared me. Just as the descents from places like Mount Everest are the times of greatest danger—80 percent of accidents on the mountain happen on the way down—the moments near the end of anything are where emotion and overconfidence can lead to error. I found out later that three people died coming down from Everest on the day I made it to the summit. It's not over until it's over. And one of the great lines from *The Alchemist*, the book I'd treasured and given to Jenna that day in Sydney, came back to me.

"Before a dream is realized, the Soul of the World tests everything that was learned along the way," Coelho writes. "That's the point at which most people give up. It's the point at which, as we say in the language of the desert, one 'dies of thirst just when the palm trees have appeared on the horizon.'"

My palm trees had appeared on my horizon in those shimmering, luminous mountains. And I knew I'd made the relaxation mistake before, when the end almost seemed in sight and the peril became most profound.

In Greenland.

I'd been on the Greenland ice cap for nearly four weeks when it happened. I was training for Antarctica, and had almost completed the east-to-west crossing—nearly four hundred miles in total. I'd arrived at my final campsite. I was feeling confident and strong, young and invincible, and I let my guard down. I saw the finish line in my head and thought I was across.

I'd religiously poked and prodded every square foot of ice around my tent space through the previous nights, searching for partially covered crevasses, which were numerous and deep. But that night I didn't, or didn't do it thoroughly enough. I'd pulled out my tent and laid it down. And then just a few steps from the tent door, I fell.

Within an instant, I felt nothing below my legs but air. I'd caught myself with my outstretched arms as I went down, which kept me from falling farther, but everything beneath my armpits was dangling in the crevasse. My legs had nothing to get purchase on. They kicked into empty nothingness as I desperately held on, fearing that my mittens might start to slide toward the chasm. Finally, I managed to swing to one side and climb up, and only then, in looking back down, did I truly grasp the danger my overconfidence had exposed me to. The crevasse was blue-walled deeper than I could see. It went down into the ice's inky darkness and would have spelled almost certain death if I hadn't caught myself.

I now stood on an even larger expanse of ice, staring at the Transantarctic Mountains, determined not to forget the lesson learned. The ends of things, in descending from great mountains or in the distraction or elation that comes from feeling almost there, are where hope and peril can combine in the cruelest ways, and I knew I'd have to be vigilant.

"It's not over, Colin," I said aloud. Then I said it again, whispering it out toward the mountain ridgeline as the skies grew clearer and bluer. "It's not over yet."

* * *

WHEN I CALLED JENNA the following night, Christmas Eve, day fifty-two, I had a million things I wanted to share about my journey-within-a-journey through the previous few days—the crashing low, the new sense of resolve, the parting of the clouds to reveal the great mountains at a moment when my soul desperately needed a reminder of Oregon. But she cut me off before I could start.

"Oh my God," she said. "How bad is it?"

"What do you mean?" I asked, blinking up at my tent roof, which was about as quiet as on any night I'd experienced so far. My solar panel lay almost completely still in its little pocket.

"*The storm!* I thought you just got out of it, and now it's back?"

"There's no storm. It's about as clear as I've ever seen. What makes you think . . ." I glanced around the tent again, feeling suddenly uncertain. But all was calm, all was bright. No roaring flap of the tent, no pelting slap of ice crystals. Strong 10 p.m. sun.

"Lou's live map is down because you guys are experiencing such severe weather conditions," she said. "That's what his website says."

"Hmm . . ." I said. "What do you think?"

"I don't know—would the weather be any different where he is?"

"No, I don't see how. . . . It's clear for a long way in every direction," I said. "The mountains are just amazing. . . . But it's Lou . . . so I don't know. Do you think he has something up his sleeve?"

"Well, I don't think he can catch you, Colin—he was more than twenty-one miles behind you when his tracker last reported."

We were both silent, thinking.

"Weird though," I said.

"Definitely weird," she said. "But don't let this spook you—you've got this." And I heard in her words an echo of that night when I'd been preparing to join the chain gang of climbers. "Listen to what's inside you, Colin," she said. "Trust that voice."

CHAPTER FIFTEEN

Infinite Love

DAY 53

A s a son of the Pacific Northwest, I've always thought of Christmas as a day with a split personality. The region's famous gloom
burrows down to its deepest place—not just in the darkness of short
winter days, but in the damp, gray chill that rolls in off the Pacific
Ocean and seeps into every undefended corner. And yet at the exact
same moment, the power of family, community, and holiday cheer
is at its most radiant. So the day, it seemed to me, celebrated opposite forces equally, and I always loved that about it—darkness and
light, chill and warmth, solitude and solidarity—both sides of the
equation so rich and powerful, and neither one understandable
without the other.

I'd set my alarm for 4:30 a.m. that Christmas Day—my fifty-third
morning on the ice—following my head-scratching conversation
the night before with Jenna about Rudd's tracker. The sun glinted
its red rays through the roof, and all the worn, patched, frozen, and
frayed pieces of my life gently swayed around me and over my head,
and when I checked the inReach there was a text from my dad. His
words underlined everything I'd just been thinking about choices
and darkness and light.

"Merry Christmas," he wrote. "Remember the most important thing."

I read the line over and over. I could hear those words echoing from my earliest childhood memories through every major athletic event of my life. He always spoke them the same way, whether we were heading to a swim meet or a soccer match, looking deeply into my eyes when he did, and he'd repeated the phrase often enough that he no longer even needed to say the two words that would complete the thought: "Have fun." They now came from inside me. Enjoy the journey, my dad was saying. The pursuit of victory and the finish line isn't the only thing in the world.

I'd already made one choice prior to going to sleep. The weather forecast I'd received from A.L.E. before turning in had said that Christmas, and perhaps the day after as well, was likely to feature clear weather. After so many days of storms, I wanted to get an early start.

Dad's message resonated in my head as I pulled down my hanging line of gloves and neck warmers and put on my boots, bringing back a flood of memories. And the unspoken part, the words he didn't need to write, seemed most powerful of all—filling emptiness with memory and love and producing an energy that I could draw strength from.

But then I reached down to grab my orange duffel bag to exit the tent—and staggered back in shock. The bag felt like it had been loaded with rocks, twice as heavy as it had been in days past. My body had been changed, gradually but profoundly, by my weeks on the ice, and the unexpected effort of lifting the bag was the signal flare.

I unzipped my jacket and reached inside, feeling the bony row of ribs, then to my protruding hip bones. I ran a hand down the snow skirt I wore around my waist, across the clumsy stitch repair I'd made two weeks ago, taking it in by three inches to keep it from falling off. The hand kept going, down to my thighs, thin as arms, and the calves like deflated bike tires, all the muscle definition I'd built up in training eroded to nothing. I felt as though I'd become the scarecrow from *The Wizard of Oz*, a paltry man stuffed with straw, ready to spill out and blow away with the wind.

From earliest childhood, I've wanted to know what my body and mind are capable of. It sounds like a simple question, but it never really is, because none of us knows. Too often, answers or assumptions are thrust on us by others who say what our limits are, what our frontiers and boundaries should be, what we can accomplish or not. And then we come to believe those limits and boundaries to be true, and the more we believe them the truer they become.

That morning—as I contemplated my weakened body—everything was up for grabs all over again, reducing down to a single question: What have I got left? I knew that much of what I'd started out carrying across the ice, however heavy it had felt, was gone—eaten or burned up as fuel to keep me alive. And maybe that had happened to me, too, I thought. I was a reduced man, stripped to his essence. *Burned clean* was a thought that came to me.

And so, feeling both filled to the brim and yet at the same time emptied completely, I stepped out onto the ice, certain of only one thing, that the path I'd started on nearly two months ago was about to go to its deepest, most powerful place—and the most vulnerable one of all—inside my mind.

THE MOUNTAINS AND THE LEVERETT GLACIER beckoned to me like sirens in some ancient Greek myth as I climbed into the harness. Their presence in the distance, after so many days of flat and featureless ice, made everything feel different and, it seemed, *smell* different—something in the air of rock and earth. But my arms and hands were the first signals to me that I'd found it, that I was at the banks of a truly deep flow state that morning as I pushed north.

My arms swung as usual. My hands gripped the poles as usual. What was new was that I felt I could see beyond those simple functions, down into the muscles and tendons. From the arms the wave of awareness moved up through my shoulders, and then through the muscles of my neck and then up through the back of my head and down my back. Every physical place that the wave touched was weakened, I knew, but it was almost as though the awareness itself was becoming a strength—that knowing what I had inside was the source of power.

And all of it was tied together with the muscle that felt most focused of all, and the true key to the flow state, the muscle six inches between my ears. My body might be more exhausted than ever, but my mind could override that weakness, making me stronger than ever. My thoughts were anchored in place, moving across the ice, seeing and feeling every aspect of that movement, and yet at the same time roving out far beyond me, unbound and uncontained.

After about an hour of pulling my sled, and realizing with every breath and stride the depth of what I'd tapped into, I was moving differently, and thinking differently, and I started calculating: I had seventy-seven miles to go to the finish, and I'd gone an average of sixteen and a half miles a day through the course of the expedition, doing twelve-hour days. The fact that I could even think of the hours remaining to the finish—and the solitary wooden post that I knew marked the edge of the continent—was itself astonishing. Weeks had become days, had become hours, almost before my eyes, though it felt like a lifetime.

And from that new sense of time and the strength I felt as I waded deeper and deeper into the flow state, a curious question began to grow in my mind: What if I didn't stop? What if I just kept going all the way to the end in one last push? What other frontiers might be out there that I'd find and cross along the way? And so my math game continued. If I'd averaged sixteen and a half miles over twelve hours—and more than that in recent days with my now lighter sled—a final push to the end might be doable in forty hours or so in a continuous run.

Forty hours. The number rolled through my head. I had ultramarathoner friends who'd done hundred-mile races in less than that. People worked forty hours in their jobs every week, and slept even more. It started to seem like a number I could get my head around.

And then I began to add up my food. I had about twenty thousand calories remaining of the Colin Bars if I stacked them all in a pile. After all these weeks I still craved them with their perfect balance of nutrition and flavor designed specifically for my body. The bars required no cooking, so I could carry them and eat as needed—though that would certainly also be a risk. If I pushed hard, ate through my food supplies, and then had an accident or didn't get to the end, I'd have a serious food crisis.

Rudd's wily ruse with his GPS tracker was part of my thinking. That he was still out there, playing another card, added a wrinkle of uncertainty, if only because I'd gotten used to knowing exactly where he was. I'd seen how quickly things can change with a single bad day.

But a bigger, deeper part of me was hungry to push because I'd reached a place on the ice where all the old boundaries of Antarctic math—miles, calories, hours, days—seemed up for renegotiation. It was time for me to explore the furthest boundaries of my potential.

I knew, even without the flow I felt in my strides toward the mountains—looming closer every minute—that I could function in a place of deep fatigue. I'd seen that the summer before coming to Antarctica, when I set out to break the world record for reaching the high point of every state in the US in the shortest time.

The Fifty High Points challenge tested my strength and stamina in preparing for the biggest goal of my life, the Antarctic crossing. I wanted to see how my body and mind worked through day after day of constant, intense effort, so I climbed forty-two of the high points in a whirlwind two weeks, from Alaska to Hawaii, and all the smaller peaks on the east coast. But the eight mountains that were left were the biggest ones in the lower forty-eight states—including Mount Whitney in California and Mount Rainier in Washington—and the seven-day push to the finish included more than 150 miles of trail running and more than 60,000 feet of elevation gain, the equivalent of climbing Everest twice from sea level. I was utterly exhausted and sleep-deprived—resting between mountains as my dear friend and collaborator Blake drove our rented RV to the next trailhead. But I found something inside me, in getting through it in a record twenty-one days. It was an ultramarathon that convinced me I could keep going in Antarctica.

And almost without deciding it consciously, I realized I'd made a Christmas choice, and I wanted to tell someone. So I pulled out Cam, pushed record, and watched the GoPro come to life. I'd sobbed into my little lens. I'd jumped around dancing on the ice to *Graceland*. I'd been ready to collapse over and over in talking at night, recording sometimes bleak and exhausted thoughts.

Now I heard a different voice coming out of me.

"I'm going for it," I said quietly, pulling the eye in closer to my face. "I'm going to try to finish this thing in a final push, all the way. The Antarctica ultramarathon." I looked around the ice, feeling a confidence and serenity that was, strangely, connected to the deep weakness I felt in my body. Everything was connected. I'd been altered by my journey in both mind and spirit, and that new person stood there with his face in Cam's lens. "I need to see what I've got inside," I said.

THE LEVERETT GLACIER had sat on a corner of my mental map from the beginning, but through those long weeks on the ice, I'd mostly tried to avoid thinking about it, because it seemed too far away. My journey across Antarctica had been, until that morning, about waypoints and days and hours, about the exactitude of calories and hours in the harness, about improvising when crisis hit and adapting when improvisation failed. I thought in incremental goals—making it to the South Pole, getting through with enough food, surviving the constant cold.

After six hours in the harness that morning, still locked in the flow, I arrived. I stood at the top, staring down at the great glacier that had so filled my imagination. I felt ready. That 4:30 a.m. sense of curiosity and clarity had deepened, and my body, for all the weight loss and weakness I felt, had responded with a cadence of muscle memory. I felt a resolve, a firmness, and a calm deeper than at any moment since I'd arrived on the ice. The Leverett would mark a downhill run toward the Ross Ice Shelf and the finish. It would be my passage through the Transantarctic Mountains. It was the passageway to the end.

I wanted to begin the descent immediately, but also to stand there and take it in. The jagged skyline itself was staggering, with mountains that seemed to grip the great glacier—only three or four miles wide through most of its length—like fingers around a giant icicle. And those massive peaks, some higher than fourteen thousand feet, glowed in their majestic tapestry of shadows, rock, snow, and brilliantly reflected light.

From studying the maps of my route, I knew that the top of the Leverett had a brief stretch—perhaps a mile or so—that was relatively steep downhill. I'd fantasized about that, after weeks of pulling a heavy sled, and as I stood there looking down, I thought of Dad. I'd go faster than I ever had on any past stretch of ice. I'd have fun. I'd honor him with my Christmas choice.

But as I started picking up speed on my skis, I also quickly realized that the physics, in this part of my ultramarathon at least, would be different, too. The sled, no longer really being pulled by me at that point, but proceeding downhill from its own weight, slammed me from behind and almost immediately knocked me down with a hard fall onto the ice.

I got up and looked back, almost wanting to have an argument with the sled. It had been like a vast dead weight behind me at the start, and never had it gone easily anywhere, even as it got lighter over the weeks. And this felt almost like payback, as though the sled had had enough of being pulled and now had a mind of its own.

And no matter what I did, it happened again and again. I'd start down, only to feel the sled smashing against my legs—gently at first, just a touch—then often with a jolt and a shove that sent me sprawling.

When the glacier finally flattened, I let out a sigh of relief, which surprised me because of how much I'd looked forward to that down-hill mile. But almost immediately I began to hit patches of exposed blue ice, which became its own trial. I wasn't being thrown down at that point by an out-of-control sled, but my skis could barely make traction on the intensely slick surface, and so the falls continued and felt even harder with no cushioning of snow on the rock-hard ice. But I was also so deep in the flow state, aware of everything around and inside me, that the falls became simply an aspect of the experience, one I could observe as much as be a part of.

After one particular fall, I realized that at almost every other moment of my journey across the continent, a day like this would've seemed hard, painful and frightening. A hundred miles back, or five hundred miles back, I would almost certainly have gone into a fear loop, my mind racing with the potentials and implications of a bad fall, a broken bone. I knew too well that place of obsessive what-if fears.

But now, though I knew I was bruised all over from my tumbles that day, those fears seemed entirely burned away. Climbing up onto my knees, still in the harness, the sled askew behind me, I lifted my face up toward the sky and felt a wave of energy breaking over me and through me.

And more than just energy. Clarity. The stark emptiness of Antarctica that had drawn me and captivated me, the silence from deleting my music, and the stillness that can come from meditation had all combined to create a moment when it felt like everything unnecessary in the universe was gone. What was left was crucial and shimmering and perfect.

I'd never felt anything like it—as though something ancient, but instant and brand-new at the same time, had come down out of the Antarctic sky, or up through the millions of years of ice.

I opened up my arms and arched my back, face thrust up toward the sun, to absorb and accept the gift. My arms and chest felt as if they were forming a kind of mirror, or a satellite dish, that was collecting the positive energy so many people out in the world were sending toward me, in wishing me safe passage. I was a mere speck on the ice, invisible to all the world, no one to see me or hear me, as isolated and alone as a person can be on a crowded planet where crowds are often the loneliest places of all. People right then, at that moment, were riding in elevators avoiding eye contact or burying themselves in their phones on the subway—I knew that place myself, feeling utterly alone in the middle of a big city.

But it struck me as both powerful and strange that I'd gone so far and so deep to the edge of emptiness and solitude only to find myself feeling more connected than ever, and the phrase that came to me had to be said aloud.

"Infinite love," I said quietly, then repeated it, louder. "Infinite love!" And a third time, louder still, shouting now. "Infinite love!"

In that moment, I felt compelled to send some of that positive energy to the great Captain Louis Rudd.

"You're out there somewhere, Lou, and I'd like to express my gratitude," I said, out into the endless white. "You've pushed me, and made me better for it. I hope your passage is safe."

Then I grabbed Cam and pushed the button, the little red eye peering back at me. I stopped and looked around. "But right now it's just you and me, Cam, here in the middle of a huge glacier, in the middle of nowhere," I said, holding up my hand to touch the lens with my mitten. "Yet, somehow I don't feel alone. I think the world is reaching right back." I pulled the lens closer to my face. "I'm not alone. None of us are."

BY THE TIME I LOOKED AT MY WATCH and realized that it was almost time for my 8:50 p.m. call to the A.L.E. Comms Box, I'd been going for nearly fifteen hours, my longest day by far, and I'd probably eaten at least ten thousand calories of the Colin Bars. I'd been eating as I'd been moving, with a flow of awareness that said my body would tell me exactly when it needed to be fed, just as it was showing me how to move. And though I'd always been in my tent for the 8:50 p.m. check-in, that night the boundaries were gone.

I had no intention of stopping, still brimming with the curiosity of what could happen out there at the edge of performance and possibility, and I called the Comms Box from the ice.

Tim answered and I saw him in my thoughts, sitting there in front of his keyboard, and felt a sudden deep affection for him. If I could somehow keep going, I realized, this might be my last ever conversation with him.

I gave him my coordinates and mileage so far that day—nearly forty miles, my best day ever on the ice by far. He began asking how I was doing, issues to report, conditions of where I'd camped, the usual Tim line of questioning.

"Actually, I'm not camped," I said, staring out at the mountains. "I'm planning on going on a few more hours."

"Wow," Tim said. It was one of the few expressions of personal interest I'd heard through our many exchanges.

"Weather has been beautiful," I said. "Decided to take advantage of it."

"Okay, got it, just send me your coordinates when you make

camp," he said, immediately back to business. Tim was Tim and I hung up the phone smiling.

I'd noticed, even as I stood there with the phone, that the winds were starting to pick up around me. On the upper part of the glacier, the protective embrace of the mountains had shielded me, I realized, and as I'd moved back into the open that shield was gone.

As I continued on, things intensified, and I was very quickly in the middle of a serious squall, which evolved into a full ground blizzard. A ground blizzard isn't a regular storm, and this was the worst I'd ever experienced. Regular Antarctic storms pummel you with the load of snow and cold they bring with them. They carry their freight with a force that feels as though they want to pick you up and haul you off with them to some netherworld of cold. A ground blizzard is worse in some ways because it swirls from every place, a chaotic maelstrom blown up from the ground and whipped into walls of snow that close in from every side. I decided that it must feel something like this to be inside a blender or a vacuum cleaner.

You could lose your way very quickly in a storm like that, and there were many moments of my journey across Antarctica when a storm of such severity would probably have seemed like the great demon itself, a storm beyond the limits of terror. But now, as I peered out into the thick, swirling wall of white, I felt a calm that said this storm would not touch me, not in the places that mattered. I'd staked it out and claimed it. I'd transcended the physical discomforts of the external world in all its raging chaos, and found a deep inner peace.

I was certainly aware of the storm's deep cold, and I knew that my body could be knocked over by a ferocious gust of wind, but with every step, as I moved further into it, I felt the fortress of calm protecting me. My mind couldn't be knocked down.

* * *

AT MIDNIGHT, after eighteen hours of pulling the sled nonstop, the storm still raging, I realized that I was running out of water. Water was a different variable than food. It could only be made over the stove, and the stove—especially in blizzard conditions—would only function in the tent. So I'd need to stop. As I pulled the tent off the sled, my near disaster only a few days before flashed through my mind. My hands hurt just as much as they had that night. The cold was penetrating me just as much or more. The winds were certainly more severe. Risks and unknowns were all around me, swirling like the snow itself.

But this time was different. Even with all those things being thrown at me, I knew with a certainty and absolute confidence that I could accomplish the task and put up the tent. As I laid it down on the ice, the fabric flapped and whipped, and I knew that the possibility was real that through error or accident, should I lose my grip, the tent could be gone into the storm, with fatal consequences. Fear and distraction had been my enemies on that night when it almost happened—they'd been in control. But now I was in charge, and I knew what to do to keep the fear and distraction at bay.

I anchored the tent to the sled and followed through with all the steps to secure it, feeling my hands gripping the fabric, but also knowing exactly how hard I needed to grip, and no harder, and seeing every step with a smooth efficiency I doubt I'd ever mastered before. I carried over the stove and zipped it in.

And then I stood outside the tent door, the storm swirling and howling around me.

"Colin, you are strong and you are capable," I said aloud, to the storm and to myself. And even as I said it, I realized that the phrase, repeated every morning on the ice, was no longer a mantra to bolster my confidence. Nor was it a statement in defiance of the storm, which I'd also done a few times. I wasn't afraid anymore. It simply, at last, felt true. I no longer had anything to prove.

*   *   *

IT WAS ABOUT 7 P.M. IN OREGON—midnight my time—when I called Jenna from inside the tent, right in the middle of Christmas dinner at my sister Caitlin's house in Hood River. I could almost smell the ham and salmon on the table, the gluten-free sage stuffing, and the pies in the kitchen, laid out by the stove to cool.

"What a day you had!" Jenna said when the call went through. "Forty-eight miles! It's amazing—we kept watching you on the tracker, and watching, and you just kept going. Your mom called you her 'unstoppable little blue dot.'" She stopped and I heard her breathe. "We're missing you here for Christmas, baby, but I'm so happy to hear your voice, Colin. When you didn't call at your usual hour, we all started to wonder, but I knew..."

"I'm good, Jenna. I tapped into a deep flow state. There's so much I want to tell you..."

"I could feel it. And now I hear it in your voice... So you're in the tent then, stove on and fed?"

"I'm in the tent," I said, watching it heave and flap around me.

She was silent for a moment, absorbing that. I could almost see her expression, see her listening. "The tent's rattling around. You're in a storm? I know what that sounds like after fifty-three days." She paused to listen again. "We thought, when you didn't stop, that you were probably having great weather."

"It's actually one of the worst storms I've seen, full ground blizzard. It's like a shaken snow globe out here." I paused for a second. "But I'm not stopping. I'm just melting snow for water, and then I'm going to keep pushing to the end," I said. "I've hit a place that says I need to keep on, go back out. I need to see what's in there. In me."

She was silent for only a beat. "I hear it, Colin," she said softly. "I hear the strength in your voice.... I know you've got what it takes to keep pushing.... Wait, hold on, here's your mom."

Mom's voice suddenly filled my head. "You're really doing it, Colin," she said. "I just want to say how proud of you I am, and Merry Christmas."

"And I want to say thank you," I said. "For . . . everything."

"It's wonderful, this thing I'm hearing in you, in all of us," she said. "It's like a choir or something, like a hallelujah chorus." She stopped and laughed. "Too much Christmas music around here maybe. . . ."

Then Caitlin picked up the phone, my big sister's supportive words always meaning the world to me, and Brian, and other members of my family, all of them shouting to say they wished I was there with them. And finally Jenna came back.

"I know you've got to the place you dreamed of all this time. The frontier of the possible. And that I shouldn't be worried about you. I'm so happy for you, for us."

"Yes," I said. "I feel your strength in here with me right now in the tent, Jenna. You're walking with me through this storm . . . inside me more than I know how to describe. Strength . . . yours, mine, the amazing energy I feel from people out there following my journey—it's a village, not just me at all."

I'VE NEVER SET OUT to be a conquering hero. In the books my mom and dad read to me as a child, the characters I always loved best were the scouts, the seekers of truth going out to survey and report back from the frontier, sharing lessons learned and the maps they'd drawn. The point of The Impossible First was to push the edge of the possible and to bring back what I learned to perhaps inspire others to take their own scouting expeditions to their own Impossible Firsts.

As I packed up my tent and prepared to continue on into the storm, all the pieces of my life's journey began rolling through me.

I was there because of all the people who'd supported me, who'd made sacrifices for me, and who'd never stopped believing in me.

I saw David, sitting near the back of the classroom, where I was, on that first day of high school, and there again next to me in Thailand, holding me up and trying his lamest of jokes. "More hospital," he said as he'd carried me in.

My mom was there in the storm, too, and I could see her face and eyes in a thousand ways and at a thousand times—at the foot of my hospital bed and there across the kitchen, hand on the wooden chair, her eyes demanding that I rise up and walk, and dancing through our house to Paul Simon like a wild woman. And my dad was with me, hiking at my side through some damp and fern-wrapped trail in the Cascades, teaching me about stewardship and responsibility and the annual rate of retreat of his beloved Mount Hood glaciers in a warming climate, and most of all showing me through his life's example that loving the earth was about caring for it.

And Brian, grinning across the front seat of his pickup truck on the way to my first Vipassana retreat, and Caitlin, holding my hand on my first day of school, and always beside me in the car on Switch Day.

Mr. Gelber was there, rubbing his chin and looking at me with his brilliantly perceptive gaze across the table at his backyard barbecue. I could even smell the brats on the grill. Mr. Boyle was with me there in the storm, and I saw him staring up at the ceiling from his conference table at Columbia Sportswear, deciding the fate of the project Jenna and I had brought to him.

And Jenna. I felt I could almost reach out into the storm and touch her. I saw exactly how she'd looked in the bar that day in Fiji, and the little dark brown line that runs across the iris of her left eye, which I'd fallen in love with the first time I saw her.

I felt stuffed with all those things, like a symphony was playing through me and inside me and every step through the storm was the space between the notes. Strength came from that boy I once was, jumping up and down on the couch watching Pablo Morales win Olympic gold. And from that nervous teenager showing up for school on the wrong side of the river, and the high school grad arriving at Yale full of Pacific Northwest attitude. And from that wounded twenty-two-year-old, crying in his bed in a Thai hospital. And from that fool who drove away into the steamy July heat of Portland and had to experience the pain of intense loss before becoming the man who would "pop the question" on a mountaintop in Ecuador.

THE STORM LIFTED AROUND MIDDAY as I approached what I knew was the end of the continent. A wooden post, put in place by the United States Geological Survey, marks the place where the continent ends and the Ross Ice Shelf begins.

My GPS told me I was near. And it seemed I could almost feel it, too, in the fatigue of my body, and in the heaviness of my eyes inside my mask, as though a whole life had been lived in that compressed window of time. My dad's text, my decision to push on, my call to Jenna from inside the tent, my transformative moment kneeling on the ice with outstretched arms in the middle of the Leverett Glacier—they all seemed like pieces of a story I couldn't yet quite tell or get my head around.

When I finally saw in the distance the actual wooden post where the landmass ended and the sea ice began, the finish line goal I'd poured so much into, it still felt like a shock and I had to blink back a feeling of disbelief that it could be real. I'd gone seventy-seven miles in the past thirty-two hours, faster than my math had predicted. I'd visualized reaching this place countless times. I'd pictured how the weather would be, and what the sky and the ice would look like. I'd imagined how my body might feel, and even how it might look. I'd played a made-up movie in my head of the finish-line moment over and over. And now here I was, on the afternoon of December 26, 2018, with the end in sight.

The post even had a name, which I'd entered into my GPS as the end point of the journey. It was called LOO-JW in the mystery speak of USGS government geographers. More than a few times at night in my tent, in moments when my mind had wandered into a place of despair or doubt, I'd pulled out my GPS and studied that little five-digit code name, running my finger across the screen, trying to believe I'd reach it.

But now, when I finally saw it on the horizon, the post looked so tiny and insignificant, an isolated little stick in the middle of nowhere, that it seemed almost absurd. There'd be no one there to welcome me, or congratulate me. No cheering crowds or medals. Just a solitary hunk of wood.

A thousand huge forces, a single mistake, or a moment of bad luck could've stopped me from reaching this place.

A part of me wanted to charge on to the post, finishing what I'd started. I was a quarter of a mile away at most—a lap around a high school track. I could be there in minutes. But a bigger part of me wanted this moment to last forever. The post wasn't going away. I'd reach it soon enough and touch it and perhaps cry at the touch of it. Rudd was far behind. I'd achieved what I set out to do, to complete the world's first solo, unsupported, unassisted crossing of the Antarctic landmass. I knew I'd never be in this place again.

So I stopped, wanting to stretch out this moment, with more than 931 miles behind me, and just a few hundred yards to go. I unclipped from my sled. I put on my extra parka layer and sat down. I looked out toward the post, then back south toward the Pole and the direction I'd come, and finally down at the sled.

The sled.

I reached over to touch it, running a hand across the yellow cover, almost near tears. All these weeks, the sled, despite having been essential to my survival, had been my hated and burdensome shadow. Suddenly, I felt all over again the ache of that first day when I'd barely been able to budge it. I smelled again the white gas spilled down inside, and the memories that had roared out at me about the fire and the burns. I saw again the shape of it looming over me, teetering and ready to fall on me as I lay there twisted and sprawled by the huge sastruga. I felt it knocking me over going down the Leverett Glacier earlier that day.

We're all occasionally weighed down by our burdens, I thought, giving the sled a little pat. But we also need a place to hold the great gifts life offers along the way. My burden, it seemed, was also my salvation. As I trudged through the miles and weeks of my journey across the frozen continent, consuming food and burning fuel, empty space began to appear in my sled. At first, it was just a small sliver of a space, but that space grew larger and larger as the days passed.

Through the nine hundred odd miles I'd covered, I'd filled the empty spaces of the sled every day, little by little, with every memory, every lesson learned, every bit of love and wisdom that I'd gathered along the way. Now, stacked high with the treasures of my life, the sled was more full than ever.

As I'd set out on this journey, people asked me, "Why would you choose to suffer like that by yourself in Antarctica?" Now my answer was in the sled, next to all the other lessons learned. Through my crossing, I'd come to measure the highs and lows experienced in life on a continuum between one and ten.

I'd experienced the full spectrum in Antarctica; many "one" days alone full of fear, crying in my tent and wanting to completely give up. But in stepping out beyond my comfort zone, daring to dream beyond what most people thought was possible, I'd arrived at this moment. This flow state. This "ten." I was there in that moment not in spite of the "ones," but because of them.

Antarctica taught me that life isn't about maximizing our time at "five," in the zone of comfortable complacency, hedging against fear, loss, and pain. But rather, life is about having the courage to embrace the full spectrum—the tapestry of all the "ones" and "tens" and mundane moments in between. It's the key to unlocking potential and living fully.

The post sat there a quarter mile away, a solitary beacon at the continent's edge. And everything after that, I knew, would be different, after I'd finished the crossing. I was a man between worlds.

Finally, I'd sat there long enough to start getting cold.

I needed to get moving again, if only for that. I needed to go forward because my mind and body said it was time, and I'd learned how to listen. And so I stood up, walked for the last time to the front of my sled, strapped on my harness, and headed toward home.

Epilogue

I t was early morning and a thick layer of gray slush covered the sidewalk outside our midtown Manhattan hotel as the black four-door town car pulled up out front. I'd been off the Antarctic ice for less than a week, making my way to New York City from Chile, and as I stood there holding Jenna's hand, my feet were getting wet. In leaving our room, I'd worn the wrong shoes.

"You are Mr. O'Brady?" the driver asked as he climbed out. He was a thickset man in his forties with bristly gray hair and a heavy Slavic accent. I waved and nodded, but when he got around the car to the sidewalk, he immediately looked down, then back up at us. "This will not fit," he said, glancing at the car and back down again.

"I am sorry for this," he said. "They gave me wrong car. I did not know about . . ." He glanced back at his car for a few seconds and scratched his head, as though further rumination might conjure up a giant rear storage area he'd forgotten about. "I will call and they send another car," he said.

"How far is it?" I said, turning to Jenna. She glanced down at her phone and tapped in the address. "About three-quarters of a mile—point seven six, which would be about . . . ten blocks."

I looked down. My sled, dinged up and battered, lay there mired in the slushy muck, stuffed into an oversized surfboard bag with a handle and wheels. The concierge at the hotel had helped me carry it out to the street from the storage room where they'd held it for me overnight. "I think we'll be fine," I said to the driver. "Thank you."

"Ten blocks to the next waypoint!" I said, smiling over at Jenna with a message only she, of all the people in New York City—or maybe the world—could understand.

She laughed and signaled the driver that he could head out, then took my hand. I grabbed the handle at the end of the sled's carrying case, pulled the sled up onto its wheels at the back, and off we went.

People bundled up in winter coats walked by us on the way to work, deep in their earbud solitude. A huge red tourist bus roared by full of people, faces and mobile phones pressed up to the windows. I could smell pizza-by-the-slice from the twenty-four-hour joint next to the hotel and metal-tinged steam that pumped like smoke signals from a manhole cover in front of us. A giant neon billboard loomed from the top of the building at the next intersection, telling us in overwhelmingly brilliant colors about a Broadway show I'd never heard of, but that the *New York Daily News* said shouldn't be missed.

The great city throbbed, flashed, and heaved around us, hurtling through the routines of a typical winter workday morning, and the sled trailing along behind us, bouncing on its wheels, sticking occasionally in the slush, felt like the one familiar thing.

THE STUDIO GREEN ROOM was laid out with pastries, bagels, and fruit. A pot of coffee sat on a table, next to half a dozen daily papers, splayed out like a fan. But I was barely there, staring down at my hands, peeling off bits of glue. I knew that every little crumbling piece I pulled off had a story and a moment, and bit by bit they were taking me back to those days and weeks on the ice.

Jenna's elbow, nudging me in the ribs, brought me back to the present. A smiling, middle-aged woman with a ponytail had come into the room.

"Colin and Jenna!" she said, holding out her hand. "I'm one of the producers. It's so great to meet you, and thank you for coming. I followed every moment of your project and . . . just wow, couldn't get enough. Amazing! Congratulations! And the way you finished it there at the end was really powerful. It really moved me. It just about made me cry when I read about it."

I blinked and smiled at her, trying to come back to the moment. "Yes, that push at the end was a wild experience. I learned a lot—"

"No, I mean Captain Rudd," she said, looking a little confused. "How you waited for him there at the end, after you'd crossed the finish line . . ."

"Oh, right," I said, shaking my head.

And with those words, my mind torn between past and present, I was again back on the ice, waiting for Rudd. After crossing the finish line, a part of me was dying to leave Antarctica immediately. The idea of a huge meal, a hot shower, and a clean set of clothes sounded like heaven. Most important, I wanted to get back home, see Jenna and my family as soon as possible, but there was an equally strong part of me that wanted and needed to complete the circle that had begun on the Ilyushin flight. I wanted to see Rudd again, to make a statement of respect, to honor a worthy competitor. I wanted to congratulate him in person. Out of seven and a half billion people on the planet, he was the only other one who knew what it took to complete that crossing. So I waited, calling off the plane that was on standby to pick me up.

I knew there might be some awkwardness to the reunion given the intensity of our competition. Rudd arrived two and a half days after my finish at the USGS post, giving me some time to think through what felt like a protocol for how he should be greeted and acknowledged. I'd set up my tent about a mile beyond the post, near where the plane would land. He should have his own finish, I'd decided, his own moment to absorb what he'd accomplished. I didn't want to be standing there like I owned the place just because I'd gotten there first.

A few hours after he'd reached the finish and had time to set up his own tent, we finally reunited. He looked horrible and radiant at the same time, like the soldier he was, still firmly erect in posture but with an aura about him that was different now, too, than the man I'd met on the plane. The scruffy tatter of his jacket and the wounds on his face from the cold—scabby, frostnipped cheeks and lips—made him seem like a knight from an ancient story, coming in off the field of battle, bloodied but valiant. We both said congratulations at the same time and laughed.

And over the next two days, as we waited to fly out together, we mostly spent time on our own, reflecting on where our respective crossings had left us. But the second night, sitting outside his tent, swapping stories with me about our journeys, he generously offered me one of his extra freeze dried meals, knowing I was very low on food. His gesture underscored an unspoken camaraderie that had formed over the last couple of months. He then went silent for a moment, and I thought of that morning in the mess tent at Union Glacier when he'd blurted out his changed plans about where he'd start.

Breaking the silence and looking at me with kind eyes he said, "You know, Colin, I pulled longer hours in the harness than in any of my previous expeditions because of you and never took a rest day, wanting to keep the distance close. But to be honest, most of the time until the very end, I wasn't too worried about you being out in front of me. I was convinced that, in your inexperience, Antarctica would take care of the race for me and I just had to hold on."

Despite the differences that separated us and always would,

we now had a bond that would last forever. We both leaned in and shared a warm hug.

"GEEZ," I SAID when the producer had left and I was sitting back in my seat and looking over at Jenna, feeling overwhelmed by the swirling memories and emotions that were rolling through me. "What a journey, huh?"

She took my hand. "To think that less than a week ago you were on the ice, then Punta Arenas . . ." She gazed off for a second and shook her head.

I turned fully to face her and took both her hands in mine. "I was never alone out there—you walked every mile with me, Jenna. I was happy and proud of myself down there on the Ross Ice Shelf, of course. But it was only when I got down off that plane in Chile and you ran toward me and I had you in my arms, smelling your hair, going deaf with your screaming, that I could finally say, 'Yes we've done it, we made it across!'"

Overwhelmed with emotions, I held her for a minute, then went on. "You were the real finish line and I couldn't have done this thing in a million tries without you. None of this is possible without you."

I put my hand on the side of her face, and inched closer to give her a kiss.

"Sorry to interrupt," a young production assistant said in a brisk strictly business way that reminded me of Tim from the Comms Box. "They're ready for you."

He led us down a corridor where people were rushing around us in both directions, and then through the doorway leading onto the set.

The production assistant tapped me on the shoulder. "Two minutes," he said. A cameraman stood next to a whiteboard on the wall near the door. The show's name was printed neatly at the top, with a handwritten list of guests below. An eraser sat in the tray at the bottom. And there I was. "Colin O'Brady, The Impossible First, (w/sled)," my line said, with the last word presumably included as a reminder to the production crew that what Jenna and I had dragged down to 30 Rockefeller Plaza needed to be on the set, too. My sled, now empty, never felt more full. Jenna and I glanced at the whiteboard and we smiled knowingly at each other.

Whiteboard into reality.

Acknowledgments

First and foremost, I want to give a standing ovation to Jenna B, my wife, my love, my business partner, my co-creator of magic. Although it's my name on the cover of this book, none of this would have ever been possible without you. This is *our* story. Thank you for your strength when I was weak, your endless patience, your boundless creativity in making the impossible possible, and your infinite love. I look forward to a day, many decades in the future, when I can sit in a beautiful place with you, smiling back on all of the memories we've created together.

Blake Brinker, my right-hand man, creative collaborator, and dear friend: I'm grateful that serendipity brought us together on that fateful evening in 2016 when I was first learning how to share my story. You're a brilliant storyteller and exceptional human being. Your unwavering support in ways big and small has meant the world to me. Thank you for all you've taught me. This book wouldn't be what it is without your tireless dedication and creative genius.

Kirk Johnson, thank you for your assistance in writing this book. Your ability to listen, research, distill, and rework over and over again certain sections without complaint made *The Impossible First* better than it would have been otherwise. You're a consummate professional.

Jenna, Blake, and Kirk, the collaboration between the four of us to bring this book to life has been one of the great joys of my life.

Sarah Passick and Celeste Fine, my literary agents: you two are forces to be reckoned with. I can't think of a better team to have my back through this process. Thank you to Amber Rae for introducing us. Sarah, you believed there was a book inside me, even before I set foot in Antarctica.

I want to extend a huge thanks to the entire Simon & Schuster and Scribner team. Jon Karp, you were the first person to believe in this book, reaching out to Jenna before I'd even left the ice. Rick Horgan, my editor, thank you for your editorial help and for walking me through the publishing process as a first-time author. Nan Graham, thank you for championing this work and pushing me to make it even better.

To my mom, Eileen Brady: your unconditional support and love have made all the difference. The words you whispered to me as a baby and thousands of times throughout my life, "Colin, you can do anything you set your mind to," spurred me to take action to realize my wildest dreams.

To my dad, Tim O'Connor: thank you for opening my eyes to the great outdoors and for always reminding me to remember the most important thing.

To my stepparents, Brian Rohter and Catherine Downey: many in blended families try their best to simply tolerate each other. You've both done so much more. Thank you for loving me and accepting me as if I were your own child. You both have had a profoundly positive impact on my life.

To my sister, Caitlin: before we had this big Ohana blended family it was just me and you. You've loved me on my best and worst days. While I was in Antarctica you were one of the true rocks on the home front, diving deep with the maps, tracking the race progress, and providing crucial emotional support. Thank you for always being there for me through all of the phases of life. I'm proud to be your little brother. I don't tell you this often enough: I love you.

To my four stepsisters, Sadie, Casey, Eva, and Lili: I hate even using the word "step" to describe our relationship. You're my sisters, my family, my blood. I can't imagine my life without any of you.

To Richard, my one and only brother: although we grew up with different moms and on different sides of the world, you've always been an important person in my life. Thanks for teaching me all of the things only a big brother can.

To G-Sue, my grandma: I wish you were still with us so that I could share this book with you. You've been one of my biggest advocates and role models. Our beloved extended family is strong as ever today because of your legacy as the matriarch.

To Mike McCastle: just calling you my strength coach would be minimizing your role in the success of *The Impossible First*. Yes, you came up with some of the most unique and innovative ways to test my body and mind ahead of my expedition—and your own four world records are astonishing—but more than anything I've found in you a kindred spirit and brother. Thank you for always believing in me. I look forward to many more years of supporting each other's dreams.

I've had many coaches throughout my athletic career. I want to give a special mention to Beth Winkowski, who coached me in swimming from a young age and somehow managed to channel my energy in a positive direction. You were the first person who showed me what it meant to set audacious goals and put in the work to achieve them. Other impactful coaches I'd be remiss in not mentioning are Mike Taylor, Phil Claude, Frank Keefe, Ben Gathercole, Siri Lindley, and Greg Mueller. I've learned many important lessons about life and sport from you all.

Cheryl GreatHouse, master bodyworker, with all of my training over the years you've always been there to help keep me healthy and moving forward. More important, I feel deep gratitude for the wisdom you've bestowed and the compassion you've shown me over the past decade as I've shared my dreams with you through all of the ups and downs.

There are several communities, teams, and groups of friends who have had an outsized positive impact on my life. I want to give a special shout-out to: REALITY, Burning Man, BZ, Yale Swimming, BREAKOUT, Space Odyssey, The Fellas, 29029, and the Boundless 8.

To the staff at Antarctica Logistics and Expeditions (A.L.E.): your expertise and skills played a huge role in the safety and success of both my Antarctica crossing and the Antarctica portion of my Explorers Grand Slam world record. A special thanks to Steve Jones, Devon McDiarmid, Simon Abrahams, Dr. Martin Rhodes, Tim Hewette, Julia Doyle, Carolyn Bailey, Marc De Keyser, Roxanna Serrano, Tim McDowell, and Fred Alldredge.

There are many people who have taught me how to be a better outdoorsman, mountaineer, and polar explorer. A special thanks to Glynn and Sue Thomas and Steven Stark for taking me on some of my first "bigger" climbs when I was a teenager. Thank you, also, to National Outdoor Leadership School (NOLS). My semester in Patagonia in 2004 had a huge impact on my life and instilled confidence in me to explore wild places. Thank you to Guy Cotter for introducing me to eight-thousand-meter peak climbing and your help with my Everest logistics in 2016. Russell Brice, you are a legend; your expertise and friendship in 2015–16 played a huge role in my success with the Explorers Grand Slam. Masha Gordon, the day we climbed together on Manaslu in 2015 still stands as one of my all-time favorite days in the mountains. It's a great reminder that sometimes just being up high, and not making the summit, can be deeply joyful and fulfilling. Vern Tejas, the biggest Seven Summits badass of them all and my March 16 birthday twin, you opened my eyes to Antarctica for the first time. You've literally been there in some of the biggest moments of my life, at Union Glacier after I crossed Antarctica and on Denali at the end of the Explorers Grand Slam. Seeing you that day when I was descending from Denali was surreal. The kindness in your eyes as you hugged and congratulated me that day, even though I'd just broken your record, taught me one of my life's most important lessons about humility and grace. Dixie Dansercoer, your mentorship from the beginning to the end of my solo crossing was remarkable. You're one of the most accomplished, yet humble polar explorers ever. You and Julie have laid an incredible blueprint for how to operate as a husband-and-wife team in this world. Pasang Bhote, I'm not sure I know anyone stronger than you are in the mountains. Your calm in the midst of chaos on Everest, and your perseverance to help me get to the summit, taught me about the power of the human spirit. Tucker Cunningham, we formed our bond long ago swimming endless laps in a pool together. Who knew you'd be the one standing beside me on the summit of Denali in a crazy storm as I finished that project? Both you and Drew Pogge played such a huge role in making that Everest- Denali back-to-back possible. Dr. Jon Kedrowski, there is so much I can say about my favorite climbing partner, but I'll just leave it at this . . . Suuuummiiiittt!

There is a long list of polar explorers whose courage and desire to push the envelope one step further over the generations have inspired me along my journey. They're too numerous to name, but a special hat tip goes to: Ernest Shackleton, Captain Robert Falcon Scott, Roald Amundsen, Reinhold Messner, Børge Ousland, Mike Horn, Ryan Waters, Cecilie Skog, Felicity Aston, Ben Saunders, and Henry Worsley. I can't wait to see what the next generation of polar explorers dreams up to push even "farther south."

Thank you to the Explorers Club for granting me flag 109 to carry on my journey. It was a great honor to add a small piece of exploration history to the storied life of that flag and the club.

Lucas Clarke, when I met you in first grade, I knew we'd be

friends forever. So much of who I am today stems from our lifelong bond. I love you.

David Boyer, you saved my life that day in Thailand. No words can fully express my gratitude for what you endured to support me. I know you were just as scared as I was, but your courage and unconditional love gave me strength to keep fighting. Although the burn was a significant moment in both of our lives, it by no means sums up our friendship, which has included everything from playing soccer, to building our first business together painting houses as teenagers, to endless laughs over Ping-Pong and pool. I'm so glad you married my sister Lili, because now I can officially call you my brother.

I'm beyond grateful for the many other friends that have made me the person I am today. There are too many to name. You know who you are, and I'm incredibly fortunate to have you in my life.

In 2015, when Jenna and I were trying to get our first project off the ground, there were many doubters. However, there was a small number of people who believed in us and took action to ensure our success. Deep gratitude to Mark and Kathy Parker, Tim Boyle, Angelo Turner, and Bill Silva for taking a chance on us.

Brian Gelber, you and your family's support all these years means more to me than you'll ever know. None of this story gets written without your taking the biggest chance on me in 2009. Moreover, as you well know, there were many low moments during my athletic career when others would have backed away, but you stuck with me through it all. You've been my steadiest mentor and supporter, and are now a cherished and lifelong friend.

Charlie DuBois, Dr. John Troup, and the entire Standard Process team, thank you for your unwavering support of my goals with both Fifty High Points and The Impossible First. Optimizing the food and nutrition was the key innovation to making this "impossible" crossing a reality. The Colin Bars were pure magic. Your incredible team at the Nutrition Innovation Center is largely responsible for the success of this project, and I take great pride in knowing that we solved my nutritional needs in the healthiest way possible through organic, plant-based, whole-food solutions.

Thank you to Sleep Number and Grand Rounds for your sponsorship support to help me prepare for and execute on this dream.

I'd like to thank the many members of the press and media. I wanted to give a special thanks to Rich Roll for casting an initial spotlight on my work in 2015 when you granted me one of my first long-form interviews. Adam Skolnick, thank you for your superb coverage in the *New York Times* of the Antarctica journey. It was an honor to have you so intimately involved. Tamara Merino, thank you for your exceptional photography for the *New York Times* and the many images from Antarctica that were selected for use in this book. Almost all of the images from the actual journey I had to take myself since I was making the trek alone, but you captured some exceptionally poignant moments of Caption Rudd and me before and after, as well as Jenna's and my prep pre-expedition and our reunion in Chile. Sandy Friedman, your storied legacy in PR is unmatched. Thank you for pouring your heart and soul into supporting and collaborating with Jenna on the media front all these years.

Aaron Bergman, you were with me during the dreaming and planning phases of Fifty High Points and The Impossible First, and you gave up any hope of rest over the holidays to help Jenna with the barrage of attention after I finished over Christmas. Thank you for your tireless work and belief in me early on.

Ryan Kao, I knew nothing about photography when I met you, but you pointed me in the direction of my first camera to capture these adventures so I could share them with the world. I'll never forget bouncing around in the back of an RV with you as you documented my race through fifty states. You are a talented videographer.

Marianna Brady, my cousin, you elevated the Explorers Grand Slam with your creative talent, pushing me to share my story in ways I hadn't before. Shunryu Suzuki said, "In the beginner's mind there are many possibilities, but in the expert's mind there are few." Thank you for diving in with Jenna and me in the beginning even though none of us knew exactly what we were doing.

Ece Anderson, you made an offhand suggestion in 2011 that I should try a ten-day silent Vipassana meditation retreat. Your suggestion ended up leading to one of the most profoundly significant moments of my life. No words can ever express the gratitude I have for the benefits Vipassana has given me. In wishing to pay this gift forward, I highly recommend Vipassana to anyone looking to find the next level of mental peace and strength. It's completely free to attend a ten-day retreat and there are centers all around the world. There's nothing I've done that has given me as significant a return on time invested. www.dhamma.org.

Dr. Joseph Pulito and the staff at the Legacy Oregon Burn Center, thank you for the care you provided me both in person during my recovery in 2008, as well as your counsel while I was still hospitalized in Thailand. Thank you to the many doctors and nurses in Thailand who played a role in my recovery. Thank you to everyone in the medical community who crossed my path during my immediate care and long road to recovery after my burns. You all played a significant role in helping me beat the odds of my initial prognosis.

To Shannon Pannel, my first-grade teacher and hero: many in your shoes would have found my energy and curiosity at that age to be disruptive and cause for discipline, but you found a way to harness my rambunctiousness toward learning and growth. The foundation of my life was built on the principles you inspired in me. May you rest in peace, but may your spirit live on in educators across the world. In my nonprofit work in schools I've come to realize more than ever that the unsung heroes of our world are the teachers. Kristi White and Alice Atha, you were the first two teachers to invite me to speak to your students. I've connected with thousands of classrooms since then, but you two stand out as all-stars of the profession. Thank you for all that you continue to do, and for the young lives you've positively impacted. Thank you as well to the Alliance for a Healthier Generation for broadening my platform to reach students around the country and for your ongoing commitment to instilling health and wellness principles in kids. Dacia Jones, aka Dr. Drizzle, you've helped me impact students engaged in STEM education through our virtual field trips and curriculum around the world. I can't wait to continue our work together inspiring and uplifting the next generation.

Captain Louis Rudd, my reason for attempting The Impossible First boiled down to a desire to unlock the depths of my potential. Little did I know that having you out there would be the catalyst for tapping into that. Your presence in Antarctica pushed me harder than I ever imagined I could push myself. I have the utmost respect and gratitude for you. I'm so glad that after all of the intensity of the competition, we've been able to maintain a bond and friendship. As a symbol of that camaraderie, it was deeply meaningful to share a cup of tea with you in London nine months after we finished and to laugh and reminisce about the adventure of a lifetime.

I took on this project for anyone who has ever been told their dreams are impossible. I've received countless kind messages from people of all ages about the impact that The Impossible First journey had on them. Of those, the ones that have most touched me have been from people reporting the actions they've taken in their own lives as a result. Your actions are what inspire me. So thank you, for daring to dream greatly and live boldly in pursuit of your own "Impossible First."

#BePossible